The Power of Partisanship

The Power
of Partisanship

JOSHUA J. DYCK

AND

SHANNA PEARSON-MERKOWITZ

OXFORD
UNIVERSITY PRESS

OXFORD
UNIVERSITY PRESS

Oxford University Press is a department of the University of Oxford. It furthers
the University's objective of excellence in research, scholarship, and education
by publishing worldwide. Oxford is a registered trade mark of Oxford University
Press in the UK and certain other countries.

Published in the United States of America by Oxford University Press
198 Madison Avenue, New York, NY 10016, United States of America.

Library of Congress Cataloging-in-Publication Data
Names: Dyck, Joshua J., author.
Title: The power of partisanship / Joshua J. Dyck, Shanna Pearson-Merkowitz.
Description: New York : Oxford University Press, [2023] |
Includes bibliographical references and index. | Contents: Introduction—
Partisanship and Ideology in Political Decision-Making—Elite Cues,
Negative Partisanship, and the Changing Media Landscape—Partisanship,
Policy, Compromise, and the Non-political—Partisanship, Race, and
Intergroup Contact—Prospect Theory and Partisan Cues—Political
Responsiveness to the Lived Experience—Independents, Knowledge, and
Alienation—An Elite Problem Calls for an Elite Solution.
Identifiers: LCCN 2022058195 (print) | LCCN 2022058196 (ebook) |
ISBN 9780197623794 (Paperback) | ISBN 9780197623787 (Hardback) |
ISBN 9780197623817 (epub)
Subjects: LCSH: Political parties—United States. | Ideology—Political
aspects. | Political culture—United States. | Political participation—United States.
Classification: LCC JK2265 .D93 2023 (print) | LCC JK2265 (ebook) |
DDC 324.273—dc23/eng/20230118
LC record available at https://lccn.loc.gov/2022058195
LC ebook record available at https://lccn.loc.gov/2022058196

DOI: 10.1093/oso/9780197623787.001.0001

Paperback printed by Marquis Book Printing, Canada
Hardback printed by Bridgeport National Bindery, Inc., United States of America

To my parents, Dennis and Susan
To my children and husband, Sabine, Matcha, and Erik

Contents

List of Figures and Tables   ix
Acknowledgments   xiii

Introduction: Misinformation, Partisan Gamesmanship,
and Toxic Politics   1

1. Partisanship and Ideology in Political Decision-Making   10

2. Elite Cues, Negative Partisanship, and the Changing Media
   Landscape   23

3. Partisanship, Policy, Compromise, and the Non-Political   47

4. Partisanship, Race, and Intergroup Contact   69

5. Prospect Theory and Partisan Cues   99

6. Political Responsiveness to the Lived Experience   115

7. Independents, Political Knowledge, and Alienation   146

8. An Elite Problem Calls for an Elite Solution   163

Appendix   181
Notes   201
References   205
Index   225

Figures and Tables

Figure 2.1 Proportion of the Electorate Who Identify as Strong
Partisans, 1952–2020   26

Figure 2.2 Feeling Thermometer Ratings by Partisans of the Other
Party, 1978–2020   29

Figure 2.3 Percent Likes/Dislikes about the Parties, 2020   30

Figure 2.4 Ideological Categorization of the Other Party by Strong Democrats
and Republicans   31

Figure 2.5 Polarization in the House, 1880–2019   33

Figure 2.6 Campaign Information Sources, 2020   39

Figure 2.7 Polarization of Viewership   40

Figure 2.8 Trust in the News Media by Party Identification, 1996–2020   41

Figure 3.1 Preferences for Compromise, 2010–2017   57

Figure 3.2 Effect of Democratic/Republican Majority Status on
Candidate Preference   61

Figure 4.1 Type of Contact with the Closest Black Contact by Party Identification
among Whites, 2020   83

Figure 4.2 Intergroup Contact and Views of Fairness, Discrimination, and Racial
Resentment, 2020   86

Figure 4.3 Intergroup Contact and Views on the Role of Race in Discussions
of Police Shootings, 2020   89

Figure 4.4 Intergroup Contact and Support for Redistributing Police Budgets
to Better Fund Social Services, 2020   90

Figure 4.5 Intergroup Contact and Government Role Scale, 2017 and 2020   91

Figure 4.6 Contact with Black Americans and Support for Affirmative
Action, 2014 and 2020   95

Figure 5.1 2020 County Vote Share and 2021 Year-End Vaccination Rates   105

Figure 5.2 Support for a Free Vaccine by Treatment Effect and Party Identification 109

Figure 5.3 Results of the Prospect Theory Experiment with Partisan Cues   112

Figure 6.1 Context and Concern about Violence (Independents)   128

Figure 6.2 Context and Concern about Violence (Partisans)   130

Figure 6.3 Context and Attitudes about Gun Policy (Independents)   132

Figure 6.4 Context and Attitudes about Gun Policy (Partisans)   133

Figure 6.5 Context and Perception of Open Space   137

Figure 6.6 Context and Support for an Open Space Bond Proposal   139

Figure 6.7 Personal Financial Struggles and Support for Affordable
Housing and the Minimum Wage   143

Figure 7.1 Political Knowledge by Party Identification, 1988–2016   153

Figure 7.2 Average Feeling Thermometer Ratings of the Two Parties by Pure
Independents, 1978–2020   156

Figure 7.3 External Efficacy by Party Identification, ANES, 1952–2020   159

Figure 7.4 Regression Predicting Political Knowledge, 2020 ANES   160

Figure A5.1 Support for a Free Vaccine by Willingness to Pay   191

Figure A5.2 Support for a Free Vaccine by Willingness to Pay and
Party Identification   192

Table 3.1 AIC/BIC Statistics for Pre/Post Election Models, Party
Identification → Policy Issues, 2014   50

Table 3.2 Partisan Policy Cue Experiment Results, 2018   52

Table 3.3 Partisan Food Experiment Results, 2017   66

Table 5.1 Vaccine Cue Experiment with Willingness to Pay Cut Points   107

Table 5.2 Prospect Theory Experiment with Partisan Cues   111

Table 7.1 Political Knowledge by Party Identification, 2020   152

Table 7.2 Federal Spending Knowledge by Party Identification, 2020   154

Table 7.3 Trust in Government by Party Identification, 2020   157

Table 7.4 Views of Government Corruption by Party Identification, 2020   158

Table A3.1 Regression Analyses Examining Policy Position Stability Pre- and
Post-Election, 2014   184

Table A3.2 Multinomial Logit Model Predicting Candidate Preference, 2014   186

Table A4.1 OLS Regression Models for Discrimination, Fairness, and Racial
Resentment Scales, 2020   187

Table A4.2 OLS Regression Models for Attitudes toward Race and Policing, 2020   188

Table A4.3 OLS Regression Models for Support for Government Help to
Blacks Scale, 2017 and 2020   189

Table A4.4 Ordered Logit Models for Support for Affirmative Action,
2014 and 2020   190

Table A5.1 Vaccine Cue Experiment Results, 2020   191

Table A6.1 Ordered Logit Models for Concern about Gun Violence and School
           Shootings, 2014   193

Table A6.2 Ordered Logit Models for Policy Attitudes about Guns, 2014 (1)   195

Table A6.3 Ordered Logit Models for Policy Attitudes about Guns, 2014 (2)   196

Table A6.4 Ordered Logit Models for Attitudes about Open Space, 2016   197

Table A6.5 Ordered Logit Models for Attitudes about Affordable Housing
           and the Minimum Wage, 2016   198

Table A7.1 OLS Models for Political Knowledge, 2020   199

Acknowledgments

This book was born out of years of discussions between us and others, many of which started during our time at the Department of Government and Politics at the University of Maryland at College Park (2001–2006 and 2004–2009, respectively). We met in Geoff Layman's Advanced Quantitative Methods class in which Shanna drove Josh, the course TA, slightly crazy trying to understand minutia of the material. We first worked together in 2009 on our first article, a journal article on context and support for gay marriage—a paper that can be directly traced to the work of several of our graduate school advisors and that laid the groundwork and some of the foundational thinking on this book. The paper was the result of a cold email from Shanna to Josh while he was an Assistant Professor at the University at Buffalo, SUNY. That email was the start to what has become an important and wonderful friendship and a fun and productive professional relationship. Over the years, we have spent countless hours together in coffee shops, a grocery store food court, the lobbies of conference hotels, on the phone, and lately on Zoom, grabbing every chance we've had to develop research ideas and survey questions, and write together. As a result of that process, this book is a true collaboration. We can no longer sort out who wrote what or which idea was whose. It is the product of a decade of brainstorming and building on each other's work. As a result, we owe each other a great deal of thanks and acknowledgment. Following standard political science tradition, authors are listed in alphabetical order, but the contribution is equal. Neither of us feels as though we could have written this book without our co-author.

This friendship would never have been possible were it not for the culture of co-authorship, collaboration, and creativity fostered in the University of Maryland at College Park's Department of Government and Politics. We owe a great debt to our mentors and teachers at the University of Maryland, especially Jim Gimpel (to whom we yell, "Let's do some political science!"), Karen Kaufmann, Geoff Layman, Irwin Morris, and Frances Lee. Our graduate school friends and colleagues (and sometimes co-authors) John McTague, Laura Antkowiak, Nate Bigelow, Jenn Lucas, Juliana Menasce Horowitz, Chris Whitt, Becca Thorpe, Anne Cizmar, Mike Evans, Julia Jones, Ozan

Kalkan, Annie Leonetti, and Adam Hoffman also contributed a great deal to our intellectual development and to the way we view the world.

We are each especially beholden to Thomas Carsey, who passed away in 2018. Despite the fact that neither of us was his graduate student or his colleague, he spent countless hours mentoring us and engaging each of us individually in critical analysis of public opinion and partisanship. It was also likely his research on conflict extension with his co-author and longtime friend (and our professor and friend) Geoff Layman (Carsey and Layman 2006; Layman and Carsey 2002) that lit the match that sparked this project. Without their critical contribution to the field of political polarization and partisan behavior, this book would never have been possible. Tom and Geoff are two of the nicest and most supportive scholars in political science, and the hole that Tom left when he passed away will never be filled. We miss you, Tom, and are forever thankful for having had the chance to know you. For those who did not know Tom, we encourage you to read the artful biography written by his friends and graduate students published in *PS* (Banda et al. 2018).

We also thank the many scholars who indulged us in our development of the ideas in this book and gave us helpful feedback along the way, including Alexandra Filindra (who co-authored with us one of the articles that led to the ideas in Chapter 4), Ted Lascher, Liam Malloy, Janine Perry, Gregg Johnson, David Barker, Jeremy Pope, David Hopkins, Melissa Deckman, Stella Rouse, Don Haider-Markel, Mark R. Joslyn, Marc Hutchison, Brendan Skip Mark, and Corey Lang (who co-authored the grant that produced some of the data in Chapter 6). We are also indebted to the Political Communication Working Group at UMass Lowell, including John Cluverius, Morgan Marietta, Mona Kleinberg, and Jenifer Whitten-Woodring.

While we don't know the blind reviewers that reviewed this book or the journal articles we published that helped in its development, we thank these anonymous social scientists for their constructive and helpful feedback. As a result of this thankless work, we were able to gain critical feedback from smart people that made our work better. We also thank our former students who helped us with various data components of the book, including Makayle Washington, Michael Coates, and Patrick Prendergast. Oxford University Press was an absolute joy to work with on this project; we especially thank our acquisitions editor, Angela Chnapko. On this note we are particularly thankful to our free editors: Shanna's father, David Merkowitz, and Shanna's husband, Erik Christiansen.

The Center for Public Opinion at UMass Lowell provided the funding for much of the data in this book. This would not have been possible without the continued support of former Chancellor Jacquie Maloney, former Senior Vice-Chancellor for University Relations Patti McCafferty, Provost Joe Hartman, Dean Luis Falcón, and former Center Co-Director Frank Talty. Some of the data in Chapter 6 was also collected as part of a grant from the USDA National Institute of Food and Agriculture, Agricultural and Food Research Initiative Competitive Program, Agriculture Economics and Rural Communities, grant number 2015-67024-22937.

Although most of the data in this book is original and has not previously appeared in print, several of the ideas were developed in previous publications. The ideas in Chapter 4 were first developed in several of our previous publications, including "The Conspiracy of Silence: Context and Voting on Gay Marriage Ballot Measures," published in *Political Research Quarterly*; "To Know You Is Not Necessarily to Love You: The Partisan Mediators of Intergroup Contact," published in *Political Behavior*; and "When Partisans and Minorities Interact: Interpersonal Contact, Partisanship, and Public Opinion Preferences on Immigration Policy" (with Alexandra Filindra), published in *Social Science Quarterly*. However, all the data and analyses in Chapter 4 are new. Some of the data and ideas we present in Chapter 6 are in common with, and grew out of, a publication with Corey Lang and Patrick Prendergast, "The Individual Determinants of Support for Open Space Bond Referendums," in *Land Use Policy*, but the models presented in Chapter 6 are unique to that publication. Two of the models presented in Chapter 6 on gun control appeared in "Crime and Partisanship: How Party ID Muddles Reality, Perception, and Policy Attitudes on Crime and Guns," which appeared in a special issue on gun control in *Social Science Quarterly*.

Seventy-five percent of this book was written and completed between March 2020 and February 2022, during the Covid-19 pandemic. We are indebted to the front-line essential workers: the employees in essential industries who must physically show up to their jobs including but not at all limited to the grocery store clerks and storeroom workers, the meat packers and food factory workers, the mail delivery workers, the safety and security workers, and those who worked to keep trash picked up, electricity on, and to make sure the elderly were cared for. You put your lives and your loved ones in danger so that we could all eat, work, and be as safe as possible in the pandemic. We are further indebted to the health care workers who also put their lives and families on the line working long, thankless hours helping others survive. Finally, we thank the scientists who developed lifesaving tests, treatments, and vaccines, not just for Covid-19 but for all the potentially curable illnesses cutting lives short. Thank you all for your service to this country and the world.

From Shanna:

I owe a great debt of gratitude to my father, David R. Merkowitz, and my mother, Carol S. Pearson. They have contributed to my work in more ways than I can count. My father volunteered on every presidential campaign from 1980 to 2016, often in battleground states far from our home, including New Hampshire, Maine, Florida, Colorado, and Iowa, and countless state and local races in between. His interest and passion for politics got me interested in politics in the first place, and his shared *New York Times* articles often became the examples we used in this book. My mother was a pioneer in the academy and managed to use her academic work to improve the lives of people, businesses, and government institutions in the "real world." I can only hope to come close to my mother's passion for helping others and her dedication to academic research. I also thank my brothers, Jeffrey and Stephen Merkowitz, for their ability to fight about politics despite agreeing on the vast majority of political issues. I'd also be remiss if I did not thank my great aunt Nina Silberstein, who, at 100 years old, is still a huge MSNBC fan. Her views on politics and how they changed during her lifetime is positively captivating when we can get her to talk about it. Several dear friends also deserve their own thanks: Gillian Powers, Rachel O'Reilly, Liam Malloy, Skye Leedahl, Scott Jensen, Craig and Liz Odar, Melissa Loh, Erik Loomis, Katie McIntyre, Laura Pomerance, Maryland State Delegate Ariana Kelly, and Abby Godino, Jill, Jim, and Micah Greenberg, and my sisters-in-law Grettel Bustos Galeano, Molly Savitz, and Amanda Hency. This last year would have been impossible without you. I am also indebted to Maryland State Senator Brian Feldman for giving me the opportunity to spend several years in the Maryland State Legislature learning the ins and outs of the inside game of politics. This multi-year behind-the-scenes experience helped craft my early ideas that eventually landed in this book.

Most importantly, I simply cannot adequately thank my spouse and partner of 20 years, Erik Christiansen, for his love and support. He is, by far, my biggest cheerleader and the reason I was able to write this book during a pandemic. We have biked across countries together, and now we have each published our first book. I cannot wait to see what life has in store for us next; whatever it is, Erik, I have no doubt you will have my back (hopefully on many more cross-country bike rides). Finally, I thank my children, Sabine and Matcha, who made sure I never spent too much time writing uninterrupted. I look forward to spending a lot more time with you. Your smiles, hugs, and laughs bring me endless joy. I hope you grow up to a country in better shape than the one we describe in this book.

From Josh:

I feel very fortunate to get to do the job that I do. Teaching students to understand where their preconceived notions about politics come from has certainly had a big effect on my thinking about partisanship over the last two decades. I want to thank my students, those I have taught at the University of Maryland, at the University at Buffalo, SUNY, and at UMass Lowell. Their willingness to listen, read, challenge, discuss, and be vulnerable never ceases to amaze me. We come to a series of fairly depressing conclusions in this book, but my interactions with young people is one of the things that continues to give me hope.

My family has been very supportive of my education and academic ventures, even when it took me far away from home. I am indebted to my parents, Dennis and Susan, for providing me with opportunities and instilling in me a love and appreciation for public education. I thank my brother Ben and his family for their continued love and support, and for sharing their Disney+ subscription with me. And to my friends Corey Davenport, Josh Jakubczak, and Bill Noland—the Dudes—I would not have survived the doldrums of pandemic life without your friendship.

Introduction

Misinformation, Partisan Gamesmanship, and Toxic Politics

High-profile Republican elected officials, major news personalities on Republican-leaning entertainment news shows on the major networks and websites, and a gaggle of conservative think tanks and interest groups claimed for months in 2021 and 2022 that President Biden's Attorney General, Merrick Garland, was planning to investigate parents who spoke at school board meetings for domestic terrorism. "The attorney general announced the FBI would investigate moms who dared to complain at school board meetings as potential terrorists," proclaimed the Fox News leading prime-time host, Tucker Carlson, on his show on January 13, 2022 ("Tucker," 2022). Elise Stefanik, the third-highest ranking House GOP leader, echoed this proclamation, telling Fox News viewers on another show, "They are considering parents who speak out regarding education issues for their children to be domestic terrorists" (Milbank 2022). This claim was repeated nightly on national news entertainment shows, shared on social media by national, state, and local Republican elected officials, and brought up in Congressional hearings by Republican Members of Congress.

The problem, of course, is that it had no basis in reality. Neither the Attorney General nor anyone in the administration ever even off-handedly said anything to this effect. The claim was based on a Justice Department memo calling on the FBI to help local police deal with real situations in which school board members received violent threats and were physically harassed and intimidated (Kamenetz 2021; Koch 2021). This was not about parents engaging in civic discourse or peacefully protesting school policy. The Justice Department was responding to an appeal from school boards across the country to help local police deal with people in and outside the community threatening school board members, teachers, and principals with violence because they disagreed with school policy—sometimes policies the school district had not adopted nor even discussed adopting. One school board

The Power of Partisanship. Joshua J. Dyck and Shanna Pearson-Merkowitz, Oxford University Press.
© Oxford University Press 2023. DOI: 10.1093/oso/9780197623787.003.0001

member in Brevard County, Florida, Jennifer Jenkins, recounted the experience of her last year: At one point, a group of about 15 people gathered outside her house shouting things like, "Pedophiles!"; "We're coming for you!"; and "We're coming at you like a freight train! We are going to make you beg for mercy. If you thought January 6 was bad, wait until you see what we have for you!" Someone called child protective services and told them Jenkins had burned her daughter as punishment, causing a days-long investigation into the safety of her home. On another day she woke up to an "FU" burned into her lawn with weed killer and the bushes in front of her house hacked down (Jenkins 2021). While this case may sound extreme, these were the issues that the Justice Department was responding to because Jenkins' case, while rare, was not unique. School board members in many jurisdictions were being threatened and harassed in ways the local police were strained to handle (Koch 2021).

The actual U.S. Attorney General's memo to the Justice Department called for the FBI to help "address the rise in criminal conduct directed toward school personnel" by "working with each United States Attorney, to convene meetings with federal, state, local, Tribal, and territorial leaders in each federal judicial district. . . . These meetings will facilitate the discussion of strategies for addressing threats against school administrators, board members, teachers, and staff, and will open dedicated lines of communication for threat reporting, assessment, and response" (U.S. Department of Justice 2021).

This is just one example of the current state of the misinformation environment created by partisan elites and its effect on the public. Today party elites engage in the hyperbolic misrepresentation of events, mudslinging, and blatant lying to paint the other side as a threat to basic human rights and democracy, with no regard for truth. Civil debate over policy has all but disappeared from elite public discourse. It has been replaced with a political addiction to hyperbole, name-calling, deception, and, most critically, fear mongering. The effect on the public has been to deepen attachments based on political identity instead of policy opinions, increase fear and loathing of the other party, and to ultimately increase the importance of partisan attachments and negative affect in decision-making. If you identify as a Republican and now you learn from the Congressperson or Governor you voted for and trust that the Democratic Party is sending the Attorney General after you if you voice concerns at your local school board meeting, a logical response is to detest and fear the Democratic Party, and double down on your attachment to the Republican Party.

As a result of this hyperbolic rhetoric, voters are stronger partisans than in the past and are more likely to view the opposition party—both its elected officials and its members—with a combination of confusion, disdain, and outright hostility (Abramowitz and Webster 2018; Mason 2018). Voters of both parties feel that the members of the other party misunderstand and dehumanize them, are fed misinformation, and pose a threat to the future of the country (Moore-Berg et al. 2020). However, little of this animosity is grounded in the specifics of policy. Instead, the United States is marked by affective partisanship—that is, partisanship driven by strong attachments to the party as a group for reasons that have little to nothing to do with policy but a lot to do with emotion, animosity, and distrust of the other party.

The central argument of this book is that the growth in affective partisan polarization, and the resulting negativity voters feel toward the opposition party, has far-reaching, often toxic effects on how Americans behave both inside and outside the realm of politics. The power of partisanship influences support for democratic norms, willingness to engage in risk in financial and health care decisions, interracial interactions, and preferences on completely non-political issues like the choice of what to eat for dinner. The power of partisanship blocks people from learning from each other, and from their neighborhoods, and even makes them blind to their own personal economic hardship. The power of partisanship ultimately makes partisans unable to respond to information not gained through partisan channels.

There is considerable agreement among scholars and political observers that we are living through an intensely partisan and negative political time, but less research is devoted to studying the spillover effects of polarization. This includes implications that directly affect how the American public engages their democracy, but also implications directly tied to other theoretical traditions in political science, psychology, economics, and sociology. This book is our contribution to this discussion; it is a concerted effort to take full consideration of the unintended consequences of polarization and negative partisanship on political behavior.

Partisan polarization is at an all-time high. Party elites are well sorted, and the "liberal Republican," the "conservative Democrat," and the "bipartisan working committee" are relics of a bygone era. Elected officials and, as a consequence, the electorate have sorted and are much more likely to have a strong commitment to their political party than at just about any other time in history. Easy access to partisan information through social media and partisan news outlets makes the distinctions between the parties easy to understand

and exacerbates the gulf that citizens *perceive* between the two parties, even if the distinction is built more on hyperbole and misrepresentations than on actual policy differences. The public has always looked to political elite cue-givers to help them make sense of political events. In the modern era, people are inundated by one-sided hyperbolic perspectives that are reinforced each time they turn on their phones or open their preferred social media apps. We are fed by algorithms designed to learn one's political proclivities so as to increase the likelihood that we will click on and share a post. For party leaders and the partisan news media, it has never been easier to deliver neatly packaged information to co-partisan constituents about the evils of the other party. As a result, toxic negative partisanship is increasing, and partisanship and elite cues now have power over decision-making both inside the realm of the political and in our basic interactions with our neighbors and within our neighborhoods.

While pundits and some in the social sciences treat policy positions as antecedent to partisanship, we argue that partisanship has the power to drive changes in policy positions since partisans in the electorate are willing to change or even reverse positions when partisan elites re-crystalize the position of the party for political purposes, or as a negative response to the other party staking out a policy position. Moreover, partisanship affects public adherence to democratic norms and principles, such as compromise.

Our ultimate and primary contribution in this text is to expose the reality that political polarization is no longer bound by the ropes on the proverbial political boxing ring. Instead, we argue, political polarization now appears in the oddest of places, well outside what historically would have been considered political. No area of human life in the United States is now safe from partisan influence.

Partisanship is so pervasive that it has disrupted the traditional ways in which social scientists believe humans process information, develop opinions, and make decisions. We argue that foundational theories of human behavior in the social sciences are disrupted among those who identify with one of the two parties, especially strong partisans who make up nearly half of the public. These theories present expectations about the way humans respond to stimuli. This is what makes up the backbone of social science theory—our ability to predict human behavior; but partisanship has spilled over to such an extent that it upends the way human behavior can be understood. Partisan cues dominate the information environment and can change the normal expectation of human responses to stimuli.

Finally, we argue that the power of partisanship in the United States today raises questions for social scientists about how we measure and treat political knowledge. As a result of the intensity and pervasiveness of partisanship in politics today, "political knowledge" has become an endogenous feature of strong partisanship and a poor proxy for anything but partisan behavior. The failure to grapple with the measurement of political knowledge has led to a severely undertheorized and underdeveloped empirical understanding of partisanship, and even more so of independents (especially pure independents). We present evidence that pure independents are, in fact, very responsive to information because they are not biased by partisan elite cues and there are many instances where political information is local, contextual, or personal, and not about naming names of important leaders.

A democratic ideal is that people will be responsive to new information and learn from their interactions with others and their lived experience. These lived experiences in our neighborhoods and in our interactions with other citizens should inform our political attitudes. Today, we argue, the small segment of America that identifies as pure independents is much more responsive to new information than partisans are.

Altogether, partisanship today is so powerful that it has broken down the walls of the political sphere and disrupted the way social scientists theorize human behavior. Americans are willing to judge just about everything, from how they feel about a policy issue to whether they should eat a certain type of food, based on partisan elite cues; moreover, they are less likely to let other social influences meaningfully affect their behavior. The political realm has no bounds, and the partisan screen is stronger than ever. That is the power of partisanship.

A natural question is whether affective polarization and negative partisanship are symmetrically distributed between Democrats and Republicans. There is some reason to suspect that they are not. In some of our own previous research that inspired us to write this book, we found evidence of polarization being driven by both parties (Pearson-Merkowitz and Dyck 2017), while in other research we found evidence that it was primarily Republicans who drive polarization (Dyck and Pearson-Merkowitz 2014; Pearson-Merkowitz, Filindra, and Dyck 2016). There also exists a long line of research documenting "asymmetric" polarization in the United States. These authors show that while Democrats have moved somewhat left and become more internally consistent, the vast majority of political polarization is driven by the Republican Party (Gainous and Wagner 2013; Grossmann and

Hopkins 2016; Hacker and Pierson 2015; McCarty 2011; Russell 2018, 2021; Skocpol and Williamson 2016). Compared with Democratic Party elites, Republicans are more consistent and more extreme in their voting records and, historically, have been more negative and attack-driven in social media communications.[1]

Our approach to this question is ultimately empirical. As we discuss in the following chapters, partisanship and mass-elite linkages work for both parties, but it is a question for the data if one party has promoted greater extremism and toxicity, and if the power of partisanship is stronger in one party than the other. While we return to this question often, and particularly in the book's conclusion, our findings largely support the asymmetric polarization hypothesis.

Data and Methods

Throughout the book, we employ a mix of causal designs using original survey data we devised and collected for this project and observational data from large, publicly available repositories. Original data were collected by the authors, and the experiments were performed on nationally representative samples of American adults using YouGov's national panel between 2014 and 2020. National data are obtained primarily from the American National Election Study Cumulative file, 1948–2020, although we draw on other reputable data as well. We describe all the data in detail in the Appendix, and replication files are available for all our statistical models in a public data repository.

Organization of the Book

Chapter 1 lays the groundwork for our contribution, situating our argument within the existing political science literature about elite cue giving, political parties and identities, and negative partisanship. In Chapter 2, we develop our argument about the information environment, demonstrating empirically the growth in strong partisanship, negative partisanship, and the relationship of these trends to the changing media environment. The data in this chapter illustrate the changes that have taken place in mass partisanship over time and highlight the partisan influence in the information environment.

In Chapter 3, we demonstrate through causal analysis how partisanship affects preferences—policy preferences, preference for compromise, and preferences for things that are not expressly political. The data in this chapter have very important takeaways for the future of democracy. For one, we find that policy views are influenced by elite cue giving, reinforcing the findings of Carsey and Layman (2006; Layman and Carsey 2002a, 2002b) that party identification can drive policy preferences and that it is not always the other way around. Our data show that partisans' policy preferences on real policy issues like the minimum wage and foreign intervention change to align with their party's positions. This chapter also investigates how people respond to the status of their party in the legislature. We find that when it comes to being on the losing end of elections, being in the partisan minority can lead to ideological entrenchment instead of a desire to work with the majority party to influence policy. This finding suggests that partisan "strategic opposition" and "gamesmanship" (Lee 2016) are alive, well, and supported by voters, not just party elites. Finally, Chapter 3 begins our investigation of the overflow of polarization into the non-political by looking at food preferences and partisanship. Experimental evidence in this chapter suggests that learning about the food preferences of partisan elites changes the way partisans in the electorate rate these food items. Importantly, this finding is driven by negative partisanship—higher ratings of food liked by the opposition party's leader decrease how partisans rate that food.

Chapters 4, 5, and 6 collectively address how party cues affect social science theories that are not expressly political. In Chapter 4, we investigate how partisan cues alter expectations derived from the intergroup contact theory (e.g., Allport 1954). We find that when partisan elite cues profess animus toward the outgroup, even close contact fails to decrease intergroup animosity and increase acknowledgment of racial inequality. Perhaps most importantly, we find consistent evidence that for white Americans, contact with the Black community crystalizes views about discrimination and systemic racism for both groups. For Republicans, contact fails to make the expected change in attitudes among white partisans that the contact hypothesis has consistently shown over time and across contexts. This chapter utilizes original data specifically designed to test this hypothesis during the 2020 Black Lives Matter protests as well as data from other original surveys.

In Chapter 5, we investigate the role of partisanship in upending the expectations of prospect theory (e.g., Kahneman and Tversky 1979). Our data suggest that a person's tendency toward risk aversion or risk acceptance can be altered if the payoffs are structured through the lens of partisanship. This chapter includes an experiment testing people's willingness to take risk around Covid-19 and the pandemic in the face of partisan cues and an experiment testing people's willingness to take financial risk for partisan gain. We find evidence in both experiments that partisanship affects the way people calculate risk.

In Chapter 6 we turn to contextual effects theory (e.g., Berelson, Lazarsfeld, and McPhee 1954; Huckfeldt 1986). Here we begin our investigation into what political knowledge means in an information environment that is expressly partisan and whether contextual effects theory works in the way social scientists have long predicted. We suggest that partisan knowledge can act as disinformation and, under certain circumstances, someone with less factual knowledge will also possess less biased knowledge, insulating them from some of the worst impulses of an ever-evolving "two-fact" society. Our data suggest that partisans no longer gain information from their lived environment and instead view their local conditions through a national partisan lens. We find that it is only pure independents who utilize their lived experience—both contextual experiences *and* personal financial circumstances—in a responsive manner.

In Chapter 7, we discuss the measurement of political knowledge and what it means in light of the findings from the preceding chapters. Here, we introduce the idea that political knowledge, like ideology, has become endogenous to party identification. Furthermore, we present evidence that political disaffection is significantly related to lower knowledge, a departure from findings presented in previous explorations of this topic.

Chapter 8 summarizes the key findings from the previous chapters and assesses the overall contribution of the work. Centrally, we claim that the effects of affective polarization and negative partisanship on political science theory are broad and significantly alter many of our theories about human behavior, incentives, and opinion-policy linkages. Finally, we address the potential that the findings of our chapters are expressive—people simply responding to surveys in ways that do not reflect how they would behave in real life. We find no basis for this critique. Instead, we argue that the behavior of partisans over the last few years suggests that, if anything, our models underestimate the effect of partisanship on human behavior. Partisans were willing to storm the U.S. Capitol and put their lives on the line in a public health crisis for partisan gain. They are willing to end friendships and avoid family gatherings. The behavior our survey experiments suggest is manifesting in the real world in ways that go far beyond what anyone could have imagined a decade ago.

We conclude with a call to elites to fix what they broke. Democracy is at risk, and it will take elected officials on both sides of the aisle to keep the country together.

1

Partisanship and Ideology in Political
Decision-Making

1.1 Partisanship and Political Behavior

Until very recently, media explanations of American elections and the political calculations of everyday Americans often stood at odds with decades of political science research that characterized everyday Americans as emotional (Sears et al. 1980), highly partisan (Campbell et al. 1960), and lacking basic knowledge about most political issues (Converse 1964; Kinder and Kalmoe 2017). These media portrayals tended to focus on hopeful and dynamic narratives about undecided voters—Americans outside the political fray who, in the media's account, decided most elections (Kaufmann, Petrocik, and Shaw 2008). The media fawning over moderate billionaires like Michael Bloomberg and Howard Schultz in the lead-up to the 2020 primary election revealed many media insiders' deep obsession with the idea that elections are ultimately about appeasing undecided centrists.[1]

Among political scientists, however, partisanship has long been the core tenet to understanding American voters. The presidency of Donald Trump presented ample opportunities to challenge the concept that voters could behave in a manner consistent with philosophical ideas of the way the world works, what political scientists often term an *ideology*, or that voters would be more beholden to their views about policy than to their party. Trump famously came out in favor of single-payer healthcare, raising the minimum wage, raising taxes on the wealthy, and imposing tariffs during the 2016 Republican presidential primary debates, contradicting several of the most firmly held positions of the Republican Party. Instead, playing on voters' fears about immigrants and pledging to "Make America Great Again," he staged a coup of the Republican Party, doubling down on massive government spending on a border wall, a ban on immigrants from majority Muslim nations, and other "America first" policies that once would have been unthinkable to the small-government, business-friendly Republican Party.

The Power of Partisanship. Joshua J. Dyck and Shanna Pearson-Merkowitz, Oxford University Press.
© Oxford University Press 2023. DOI: 10.1093/oso/9780197623787.003.0002

Republicans in the House of Representatives and the Senate decried these policies and Trump himself, but once he secured the nomination, the "Never Trump" Republican elected officials hushed over the course of his campaign, his inauguration, and his presidency and began to endorse the new brand of policies that the Republican Party had long fought against, and that Trump championed.

The adaptation of Republican elites to Trump's new party is exemplified by Republican Senator Lindsay Graham's change from calling candidate Trump "a race-baiting, xenophobic bigot" to announcing that the Republican Party had become "the Trump party" (Thrush, Becker, and Hakim 2021). But it also makes some people question how voters continued to stick by Trump. Republican primary candidate Trump called for raising the minimum wage, raising taxes on the wealthy, and many populist policy positions, but he flipped on these issues once elected—rejecting them all. And while a majority of working-class white Republicans support raising the minimum wage and other populist economic policies (Davis and Hartig 2019), they did not reject Trump when he rejected the very policies he campaigned on—President Trump consistently enjoyed an approval rating among Republicans of 90% or higher while in office, among the highest ratings in history (and 94% among white Republicans without a college degree) (e.g., Gallup Inc. 2021; Jones 2019).

Perhaps more important is the increasing evidence that facts have become a product of the information voters receive from their co-partisans. How could the U.S. end up in a situation where, months after the election and insurrection on the Capitol, over half of Republican respondents to a Reuters poll said they believed the siege was "largely a non-violent protest or was the handiwork of left-wing activists 'trying to make Trump look bad'" and 60% of Republicans believed that former President Trump would actually have won the election were it not for widespread voter fraud (Oliphant and Kahn 2021)? Immediately after the election, 99% of Democrats believed Candidate Joe Biden had rightfully won the election, and 78% of Republicans thought President Trump had (Pew Research Center 2021)—remarkable stability despite no evidence that no more than a handful of fraudulent votes had been cast and no evidence of widespread or organized fraud (Eggers, Garro, and Grimmer 2021), or that the few fraudulent votes that were cast favored Joe Biden.

How could this happen? How could a party leader with no ideological consistency with his party receive such unfettered support? How could a majority of the Republican Party voters largely reject all factual evidence and question democracy to the point that it led several thousand voters to lead an insurgency on the Capitol? While the case of Donald Trump and the Capitol insurrection is an extreme example and often seems shocking and of-the-moment, that may be because of the rapid pace and high profile of the issues on which the party flip-flopped to keep in line with their president. However, this kind of party issue-switching behavior is an integral feature of the American political system (Karol 2009). And it is not only the Republican Party; both history and contemporary events are filled with examples on both sides of the aisle.[2]

However, the unquestioning support that partisans seem to feel toward their party and their party's messaging today is only possible given the information environment in which we live and the political polarization, negative partisanship, and the strong role that partisanship plays in structuring our views of life, government, and fundamentally what is right and wrong, that has emerged over the last few decades. In this chapter, we review the literature on political parties, negative partisanship, and the role partisanship plays in helping co-partisans create positions on new issues to ground our empirical contribution in the remaining chapters and to put our argument in context of the political science literature to date.

1.2 Partisanship, Not Ideology

While there exists a longstanding debate in the literature about whether partisanship is attained by socialization (Campbell et al. 1960) or is a function of attitudes about issues, and if the public can actually be characterized ideologically (Fiorina 1978; Franklin and Jackson 1983), recent events decidedly show a public that is more wedded to their party than to anything that can be even loosely defined as ideology. The years of the Trump administration have shown this clearly.

Of course, one of the most important critiques of ideology as the underlying reason for political positions and behavior is its lack of formal mechanism for its creation, or even a formal definition. That is, *what is* ideology? And who or what decides what makes up an ideology? Said another way: Who or what decides what policy position is conservative and what is liberal? An "ideology" is a system of ideas and ideals that serve as a basis for political and policy approaches. Voters and elected officials can be driven by an ideology—such as individualism, socialism, or libertarianism—which holds together their attitudes toward any number of policy questions; but politics in the United States does not neatly fall along these formal ideological distinctions. Instead, what is "conservative" or "liberal" is defined today by the positions of the two major political parties, via their elites.

For example, a preference for "small government," consistently applied as a political ideology, would mean government should not be involved in regulating the market nor the body. Yet "conservative" and "liberal" ideologies as applied to modern politics in the United States are a patchwork of ideologies: In some ways the Republican Party is a party of small government; in other ways it is the party of big government. Likewise, Democrats have both "big" and "small" government policy beliefs. What holds liberal and conservative platforms together is their position under one party's label (Karol 2009). Certainly, one of the party's platforms could have evolved to include low taxes, low spending, and pro-choice policy positions, as was the ideology of many Republicans, from Barry Goldwater, the Republican candidate for president in 1964, to Lisa Murkowski and Susan Collins, the last two pro-choice Republicans remaining in the Senate. To quote cigar heiress and political activist Susan Cullman, on the fact that she joined the Republican Party in the 1970s while being an outspoken pro-choice advocate, "The conservative view at the time . . . was that you don't want the government in your life. The government isn't supposed to enter your home, never mind your body" (Sussman 2020). This is of course quite different from what the term "conservative" means today, which includes less government regulation of markets and the economy, more restrictions on personal behavior and morality, and tougher policies to- ward criminals—a set of positions that does not map well onto any system of ideology, as some are "large-government" social regulation and others "small-government," individualistic. The same is true of what is considered "liberal" ideology today—a conglomeration of policy positions that do not map well with a political ideology. As a result, people like Lisa Murkowski (R-Alaska) or former Congressman Collin Peterson (D-Minnesota) are labeled "moderate" even though their votes and their views are not necessarily more moderate than those of Nancy Pelosi or Mitch McConnell; it is just that their views do not align with the positions of their parties on a small subset of policies. Thus, people with "mixed" positions in terms of the political party platforms are often more consistent with an ideology but less aligned with the positions of their party.

Both political parties embrace various elements of different ideologies from socialism to libertarianism when it is supportive of the specific policy position the party has decided to embrace and when the national policy environment leans toward the other party. For example, when Democrats were in power, Republicans argued in the Supreme Court that states' rights trump federal powers, and that programs like the Affordable Care Act (better known as "Obamacare") represented a radical overreach by the federal government; but once Republicans were in power, the platforms switched sides—Trump and Republican allies in Congress enacted sweeping environmental, healthcare, and immigration policies to be imposed on all states and argued that federal law would trump state and local laws in these areas. In response, Democrats, who over the last century have defended federal laws against arguments that states should be allowed to chart their own ways— particularly in the areas of women's rights, gun control, and civil rights— began to use state's rights arguments against the new policies imposed by the Trump administration (Levine 2017). Of course, this is possibly best summarized through the images of two Republican women carrying posters in bold letters proclaiming "My Body, My Choice" and another "Government off my body" to protest mask mandates at the same moment that Republicans in Texas and several other states were passing laws to effectively end women's access to abortion (Goldberg 2021). Whether the position is state versus federal supremacy, the size of government, or the role of the government in regulating morality, the two parties choose positions that are both internally and externally inconsistent but are politically convenient.

In other words, to say ideology governs political beliefs more than party identification or that party identification is caused by ideological positions, is to say that ideology is created by something outside the party organizations. Not only are elites inconsistent in the ways we have shown, scholars find little evidence of meaningful or stable issue positions among the public. For example, when one attitude changes, other connected parts of a belief system remain stable (Coppock and Green 2022), changing information sources can drastically alter political beliefs (Broockman and Kalla 2022), and for many Americans, ideology is simply not a meaningful concept (Jefferson 2020; Kinder and Kalmoe 2017). Instead, we see ideology and partisanship as intertwined—what is conservative is that which Republicans and Democrats in their fight for political posture have labeled conservative, and what is liberal is that which Democrats and Republicans have labeled as liberal. Importantly, the party that owns the issue may not even see the issue themselves as "liberal" or "conservative," but the other party can brand it that way through messaging (e.g., the "liberal attack on moral values" or the "conservative attack on women's freedom"). What is conservative or liberal, therefore, is a product of party competition more than it is a product of a system of ideals or values. This premise is central to how we understand the role of the political parties in American political behavior and why the political party leadership is so essential to the policy and personal beliefs of partisans in the electorate.

1.3 The Partisan Perceptual Screen

As political scientist E. E. Schattschneider (1942, 35) wrote, "a political party is first of all an organized attempt to get power" and control government, not an ideological, mission-driven organization. Ideological organizations, Schattschneider explains, are interest groups, not parties. And as Lee (2009, 3) explains, even in the pre-Trump era, "there is far more party conflict in the Congress than one would expect based on the ideological content of the congressional agenda or the policy differences between liberals and conservatives." Instead, Lee argues, "parties hold together and battle with one another because of powerful competing *political interests*, not just because of members' *ideals* or *ideological preferences*" [emphasis in original] (Lee 2009, 3). The policy positions of political parties are not driven by ideology but are determined by a host of factors, including the personal characteristics of elected officials (McTague and Pearson-Merkowitz 2013), the social movements of the time that drive activists within a party to push specific issues (Layman 2001; Layman et al. 2010), the need to keep their coalition members happy or attract new coalition members in order to win elections (Karol 2009), and, critically, the need of political parties to differentiate themselves from one another in order to win political points (Lee 2009). A core feature that allows party elites to engage in this kind of behavior is that, at their foundation, most Americans lack organizing principles around issue attitudes and therefore follow their partisan identity, even if it means deviating from previously espoused "beliefs."

The examples of parties taking up the mantle of issues that did not formerly belong to them because of their expanding electoral coalitions or political circumstance are ample. The most obvious historical example of this is the manner in which the two major political parties switched positions on civil rights (Carmines and Stimson 1989; Karol 2009). But in recent years as well, we see examples of policy pushes that do not entirely fit with the party that proposed them. This is especially common in foreign policy, where Republicans are thought to exercise ownership over hawkish stances (Egan 2013; Petrocik 1996). However, Democratic presidents have also been Commanders-in-Chief in times of war and have been placed in the position of supporting military action abroad. Even in domestic policy, both the foundations of Obama-era policy proposals like cap and trade and individual markets under the Obamacare healthcare reform have their roots in Coasian economic theory and were born in conservative think tanks and Republican administrations—yet it was the same conservative Republicans that rejected the plans from the start when they were proposed by Democrats.

Meanwhile, it was a Republican president, George W. Bush, who passed the largest expansion of Medicare in decades with the addition of a prescription drug benefit passed in 2003, with the help of a Republican-controlled Congress, and the administration credited (along with Ronald Regan) for employing the first cap and trade models to control pollutants. But it is now the Republican Party that is known for wanting to shrink both Medicare and Social Security and that adamantly opposes cap and trade policies. When the Republican Party nominated Mitt Romney for President in 2012, the man whose signature policy achievement as Governor of Massachusetts was passing the policy that became the model for the Affordable Care Act, candidate Romney promised to end Obamacare on his first day in office, calling it "day one, job one." For most of the 1990s and 2000s, the Republican and Democratic Parties were conflicted on the issue of immigration and reluctant to take firm positions on most policies. However, on all of these issues, firm position taking risked hypocrisy. How could Democrats support market-oriented solutions to political problems? And how could Republicans oppose them *and* label them as socialism? All of this, of course, predates the Trump presidency, a short time that wreaked havoc on perceptions of partisan issue positions on free trade, foreign intervention, and views about American intelligence agencies.

Central to our argument is that such inconsistencies are only possible in a world where elites provide a steady stream of messaging to a receptive audience whose underlying values and ideological viewpoints are malleable but whose party attachments are strong (e.g., Carsey and Layman 2006; Layman and Carsey 2002a). In short, partisans in the electorate are more similar to party elites than is typically credited: They are more oriented toward political competition and power holding than to any clear set of ideological preferences.

To be sure, we are far from the first academics to say that members of the general public are prone to elite-cueing, or that partisan-motivated reasoning is the psychological mechanism driving the acquisition of perceptions and attitudes. As Kunda (1990, 480) explains, people strive to hold positions that are correct and reasonable, but "people are more likely to arrive at conclusions that they want to arrive at" and "their ability to do so is constrained by their ability to construct seemingly reasonable justifications for these conclusions." Partisanship provides a quick and easy way to arrive at a conclusion that will be cognitively satisfying because it has been endorsed by opinion leaders as correct and reasonable. This allows co-partisans to arrive at conclusions that feel safe without gathering information or reflecting on its actual factual basis in the larger world or its consistency with one's lived environment. Of course, politicians also have a strong motivation to portray reality in ways that will create a distinction between voting for/supporting their party and opposing the other (Lee 2009). Thus, politicians provide co-partisans with a selective, self-serving reality.

To us, partisan-motivated reasoning, or what Campbell et al. (1960) referred to as "the partisan perceptual screen" (p. 133), means that highly partisan voters now fail to learn new political information from their lives, their social networks, or fact-based news. As one set of authors put it, partisans are "driven by an inescapable motivation to defend their partisan identity" that makes them "process information selectively and actively find ways to bring real-world conditions in line with what they want to believe" (Bisgaard and Slothuus 2018, 456). And this drive for partisan identity and cognitive comfort leads to a form of democracy that is more akin to demagoguery. What does it mean for citizens to vote, protest, or engage in political action if those actions are simply the result of the outraged rants of partisan elites and not personal needs, or heartfelt worldviews? What does civic engagement mean, and is it normatively "good" if it is not motivated by the actual lived experiences of a nation's residents but by a desire to boost one's group at the expense of the other?

As a result, we take odds with the political science literature that has, by and large, equated partisan cue-taking as a rational response and a logical "shortcut" (Lupia 1994; Popkin 1991). This "rational response" explanation suggests that while the American voter may fall short of the informational ideals of democratic theory, they find their ways to "correct" votes by using

information shortcuts. The most critical of these to a voter is their party identification and the elite messengers connected to their information networks.
As we will address in greater detail later in the chapter, a key component of
this messaging focuses on fostering negative attitudes *towards the other party*.

1.4 Party Cues as Information Shortcuts

"Information shortcuts" are meant to provide voters with the necessary information to make an informed vote. Critical to political science conceptions
of knowledge and rationality is the idea that behavior is predictable, consistent, and constrained (Converse 1964; Zaller 1992). Indeed, political behavior has largely reasoned that an individual holds meaningful ideological
attitudes when they exhibit stability in their responses to iterated versions of
the same questions, and it has largely been strong partisans who are simultaneously highly informed about politics *and* who demonstrate the highest
amount of stability in issue responses. Highly constrained voters are treated
by the political science literature as the normative goal: They know their own
positions, they know the positions of the political parties, and they vote consistently for the party with the positions that match their own because they
are able to simply vote for a party or for a ballot initiative due to a party endorsement, thereby saving time and information costs.

Information shortcuts, however, can be disinformation. Facts can be
stylized versions of the truth, and our realities may be shaped almost entirely
by partisan interpretations of stimuli in the lived environment (see especially
Marietta and Barker 2019). The conflation of partisan issue constraint with
"political knowledge," therefore, presents a bit of a conundrum for social
scientists. As partisan-motivated reasoning and cue-taking behavior become
more prevalent, nonpolitical expectations of how individuals will behave can
be constrained by behavior that is expressly partisan. Put another way, the
political science definition of knowledge is endogenous to being ideologically constrained, which is in turn endogenous to being a partisan. This is
not a hopeful development and does not signal democratic health because,
ultimately, we are just talking about partisan strength.

As partisanship has become increasingly strong and increasingly defined
as "not the other party," elites have given party identifiers in the extant public
a broader language with which to reason and talk about issues that has expanded the role of partisanship in creating a perceptual screen that not only

regulates how people view politics and public policies but prevents the intake of information which social scientists have always found critical to the way humans make judgments and create attitudes. Moreover, it expands to the non-political so that partisan cues can influence the way people view the non-political world or make the non-political world inherently political. It also expands to our interactions with others in our social spheres.

With that in mind, any social theory of human behavior is susceptible to the influence of partisan-elite cueing. Such theories are also potentially incomplete without building in an explicit component of the role of partisanship in shaping attitudes. In this way, the effects of partisanship in the American mass public have subsumed many of the ways we commonly understand human social behavior to operate, in the realm of politics, and even those that are *adjacent*. Because of this, in a strange social scientific twist, it is political independents, long maligned for their inattention to politics and low levels of political awareness, who are the most responsive to information in their lived environment. Partisans, meanwhile, are so attuned to filtering information that they will resist information, even information presented through their personal social networks and their personal experiences, that does not square with the current partisan priors.

1.5 The Rise of Negative Partisanship and Partisan-Motivated Reasoning

While voters may at any given time pick a party due to a policy preference, once political identification is developed, the likelihood of defect is extraordinarily low. This is why election analysts look to the party identification trends of young voters, particularly those voting for the first time to make predictions about the future of the parties (e.g., Rouse and Ross 2018). Although people do break with their preferred candidate, as was the case with some white voters who voted for Obama, and then voted for Trump, this is another instance in which the media plays up an outlier as a rule.

In many cases, people develop party attachments as part of their childhood socialization with little to no knowledge of the issues the party stands for. Indeed, in recent studies of which political values are consistent between parents and their children, partisanship and issues with high moral components (e.g., racism, prayer in school, etc.) have the highest transmission rates (Jennings, Stoker, and Bowers 2009). Partisan identification was more likely to be the same for parents and children than religion. Several ideological areas that are considered foundational to the political parties (such as business vs. labor) have very low transmittal rates. As a result, many voters acquire political attachments without also acquiring the accompanying knowledge about political issues or how the machinations of the political process operate.

Even among the most informed, though, politics works like a game of follow-the-leader. Elites take positions on new issues, and in response to that position-taking, members of the party respond by mimicking these statements. Partisans also engage in a process in which they differentiate themselves largely on what they are not—Republicans are *not* Democrats, Democrats are *not* Republicans. In-group identity is often more defined by the distaste for the out-group than it is an acknowledgment of what is positive about the in-group (Mason 2018). Lee (2009, 3) notes this about Congress: "Fellow partisans' shared risk has wide-ranging effects on congressional party politics. It leads members of one party to support efforts to discredit the opposition party . . . it persuades members to rally around the initiatives of their own party's president, and as a mirror image, the other party to resist initiatives championed by an opposing party's presidents" regardless of whether they were once issues their own party championed. Research on voters supports this assertion: "Ingroup favoritism is increasingly associated with outgroup animus" and "hostility toward the opposing party has eclipsed positive affect for ones' own party as a motive for political participation" (Iyengar and Krupenkin 2018, 201). Scholars have also found that partisan identity is the main driver of inter-party animus (Dias and Lelkes 2021; but see Orr and Huber 2020). We address this trend through quantitative analysis in Chapter 2.

The important point here is that as the strength of the two parties has increased, voters have shown a strong tendency to vote and adopt positions more as a defense against an out-group than as a response to any specific policy positions. This behavior is largely referred to as "negative partisanship" (Abramowitz and Webster 2016). A perfect example of this is the difference in support for "Obamacare" and "the Affordable Care Act." While these are the same policy, polls show that although the individual elements of the ACA are extremely popular even among Republicans (Kirzinger et al. 2022), support for the actual law falls drastically for Republicans, particularly when associated with the Democratic administration. For example, a CNN poll in 2013 found that when they asked about support for "Obamacare,"

46% of respondents opposed to the law and 29% supported it. But when they asked about the "Affordable Care Act" only 37% opposed the law and 22% supported it. In other words, associating the law with the Democratic president increased both the positives and the negatives (Liesman 2013).

Negative partisanship explains why objective evaluations of economic performance (Duch, Palmer, and Anderson 2000) and support for generic statements such as "American politics is always an open competition" (Hanel et al. 2018), for instance, are subject to partisan incentives. In recent work Bullock et al. (2015) uncovered that accuracy incentives can decrease the willingness of survey respondents to give spiteful, non-factual answers motivated by partisanship (e.g., to be honest about the state of the economy instead of saying that economic performance is terrible when the out-party controls the presidency). This helps put some shock-and-awe findings in context. For example, in a widely publicized finding ahead of the 2020 primary election, nearly two-thirds of New Hampshire Democratic primary voters reported preferring that a giant meteor strike the earth and extinguish all human life to Donald Trump being re-elected president (Carlisle 2020). What this means is not that voters are entirely unaware of facts that contradict their partisan predispositions or that they are unwilling to agree to ludicrous things (e.g., the giant meteor), only that political reasoning is driven by "affect" and not "fact." And while, certainly, most voters would not actually prefer a meteor strike to a Trump presidency, the fact that they are willing to say so can actually translate into politically meaningful behavior (unlike the meteor), such as trolling members of the other party one disagrees with, questioning election results, seeing public health measures as undemocratic, or being unwilling to acknowledge the positive outcomes of the other party's policies.

But negative partisanship also explains civic engagement. As Mason (2018) found, threatening, angry, and emotional responses to partisan messages increased civic engagement significantly. So not only do partisans respond to partisan messages by changing their version of reality, such as believing that President Obama was not born in the United States or that President Trump won the popular vote in 2020, but hating the other party also drives people to be more active in politics.

What makes studying voter reactions to partisan stimuli interesting is the fact that parties do, in fact, change over time. The party of Andrew Jackson, segregation, and Jim Crow evolved through various realignments to become the modern Democratic Party, the party most aligned with racial equity, affirmative action, and of which the vast majority of Black elected leaders are members. The Republican Party of Abraham Lincoln was at one point the Republican Party of Dwight Eisenhower and now Donald Trump. While some changes in party leadership can lead to gradual policy change, other changes can be more dramatic, like Donald Trump's drastic shift in foreign policy and trade policy from his predecessors.

And these shifts do not alter the electoral coalitions as drastically as one would expect if they are viewing partisans through the belief that people choose their political party based on firmly held beliefs or "ideology." Instead, especially in a time of heightened negative partisanship, people respond by rejecting or blocking anything perceived as being the position of the other party.

We now turn to studying the extent to which partisanship and negative partisanship have seeped into the way residents of the United States develop opinions—both on political issues and on what were once not political issues.

2

Elite Cues, Negative Partisanship, and the Changing Media Landscape

2.1 Introduction

Political parties in the United States today are extremely effective. Once weak and disorganized, today the Democratic and Republican Parties message their positions clearly and precisely. And while there is disagreement within their ranks, the ideological difference between the parties is far greater than the differences within the parties. This gives voters a chance to understand the policies that will likely be pursued as a result of the outcome of an election, beyond who they are voting for. While once it was hard to know, without substantial research into individual candidates, which candidate was pro-choice, anti-immigrant, pro-social services, or anti-taxes (Wattenberg 2002, 66), today people can make reasonable guesses that are likely to play out correctly in the legislator's voting record with no research other than the political party affiliation of the candidate.

Armed with just that one piece of information, a voter can cast their ballot as though they had spent hours reading a candidate's website. This ease is due to effective branding on the part of the parties, and it comes with real legislative benefits for the parties as well. The goal of a political party is to both win office and control political institutions, but also to pass legislation once they hold a majority (Aldrich 1995, 2011). While co-partisans often complain that their party won a majority of seats and yet fail to deliver on policy promises, a look back at the successes under President Obama and President Trump, including the Affordable Care Act (better known as "Obamacare"), which dramatically expanded health insurance access, and the Tax Cuts and Jobs Act of 2017 (TCJA), which substantially reduced both corporate and individual taxes (in some categories by drastic amounts), and the successful placement of two socially and economically conservative justices to the Supreme Court, suggests that when one party controls both chambers and the presidency,

The Power of Partisanship. Joshua J. Dyck and Shanna Pearson-Merkowitz, Oxford University Press.
© Oxford University Press 2023. DOI: 10.1093/oso/9780197623787.003.0003

they can deliver on the most fundamental of their platform priorities, even if they can't deliver on everything in the platform.

The political parties have in many ways become what advocates of strong parties had hoped: The parties negotiate a platform, they give voters clear choices between important policy priorities and social positions, and they work within the institution to deliver results (American Political Science Association 1950). Strong parties, like the current manifestations of the Democratic and Republican Parties in the United States, allow voters to hold elected officials accountable because policy outcomes are clearly the product of just one party, so if a voter does not like the outcome, they can vote for the other party. This is the normative ideal of the role of political parties in democracy (Schattschneider 1942;Key 1956).

Unfortunately, strong parties equaling electoral accountability assumes voter flexibility and that voters collect information about their pocketbooks or the general state of affairs in the country and judge it impartially—that is, that voters follow a "retrospective voting model." The retrospective voting model (e.g., Fiorina 1978) argues that citizens hold officeholders accountable without excessive political knowledge by focusing on the state of the economy, either their personal pocketbook or the economy as a whole. As Healy and Malhorta (2013, 286) nicely summarize, retrospective voting argues that "voters just have to answer the kinds of questions that Ronald Reagan posed in his closing statement in his 1980 debate against Jimmy Carter: 'Are you better off than you were four years ago? Is it easier for you to go and buy things in stores than it was four years ago?' The answers to these questions and related ones represent easily accessible and digestible information. Encyclopedic knowledge is not needed; these shortcuts are sufficient heuristics for voters to judge overall government competence."

For a long time, the retrospective voting model was considered, in the aggregate, correct, at least partially because presidential elections could be predicted based primarily on economic factors. The most consistently correct presidential election forecast takes into account only three variables: the president's approval rating a few months before the election, a dummy variable for if the person running is a first-term incumbent, and, critically, the change in real GDP (Abramowitz 2021).

But polarization has made elections tighter and less contingent upon retrospective results, primarily because *fewer voters are willing to hold their own party accountable*. In fact, it is not surprising that recent presidential elections have been so close and so stable. The closeness and stability of elections is largely due to the closely divided and *strongly partisan* electorate (Abramowitz 2021; Bafumi and Shapiro 2009). There simply are very few people left willing to hold their own party accountable for the state of affairs instead of blaming any poor outcomes on the other party (Schwalbe, Cohen, and Ross 2020), regardless of who is in power.

Instead, today, reliable voters are far more aligned with the political parties and the party's candidates than ever before, and a larger share of the electorate identifies as a "strong partisan"—a group that is stalwart in their attachments and prone to hyperbolic attacks on the other party. These voters have different sources of information that do not overlap and are driven by negativity and a dislike for the other party. In this chapter, we show how partisanship and the information environment, including both traditional media and social media, have evolved and how they relate with each other to produce the current political polarization that currently shapes the United States.

2.2 The Changing Nature of Partisanship in the Electorate

Over the last 70 years, political scientists have routinely asked survey respondents to identify themselves using a series of questions about partisan identity. The question, posed since 1952 in the American National Election Study, has asked respondents, "Generally speaking, do you usually think of yourself as a Republican, a Democrat, an independent, or what?" If people answer independent or something else, they are then asked, "Do you think of yourself as closer to the Republican Party or to the Democratic Party?" but if they respond that they think of themselves as a Democrat or Republican in the first question, they are then asked, "Would you call yourself a strong [Democrat / Republican] or a not very strong [Democrat / Republican]?" These three questions allow researchers to create a 7-point party identification scale which ranges from *Strong Democrat* (1) to *Strong Republican* (7) with *Not strong Democrat* (2)/*Republican* (6), *Lean Democrat* (3)/*Republican* (5), and *independent* (4) in the middle (American National Elections Studies 2021).

Figure 2.1 shows the percent of strong partisans within the population and strong partisans within each party since 1952. It is useful to examine the full extent of the time series. In the 1950s and early 1960s between 35% and 40% of respondents to the ANES identified as strong partisans, but after 1964 there was a significant decrease, particularly among strong Democrats.

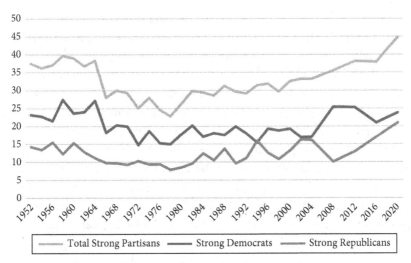

Figure 2.1 Proportion of the Electorate Who Identify as Strong Partisans, 1952–2020

Source: Data are from the ANES Cumulative Data File.

Strong Republicans also declined to a low point in 1978 when just 22% of respondents identified as strong partisans (just under 15% identified as strong Democrats and just under 8% identified as strong Republicans). The drop in strong partisanship led to the *party decline* thesis among political scientists. Writing in 1998, Wattenberg (1999) began the new edition of his book by saying that "for over four decades the American public has been drifting away from the two major political parties. Once central guiding forces in American electoral behavior, the parties are currently perceived with almost complete indifference by a large proportion of the population. Public affection for the parties has declined not because of greater negative feelings about the Democrats and Republicans, but rather because of an increasing sense that the parties are no longer crucial to the governmental process."[1]

Today these words might seem strange to most observers of the United States as the political parties are crucial to the political process and people feel very strongly about them. After 1980 and the critical realignment that followed Ronald Reagan's recruitment of the Christian Right (Layman 2001), strong partisanship began to steadily rise. And in 2020, partisan strength hit a high with 45% of the public identifying as strong partisans. Just under a quarter (24%) of Americans now identify as strong Democrats, and just over one fifth (21%) identify as strong Republicans. However, the critical change point can be seen in 2004 for Democrats and 2008 for Republicans. *Twice* the number of Republicans today identify as "strong" compared to 2008, when Barack Obama was elected. It was his election and the Republican Party's response to his election that seem to have sparked the dramatic growth in strong Republican identifiers. By 2020, the number of strong Democrats had increased slightly less than strong Republicans but still showed a strikingly large increase of 70% since 2004.

Importantly, the rise in strong partisans is not due to a decrease in people unaffiliated with a political party. The percent of Americans that identify as non-leaning independents is just about 12%. While this percentage ebbs and flows each year, it has held basically steady since 1966 when independents were 12.43% of the public. Since then, the percentage of pure independents has only ranged from a high of 16.35% in 1978 to a low of 9.2% in 1996. On average, pure independents have made up 12.5% of the American public since 1966, and they made up 12% of Americans in 2020. However, what has changed is the percent of leaning and weak partisans. Importantly, this means that primary voters and those most likely to vote Republican or Democrat are also the most stalwart in their views and most dedicated to the success of a single party. Independents have not changed, but partisans have.

2.3 The Rise of Negative Partisanship

Why are Americans identifying more strongly with their political parties? Mason (2018) argues, and we agree, that they are developing stronger attachments to the political parties due to the increasing overlap of identities or what Mason calls "social sorting" within the parties. In modern America, political party identification is synonymous with group identity/member-ship (Levendusky 2009; Mason 2018). If you are not sure what we mean, just ask yourself who comes to mind when you think of a Republican. Generally, people answer this question with a list of other group identities (e.g., Green, Palmquist, and Schickler 2008). By thinking about the parties in terms of social groups, voters create a list of in-groups and out-groups. The Republican Party has become defined as white, conservative, Christian, and straight, while the Democratic party has become synonymous with a diverse range of groups including Black, Hispanic, and other minoritized racial and ethnic groups, those who identify as LGBTQ, religiously nonaffiliated,

Reform Jewish voters, and feminists. When people think about their political party and what it means to them, they also think of these overlapping social groups. When these social groups overlap, the perceived threat from the other party can be much more powerful. White, male, evangelical Christians, for example, perceive more status threat and social distance from the other party than those who have cross-cutting social groups. But the number of people with cross-cutting social groups has drastically declined as a result of partisan sorting (Mason 2015, 2018). People are simply increasingly likely to identify with multiple groups; but, increasingly, all of those group identities tend to align with only one political party.

Strong attachment to a social group also comes with a feeling of psychological distance from the other group, and that distance drives fear, feelings of threat, and misunderstanding. When social groups do not overlap, outgroup members simply cannot understand each other and begin to see each out-group extremely negatively. This negativity is not due to actual policy or ideological distance but is affect-based (Iyengar, Sood, and Lelkes 2012). For example, a 2020 Pew poll found that over 40% of Democrats and Republicans saw the other party as a "threat to the well-being of the nation" (Dimock 2020).

Social scientists have long agreed that the development of in-groups and out-groups leads to conflict. And that is just what we see among partisans—they are motivated more by fear and dislike for the other party than by a passion for their own (Mason 2018). This is a phenomenon known as "negative partisanship" and one we will repeatedly come back to in this text.

The theory of negative partisanship states that Americans largely align *against* one party instead of affiliating with the other (Abramowitz and Webster 2016, 2018). A traditional measure of negative partisanship uses a question appearing on the ANES since the 1970s about the political parties called a "feeling thermometer." Respondents are asked to answer a series of feeling thermometer questions regarding a wide variety of political figures and social groups including the political parties. In these questions respondents are asked to rank the groups and people on a 0-to-100 scale and are told that "ratings between 50 degrees and 100 degrees mean that you feel favorable and warm toward the person. Ratings between 0 degrees and 50 degrees mean that you don't feel favorable toward the person and that you don't care too much for that person. You would rate the person at the 50 degree mark if you don't feel particularly warm or cold toward the person" (2020 Time Series Study 2021).

Figure 2.2 presents the average feeling thermometer ratings of the Democratic Party by Republicans and the Republican Party by Democrats, from 1978 to 2020. In the 1970s and 1980s, ratings were in the 40- to 50-point range on the scale—near neutral. But in the last decade, there has been a sharp decline in warmth toward the opposition party. By 2020, on average, Republicans gave the Democratic Party a bitterly cold rating of just 18 degrees, and Democrats gave the Republican Party a bitterly cold rating of 20. Strong partisans expressed even more negative affect—on average, strong Republicans rated the Democrats at 10, and strong Democrats rated Republicans at 15. Strikingly, 60% of strong Republicans rated the Democratic Party at zero—the lowest possible rating—and 46% of strong Democrats rated the Republican Party at zero.

Partisans are not nearly as warm toward their own party as they are cold toward the other party. Just 20% of strong Democrats and only 27% of strong Republicans gave their party the highest rating (100).

Any political observer would expect Democrats to rate Republicans at or below 50 and Republicans to rate Democrats at or below 50, given they have chosen their political party for a reason. However, ratings around 50 indicate that while they like their chosen party more, they do not hold much animus toward the other party. However, the 30-point decrease in feeling

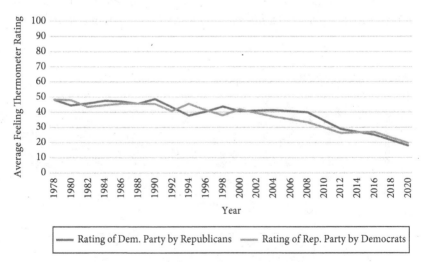

Figure 2.2 Feeling Thermometer Ratings by Partisans of the Other Party, 1978–2020

Source: Data are from the ANES Cumulative Data File.

thermometer ratings over the last few decades indicate that partisans are highly disdainful of the other party, and the disdain is felt very strongly.

Figure 2.3 uses one more measure of negative partisanship to illustrate this point. In the 2020 ANES, respondents were asked if there was anything they liked about each party and then asked if there was anything they disliked about each party. Here we present the percent of respondents saying "yes"— that there was something they liked[disliked] about the party. The overall takeaway from this data is quite interesting. Strong partisans generally say they like things about their own party but are frequently unable to name a single thing they like about the other party. On the other hand, they can name numerous dislikes about the opposition party and few likes for their own. For weak and leaning partisans, negative partisanship shows up most strongly not in their admiration of their own party, but in their dislike of the other party. Pure independents also name more things that they dislike about both of the parties than things they like, a point we will come back to in Chapter 7. Overall, these data reinforce the finding that the driving force of partisan identification in the United States today is negativity toward the opposition party.

One interesting corollary change over this period has been how strong Democrats and Republicans view the ideology of the two political parties. Each year, the ANES asks respondents how they would place both parties on an ideology scale. The categories on the scale range from 1 to 7 and in-clude: *extremely liberal* (1), *liberal* (2), *slightly liberal* (3), *moderate; middle*

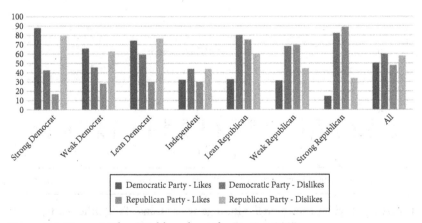

Figure 2.3 Percent Likes/Dislikes about the Parties, 2020
Source: Data are from the 2020 ANES.

of the road (4), *slightly conservative* (5), *conservative*" (6), and finally *ex-tremely conservative* (7). Figure 2.4 shows how strong Democrats and strong Republicans view the ideology of both their own party and the other party. What is striking is the consistency and the deviations. Both strong Republicans and strong Democrats view the Republican Party as some-where between "slightly conservative" and "conservative." Strong Republican respondents on average gave the Republican Party a score of 5.6 on the scale; strong Democrats responded that the Republican Party was slightly more conservative but substantively similar (5.9). But while both Strong Democrats and Strong Republicans view the Republican Party as somewhere between "slightly conservative" and "conservative," this average rating is not substantively different from how the Republican Party was viewed almost 50 years ago.

The larger divergence and substantive change over time is within perceptions of the ideology of the Democratic Party. On average, strong Republican respondents rated the Democratic Party in 2020 at a 1.58, squarely between *liberal* and *extremely liberal*. Strong Democrats, on the

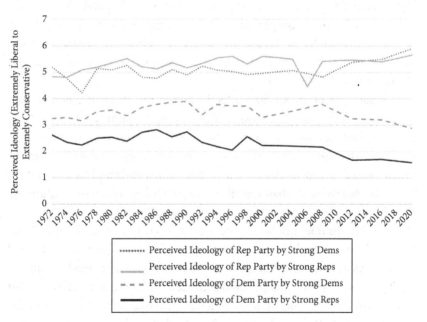

Figure 2.4 Ideological Categorization of the Other Party by Strong Democrats and Republicans

Source: Data are from the ANES Cumulative Data File.

other hand, viewed their party as much closer to "slightly liberal" (average rating of 2.88). Although strong Democrats and strong Republicans have always had divergent views on the ideology of the Democratic Party, that gap has grown over time, driven by Republicans' increasingly uniform view of the Democratic Party as very far left.

What is important and interesting about these statistics is that by all objective measures the Republican Party is much more conservative than the Democratic Party is liberal. Talk radio has coined the pejorative phrase "RINOs" to refer to "Republicans in Name Only" who break rank with their party and vote against bills endorsed by party leadership or who work with Democrats on bipartisan bills. Likewise, the left has coined their own "DINOs" to refer to Democrats who break with leadership or work in a bipartisan manner. There are far more "DINOs" than "RINOs," and the national Republican Party is more conservative in their votes in Congress than is the Democratic Party (Grossmann and Hopkins 2016; Hare and Poole 2014). In addition, measures of the ideology of the parties in Congress show that the major change in ideology in the last 60 years has been driven by the rightward shift of the Republican Party—while the Democratic Party has become slightly more liberal, Republican members of Congress have become considerably more conservative (McCarty 2011). This is illustrated by looking at the ideology estimates of polarization in the US House of Representatives using DW-Nominate scores in Figure 2.5 (Lewis et al. 2022).

The data presented so far, collectively, tell the story of negative partisanship. Americans, and especially strong partisans, are politically motivated by their disdain for the other party. Partisans have little respect for those who identify with the other party, and they see the other side as misinformed, misguided, and a threat to their ideals and to democracy. They also see them as ideologically extreme; this is especially true among Republicans.

However, this does not have to be the case—Democrats and Republicans could feel very warmly toward their party without feeling hostility toward the other side. One can certainly love one band more than another without feeling animosity and hatred toward the less preferred musical style. But today's politics is not one of more preferred, it is one defined by a hatred for the other side. In the next section we turn to changes in the information environment that have helped foster this negative, hostile, highly partisan political climate.

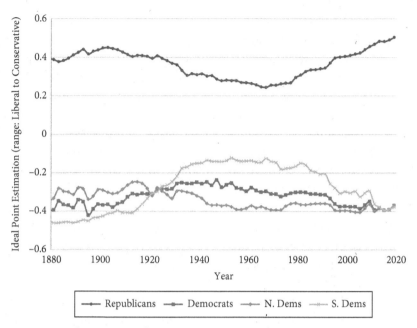

Figure 2.5 Polarization in the House, 1880–2019
Source: DW-nominate scores data are from Lewis et al. (2022).

2.4 The Changing Information Environment

The media landscape has changed tremendously in the last few decades. These changes in the information environment have certainly been contributing factors to the rise of polarization and negative partisanship. Here we highlight two changes that stand above the rest—the emergence of partisan media and the presence of social media in our daily lives.

2.4.1 The Rise of Partisan News

In the late nineteenth century, it was normal for daily newspapers to be platforms for the political parties. As Kaplan (2002, 2) explains, the press's "political advocacy extended well beyond the publication of a list of endorsements on election day, as our contemporary press is wont to do. Indeed, partisanship was a public and ubiquitous phenomenon that defined the very essence of nineteenth-century American journalism." However, in the early twentieth century, journalism changed: Papers broke free of their ties with the parties and the press created a new role and definition of the trade. This new press came with a journalist pledge of professionalism, neutrality, and impartiality, and with it a promise for a holistic approach to the news that would put the public interest above particularistic interests (Kaplan 2002). By the 1970s, broadcast television was both nonpartisan and the primary source of news for most people. The fact that TV news lacked a partisan slant and was aimed at and accessible to people without a college degree has been argued to be one reason for the centrist ideology of the era (Heese and Baloria 2017).

The age of the independent press and the nonpartisan investigative jour-nalist is not lost today. There remain nonpartisan objective outlets. However, while the objective press remains a stalwart of U.S. news, a partisan press has developed that now competes with the nonpartisan. These stations and hosts mirror the one-sided journalism of the 18th century but often present them-selves as objective journalists and appear on the same television stations as neutral news reporters.

The 1980s and 1990s transformed the media landscape. The changing na-ture of FM and AM radio, the rise of access to cable television, and the cor-responding Reagan administration's sweeping deregulations and the removal of the "Fairness Doctrine" ushered in two new forms of news and opinion to mass audiences—cable news networks, most notably the Fox News Channel (but also MSNBC) and talk radio with radio hosts such as Rush Limbaugh and Bob Grant. As political commentator David Foster Wallace explained well in a 2005 profile of John Ziegler, who was then a talk radio host in Los Angeles:

> The old, Rooseveltian logic of the Doctrine had been that since the airwaves belonged to everyone, a license to profit from those airwaves conferred on the broadcast industry some special obligation to serve the public in-terest. Commercial radio broadcasting was not, in other words, originally conceived as just another for-profit industry; it was supposed to meet a higher standard of social responsibility. After 1987, though, just another in-dustry is pretty much what radio became, and its only real responsibility now is to attract and retain listeners in order to generate revenue. In other words, the sort of distinction explicitly drawn by FCC Chairman Newton Minow in the 1960s—namely, that between "the public interest" and "merely what interests the public"—no longer exists. (Wallace 2005, para. 3)

A second large-scale public policy change, the 1996 Telecommunications Act, also transformed the information landscape. Prior to 1996, radio stations were mostly small businesses, what one might call "mom and pop" organizations that owned one or two stations in a market. They also tended to have a strong presence in community and local philanthropy and civic affairs. But after the passage of the 1996 Telecommunications bill, there was a "tidal wave of corporatization" that led to the mass sales and concentration of radio stations among a small number of corporate owners (Berry and Sobieraj 2011). For example, as of 2021, iHeartMedia, formerly Clear Channel Broadcasting, owned more than 850 AM and FM radio stations in the United States.

These corresponding policy events launched a new brand of journalism in the United States that was extremely partisan. Talk radio hosts did not ever try to hide their loyalty to a political party or ideological slant, and cable "news" personalities were branded by their ideological bona fides. Radio personality Bob Grant is largely attributed to coining the "combat talk" radio format that now is the norm among conservative talk show hosts. His show, which he pioneered in the 1970s and aired until 2013, urged listeners to call in with opinions that differed from his so that he could ridicule and fight with them on the air (Norman 1998). By the time Barack Obama was elected president in 2008, conservative talk show hosts on both talk radio and cable news were well versed in the language of negative partisanship. For example, Rush Limbaugh made headlines when he urged his listeners to engage in what he called "Operation Chaos" by switching parties and voting for Hillary Clinton in an effort to weaken Obama's chance of making it to the General Election after his campaign started to gather momentum (Walsh 2021).

Conservative and liberal partisan news is known for its negativity. Few shows highlight the policy successes of having navigated the sausage-making factory and produced real policy outcomes desired by their viewers. Instead, partisan news focuses primarily on defaming the other party's elected officials and candidates. Often these attacks are over exceptionally silly stuff, like what toppings to put on a hamburger (we will talk more about partisanship and food in Chapter 3), the color of a suit, or accidentally misspelling a word on Twitter. While in office, Barack Obama was famously called an elitist by Fox News commentator Sean Hannity for putting Dijon mustard on a hamburger.[2] Meanwhile, in January of 2019, Twitter erupted when President Trump served the Clemson Tigers football team McDonald's on their White House visit and, to add insult to injury, posted a picture boasting about it with the misspelling "hamberders."[3] President Obama was lambasted for wearing a tan suit to a press conference (as many presidents before him regularly had), but in Obama's case the color was so universally attacked by Republican partisan elites and the partisan media that it was labeled "suit gate" and for-ever changed Obama's suit color choices (Folley 2019).

While many hands have been wrung over whether partisan news is bad for America in normative terms, there have been measurable changes that can be traced to the rise of mainstream, widely available partisan news. One of the most meaningful of these studies is DellaVigna and Kaplan's (2007) research into the effect of Fox News on voting. Today, Fox News is available in over 87 million U.S. households (90.8% of television subscribers) and is the top-rated cable network, averaging 2.5 million viewers (Joyella 2021). But this did not happen overnight. Fox News was rolled out cable market by cable market, leading to a natural experiment—some towns had access to Fox News earlier than others. Between 1996 and 2000, Fox News grew from nonexistent to present in 35% of households and was watched by more than 17% of the population. DellaVigna and Kaplan made use of this natural experiment to see if towns with Fox News as part of their cable programming voted more Republican than towns without Fox News access. Their research found that towns with access to Fox News voted significantly more Republican in 2000 than the towns without access to Fox News and that the difference in support was enough to have played a sub-stantive role in the 2000 presidential election. More recent research has found similar effects on policy attitudes—while viewers today self-select into cable news outfits that fit their ideological preferences, exposure to those news outlets makes them more extreme in their policy views. For example, Gil de Zúñiga and colleagues (2012) found that even after accounting for self-selection, Fox viewers have more anti-immigrant attitudes than those who are not exposed to Fox but are otherwise ideologically similar.

Other partisan mainstream cable news media include MSNBC (launched in 1996), which caters to a more liberal and Democratic Party audience, and One America News Network (launched in 2013) and NewsMax (launched in 2014), both of which cater to strong Republican audiences.

2.4.2 The Rise of Social Media

Of course, the other change in the media and information landscape has been the introduction and mass adoption of social media apps such as Facebook, Instagram, TikTok, WhatsApp, and Twitter. These platforms introduced what had been unthinkable—widespread mass direct communication from partisan elites to those who trust them in a matter of seconds.

Prior to the introduction of social media platforms, journalists and the free press served as the "fourth estate." The press could choose what to print, fact-check, and give context to anything a politician or advocate said. Politicians could only reach a few thousand people or people who had somehow ended up on cultivated mailing lists directly. It took significant financial and time resources to get a message directly to voters. *The Phyllis Schlafly Report* is a notable example of the lengths political elites went to in order to get their message out. Starting in the early 1970s, the *Report* was mailed to her cultivated mailing list for years. The McGovern Campaign was largely credited with the advent of mass mailing for political causes on the left (Cornish 2012), just as Senator Jesse Helms was largely ascribed responsibility for starting and perfecting the move on the right (Mark 2008). But these efforts to speak directly to voters took weeks to turn around and significant financial backing.

Social media changed all of that. Facebook accounts and the like allowed social-media savvy elected officials and personalities like Donald Trump, before he was ever elected to office, to broadcast messages without the need to persuade journalists to write about them, give them credibility, or provide contrasting opinions and clarification on facts. It also allowed political elites to forego paying for and investing in traditional mass-mailing efforts. Instead, these platforms allowed politicians to interact daily or even hourly with masses of voters for free without anyone fact checking or offering a different perspective.

High-profile examples include the Twitter feeds of some of the most partisan personalities in history. For example, @realdonaldtrump, President Trump's Twitter handle, had almost 80 million subscribers before it was shut down after the January 6th insurrection on the US Capitol. As of December 2021, Democratic Representative Alexandria Ocasio-Cortez had over 12 million followers, while Republican Senator and former presidential candidate Ted Cruz had just over 4.5 million followers. Using these platforms, partisan elites can do everything from attack their opponents to endorse products to millions of people. And those tweets are shared by their subscribers to others in their social network who do not "follow" these elites directly.

2.4.3 The Consequences of the Corresponding Rise of Social Media and Partisan News

As these changes took place, many people foresaw a media heyday in which citizens could reach far more news than ever before and overcome government sponsorship and corporate media conglomeration and instead access independent investigative news. Information would bring power to the people. The "Arab Spring"—a series of anti-government protests, uprisings, and armed rebellions that spread across much of the Middle East in the early 2010s—was seen as a sign of the positive democratic surge that would result from the increased ability for people to share news and organize through social media. And while this increased ability for people to organize and march has proven true, the other side of the coin has meant that people also have much more access to reinforcing propaganda, intentional and unintentional misinformation, and an increased distrust in any news that does not reinforce their preconceived ideas.

At first, the rise of social media and cable and radio news suggested that people would have a "marketplace of ideas" to choose from; they would hear more about and from a diverse set of viewpoints. By all indications, the American public does not live in media or social network silos; it is common for people to come across conflicting ideas and information from "the other side" while online (Barberá 2020) and in their news consumption (Mitchell et al. 2014). However, there are large differences between what Democrats and Republicans watch, hear, share, and, most importantly, trust (Eady et al. 2019).

The 2020 ANES included a battery of questions regarding the sources through which respondents accessed their news regarding the election. Respondents were first asked which sources, including radio, television, newspapers, and websites, they used to access information about the election. Then, depending on which they chose, they were asked, "Which of the following [radio programs/television programs/websites/newspapers] do you [listen to/watch/read] regularly?" Figure 2.6 presents the distribution across the 7-point party identification scale for a variety of news programs and platforms. Importantly, this figure shows the difference between the news consumption of strong partisans, weak partisans, leaning partisans, and independents.

Independents are more likely to report not following the presidential campaign using any of the media asked about. Strong Democrats are much more likely than any other group, including strong Republicans, to utilize traditional print newspapers. One important note, as well, is that Democrats report getting their news from a wider variety of platforms and shows than Republicans (Mitchell et al. 2014).

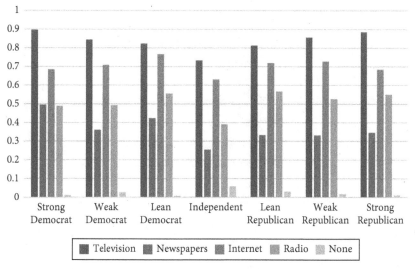

Figure 2.6 Campaign Information Sources, 2020
Source: Data are from the 2020 ANES.

In Figure 2.7, we present the distribution of media outlet choices across party identification. The data indicate not only how news media consumption can indicate a tendency toward partisan echo chambers to an extent, but also how there is some overlap in the consumption of media, even across the most partisan of news sources. For example, of those who reported reading the *Wall Street Journal*, 23% were strong Democrats and 17% were strong Republicans. Likewise, Anderson Cooper's audience was made up of 32% strong Democrats and 27% strong Republicans. These are diverse and bipartisan audiences. However, we find predictable silos as well, particularly on radio and the internet. For example, Sean Hannity's audience was 60% strong Republican, similar to that of Rush Limbaugh (57%) and Glenn Beck (53%), whereas only 1% to 2% of the respondents who said they listened to these shows were strong Democrats. For NPR, the polarization was the opposite but not nearly as strong; about 31% of the audience was strong Democrats and only 8% strong Republicans. Use of internet websites for information shows a similar polarization—Breitbart.com's audience was about 45% strong Republicans and only 3% strong Democrats, whereas the *New York Times* website Nytimes.com's audience was 38% strong Democrats and only 7% strong Republicans.

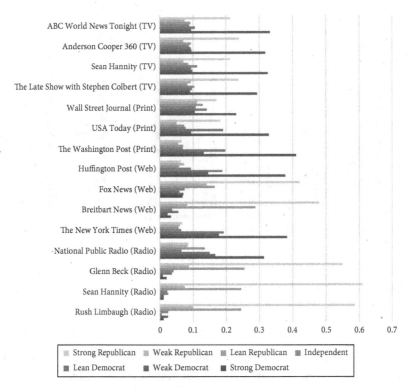

Figure 2.7 Polarization of Viewership
Source: Data are from the 2020 ANES.

To many, the distribution presented in Figure 2.7 is reassuring—the siloing of news exposure is not nearly as extreme as some commentators suggest. It is certainly not the case that all strong Democrats are nightly watching Rachel Maddow while all strong Republicans are tuning in to Sean Hannity. Even on some highly partisan shows, viewers from both sides report tuning in at least somewhat regularly.

While this could seem reassuring, the likely product of this cross-cutting exposure is not the democratic ideal most would hope for. The research had been strong and convincing that exposure to views that contradict your own can lead to moderation and understanding. However, it is critical that the contradictory information comes from trusted sources and, if at all possible, contacts with whom the person feels affinity (Mutz 2006). This is where we see Figure 2.7 as unrepresentative of the true media behavior of the American public. Because instead of listening to the different sides and weighing the arguments in a manner that democratic theorists have always seen as the ideal, the rise in negative partisanship has corresponded with a polarization of trust in media sources, largely driven by an increasing distrust among Republicans in the mainstream, nonpartisan news sources.

The ANES has not asked consistently about respondents' trust in the media over the last 40 years. ANES respondents were asked, "How much of the time do you think you can trust the media to report the news fairly? Just about always, most of the time, only some of the time, or almost never?" in 1996, 1998, 2000, 2004, 2008, and then again in 2020. Figure 2.8 presents the mean level of trust in the news media for Republicans, Democrats, and independents in each of these years. Between 1996 and 2008, trust in the media ebbed for both Democrats and Republicans, with Republicans always trusting the news a bit less than independents, and independents a bit less than Democrats. But these differences were, on par, quite small. In 2020, Republican trust decreased by 45%. As of 2020, Republicans had a mean trust of 1.73, squarely between *almost never* (1) and *only some of the time* (2) on the 5-point scale.

What Figure 2.8 does not show are the important changes in trust in media sources. While overall trust has declined among Republicans, Republicans still trust specific news sources. To evaluate this, we turn to data from the

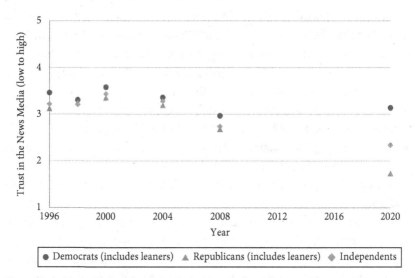

Figure 2.8 Trust in the News Media by Party Identification, 1996–2020
Source: Data are from the ANES Cumulative Data File.

Pew Research Center. In 2014 and 2020, Pew ran surveys in which they asked respondents about a variety of news outlets with substantial audiences across the different media platforms including major broadcast and cable TV networks, public broadcasters, political radio shows, high-circulation national newspapers, high-traffic digital news outlets, and international news sources with a substantial readership in the United States, among others (Gramlich 2020). First, the respondents were asked if they had heard of each of the 30 news outlets chosen for the study. If they had heard of it, they were then asked if they trusted it specifically for political and election-related news. As there is a difference between expressly trusting an outlet and actively distrusting, they asked a second question of those who said they did not trust the outlet regarding if they distrusted it. The analysis is illuminating to understand the true information environment.

Overall, while Democrats expressed active trust in a larger number of platforms (22 out of 30 sources), Republicans reported active distrust in a large number of platforms (20 out of 30 sources). Republicans expressed more trust than distrust in only seven sources. Most importantly, the most trusted four sources are the most highly partisan in the study—Fox News, Sean Hannity, Rush Limbaugh, and Breitbart. For example, in the Pew study, 65% of Republicans said they trusted Fox News while 19% distrusted it. Likewise, 30% of Republicans said they trusted Sean Hannity's show while only 10% said they distrusted it. These numbers were flipped for Democrats—61% of Democrats expressed active distrust and only 23% expressed trust in Fox News. For Sean Hannity's show, 38% of Democrats expressed active distrust and less than 1% of respondents reported actively trusting the show. The other three sources that Republicans had more trust than distrust in (PBS, the BBC, and the *Wall Street Journal*) did not have high levels of trust: 27% (PBS), 24% (BBC), and 20% (WSJ) of Republicans reported trusting these sources, whereas 20% (PBS), 16% (BBC) and 19% (WSJ) of Republicans reported distrusting these sources. Among Democrats, trust in these sources was very high—56% (PBS), 48% (BBC), 38% (WSJ) and distrust very low, with only 4% to 7% reporting active distrust in these sources (Jurkowitz et al. 2020).

Republicans' distrust in the media is largely a self-fulfilling prophecy. The demonization of the mainstream news is the *ostinato* of the sources Republicans report listening to and trusting such as Fox News, Sean Hannity, and Breitbart. Republicans tune in and largely hear that what they are told on other stations is untrustworthy "fake news" by their trusted leaders and their trusted media personalities. Of course, most notably, President Donald Trump's arsenal of attacks against the *New York Times*, CNN, and other mainstream outlets became one of the most common tropes of his time in office. And any news organization that published objective or opinion articles that did not portray his presidency in a positive light was lambasted as "fake" and as having a political agenda.

Recent research underscores that the choice of cable news channel that one watches matters a great deal. For example, Broockman and Kalla (2022) utilized a field experiment to see if one's media diet makes a difference. They incentivized (through a cash payment) a randomly chosen set of Fox News watchers to switch to watching CNN for a month. The change of station increased participants' factual perceptions of current events and knowledge about the 2020 presidential candidate's positions. It also changed what issues they thought were important, and their policy attitudes about those issues. For example, Fox to CNN watchers started caring more about Covid-19 and less about violence at protests. The problem, of course, is that it is difficult to imagine the real-world circumstances under which we could stop getting respondents to watch their trusted media sources in favor of watching something else.

The self-fulfilling prophecy has also been borne out in social media behavior. Those who subscribed to @realDonaldTrump before its permanent suspension, @AOC, or the Twitter, TikTok, or other social media feeds of just about any partisan elite, are fed a steady diet of attacks on the other party directly from trusted partisan elites (Russell 2018, 2021). To be sure, it is true that even though they number in the millions, the people who follow politicians are not representative of the general public. Twitter is not real life. Not exactly. However, research on "normal" social media users also confirms the partisan bias in the information environment (Settle 2018). Democrats and Republicans active on social media are highly likely to share posts and have posts shared with them that benefit their side and degrade the other. To quote social media researcher Chris Bail (2021), social media "distorts our identities, empowers status-seeking extremists, and renders moderates all but invisible." And when people do come across cross-cutting news and accounts through social media that challenge their side, they tend to boomerang, becoming more partisan and more extreme in their policy views. Chris Bail and his colleagues (2018) found that not only did partisans who followed a Twitter bot that was intentionally designed to give them posts that contradicted their position become more extreme in their views, the more they engaged with those posts, the more extreme they became; a finding that has been replicated and extended by others (Yang, Qureshi, and Zaman 2022).

This research suggests that exposure through social and news media to ideas that contradict one's own does not work in the same way traditional contact has and is theorized to work (e.g., Mutz 2006). Instead of cross-cutting information making people more moderate and understanding, exposure to ideas that do not support one's political positions seem to just create more polarization (Wojcieszak 2010). Moreover, and importantly, when people are exposed to a steady stream of one-sided, reinforcing information, it increases the probability that they will engage in civic or political activity (Krupnikov and Ryan 2022; Wojcieszak et al. 2016). As a result, there is an echo chamber between partisan elites and partisans in the electorate: Partisan information silos increase the likelihood that elected officials will hear from the voter through electoral and issue campaigns.

This finding is largely explained because people seek to reinforce their ideas and appear "right." Recent research by Osmundsen et al. (2021) found in their study of news sharing on Twitter that strong and leaning Democrats actually share many more news posts than strong and leaning Republicans, but those posts are just as likely to favor their perspective. Democrats share news on social media that bolsters Democrats' positions and denigrates Republicans, and Republicans share news that positively portrays Republicans and vilifies Democrats. Often, this search for reinforcing posts to share caused people to seek out and share misinformation (also see Guess et al. [2021], who find conservatives are more likely than liberals to share "fake news"). As Osmundsen et al. (2021) summarize their research:

> The sharing of false news has less to do with ignorance than with partisan political affiliation and the news available to partisans for use in denigrating their opponents. While Republicans are more likely to share fake news than Democrats, the sharing of such material is a bipartisan phenomenon. What differs is the news sources available to partisans on either side of the political spectrum. In a highly polarized political climate, Democrats and Republicans both search for material with which to denigrate their political opponent, and in this search, Republicans are forced to seek out the fake-news extreme in order to confirm views that are increasingly out of step with the mainstream media. Seen from this perspective, the spread of fake

news is not an endogenous phenomenon but a symptom of our polarized societies—complicating our search for policy solutions. (para. 3)

The changes we document in this chapter moved power from voters and groups of citizens to political elites. Elites once were in the business of recruiting voters to their side by championing policies that unaligned or weakly aligned voters preferred (Karol 2009; Layman 2001). In these times, groups of voters who felt strongly about a policy or issue could garner the ear of party officials and elected leaders. But today, party elites make their livelihoods leading policy discourse by communicating directly to their most ardent supporters—strong partisans—why the other party is a threat, why their policies are best, why they should never listen to other opinions, and how anything you may read that undermines their position is a lie. Social media allows elites to sell this bill of goods directly to their most supportive followers and have their message shared through a network of co-partisans. The rise of partisan news gives them an eager core of media personalities ready to put their message on the radio, TV, and in online and print newspapers and blogs to reach partisans not connected through social media. In turn, this creates a further hollowing of the center as few opinions are available that provide support for or objectively weigh the actual proposals of both parties. In short, polarization with the current information marketplace begets polarization.

2.5 Conclusion

In this chapter, we have shown how, over the last 40 years, the electorate has become much stronger in their partisan preferences. There has been a hollowing out of those only tangentially attached to a political party and a growth in those who are strongly partisan. A key component of the rise of strong partisanship is the concomitant rise of negative partisanship— identification against the out-party as a means of justification of party identification.

This growth has happened at the same time as the development of a cadre of strongly partisan news outlets that have allowed those who seek information about politics to find one-sided information that either supports their side or attacks and vilifies the other side. It has also happened at the same time as the advent of social media, which allows political elites to avoid the media altogether and speak directly to voters. The conflagration of these forces has led partisan elites, we argue, to have far more influence than ever before over their adherents' positions. In the next few chapters, we use a series of experiments to show just how political polarization and elite messaging can change people's opinions and how social science theories are undermined by the rise in strong and negative partisanship.

3

Partisanship, Policy, Compromise, and the Non-Political

3.1 Introduction

Right before the 2016 Presidential election, James Comey, the Director of the Federal Bureau of Investigation, announced to Congress that his organization was reviewing new emails related to Hillary Clinton's time as Secretary of State, effectively reopening an inquiry that was considered closed. For quite a time after that, Comey was blamed by many commentators for costing Secretary Clinton the election and effectively handing the election to Donald Trump (Silver 2017). The polls among the public reflect this sentiment. In January of 2017, Quinnipiac found that most Democrats who had expressed an opinion about Comey disapproved of how he was handling his job. If one divided the data by gender, education, race, or age, there was no noticeable difference between groups. The meaningful difference was by party identification: 85% of Democrats who recognized Comey disliked him. Republicans, on the other hand, were split almost 50/50 (Quinnipiac University Poll 2017).

Flash forward to April 2018. Comey had at this point disclosed that the FBI was investigating links between Donald Trump's presidential campaign staff and Russia, an action that made Comey public enemy number one in the eyes of the President and his staff. The President went so far as to regularly tweet his rage at the man he called "Lyin' James Comey." Polling at this time, also by Quinnipiac, showed that the public opinion tide had turned. As Democrats heard that Comey was investigating Trump and Republicans heard the rage out of the oval office, partisans in the electorate appeared to experience public opinion "whiplash," to quote NBC political correspondent Steve Kornacki. By that time, 89% of Republicans who had an opinion on Comey had an unfavorable opinion of him, while among Democrats who had an opinion, 71% viewed him favorably (Quinnipiac University Poll 2018).

The Power of Partisanship. Joshua J. Dyck and Shanna Pearson-Merkowitz, Oxford University Press.
© Oxford University Press 2023. DOI: 10.1093/oso/9780197623787.003.0004

The dramatic change in views of James Comey is but one example of how strong partisanship can lead to unstable viewpoints—about people and even policy attitudes—in a dynamic political environment where political elites and political parties are changing sides.

In this chapter, we transition from theory to implications. Our discussion thus far has focused on the growth of strong parties and negative partisanship, the declining value of information and the increasing relationship between elites, partisan cues, and partisan information filtering mechanisms. Our goal is to now consider the consequences of this on the mass public. What has happened to Americans as a result? We present empirical tests to demonstrate the effects of partisan-motivated reasoning and negative partisanship on policy positions, attitudes toward democratic norms of compromise, and non-political preferences. The analyses we present in this chapter suggest not only that partisan-motivated reasoning exists, but that it has found its way into the public psyche on policy issues, system values, and even seemingly inane everyday non-political preferences. The cup of partisan-motivated reasoning runneth over.

3.2 Partisanship and Policy

We begin our examination with a simple query: How strongly does partisanship shape issue preferences? We are most interested in testing this in a *dynamic* environment. That is, what ability does partisanship have to cause changes in policy positions? This research question is of particular interest because it allows us to determine if party identification occurs prior to issue positions, allowing us to show that issue preferences are indeed responsive to party identification and not the other way around. In the prior chapters, we argue that party identification structures attitude formation, and that partisans will adopt issue positions promoted by co-partisan elites even if they are inconsistent with previously held beliefs or are counter to the traditional expectations of a political ideology. Here we provide the data to test and support that proposition.

To test the ability of partisanship to drive changes in policy positions, we make use of two types of causal designs. The first involves a temporal study of attitude change during an election campaign using pre- and post-election data. The second uses an experimental framework to test whether exposure to partisan cues affects policy attitudes—each approach has its benefits and drawbacks, but together they help us go beyond correlational studies and parcel out cause and effect.

While we propose that partisanship is a critical driver of policy positions, we also expect some issues to be more resistant to change than others. Issues that are so long on the political agenda that they allow voters to have gut responses on the policy tend to be very resistant to change (Carmines and Stimson 1980; Dyck and Pearson-Merkowitz 2019). As a result, even if a voter's mind would change over several election cycles of the party branding the issue differently, we would not expect any change in a single election, particularly on morality policy issues (Carsey and Layman 2006). Thus, we would not expect positions on things like abortion, a classic "easy issue" for voters, to change if an elite like Donald Trump chose to endorse a pro-choice agenda (also because he would never have made it to the national stage with that position given the role of the religious right in the Republican Party). But on issues that are more complex and less grounded in morality or religious tenets, we expect voters to be very amenable to following elite cues.

The first test comes from a module we added to the 2014 Cooperative Congressional Election Study. The study design involved asking respondents for their opinions on a series of issues—raising the minimum wage, the auto bailout, concern with other parts of the world, free trade, and contraceptive coverage in healthcare. Respondents were asked these questions in the pre-election survey and then again after the election. We put this array of questions on both surveys with the hope that some of these issues would become salient during the presidential election and some would not, which would allow us to test our hypothesis; and, luckily, that is what happened. Our goal with this modeling strategy is to see if the campaign strengthens the association of party identification with policy attitudes. If policy attitudes are set, we should see no change in the model between the pre- and post-election surveys. If partisan elites help their voters develop policy positions, one would expect a better model fit in the post-election models than the pre-election models.

To do this, we modeled support for each policy as a function of a small set of demographic variables and party identification and assessed model fit with both Akaike's information criterion (AIC) and the Bayesian information criterion (BIC). The model fit statistics are presented in Table 3.1, and all of the regression models are presented in appendix Table A3.1. The models were restricted so that only respondents who answered both the pre- and post-election questions were included. For both AIC and BIC, a smaller

Table 3.1 AIC/BIC Statistics for Pre/ Post Election Models, Party Identification → Policy Issues, 2014

	Pre-election	Post-election	Pre-election	Post-election	Post-election model is better fit?
Policy issue	AIC	AIC	BIC	BIC	*
Minimum wage	1,927.19	1,907.12	1,999.55	1,976.49	*
Auto bailout	1,955.61	1,948.28	2,024.95	2,017.63	*
Concern with other parts of the world	1,994.75	1,955.13	2,064.09	2,024.47	*
Free trade	552.08	553.67	612.54	614.13	
Contraceptives as part of healthcare	734.24	778.01	803.38	847.15	

Notes: Data are from the 2014 Cooperative Congressional Election Survey, UMass Lowell Module. Models are restricted to respondents who answered both pre- and post-election survey. Full models are presented in the appendix, in Table A3.1.

number indicates a stronger model fit. We observe that on the issues of the minimum wage, the auto bailout, and foreign policy, the campaign appears to have amplified the connection between party identification and these issue attitudes—people's issue positions came into line with the information supplied in the campaign by partisan elites. As we suspected, there is no evidence of this for the issue of free trade, which did not play a major, if any, role in the campaign, and healthcare/contraceptives, which is long on the political agenda and is part of the larger debate about birth control and abortion that has maintained a prominent role for both Republicans and Democrats in campaigns since the 1980s.

What should we make of these results? First and foremost, for issues that appear to have been more central to the 2014 campaign—particularly the focus on the minimum wage—we see that the campaign strengthens the relationship between party identification and issue attitudes, calling attention to the issues that are on the agenda. We are cautious however, not to overgeneralize from this one year as 2014 was a relatively low-stimulus midterm election that lacked an overarching theme or national issue. However, what these results also show is that the link between party identification and issue positions is still increasing—partisans are becoming more polarized in their issue positions over time, voters have not "plateaued," so to speak. Instead, voters are becoming even more aligned across more issues. And, most critically, the results show that the information environment is the key to that process. We do not witness voters changing parties to align with elites on these issues; instead, we see voters becoming more polarized on the issues that the candidates debated. Critically, it is strong partisans who are driving these results. Take, for instance, the minimum wage. The average distance on the 4-point scale between strong Democrats and strong Republicans increases by 4 percentage points from the pre-election to post-election survey. Thus, our results so far suggest that while candidates clarify issue positions of the party, this also helps co-partisans in the electorate, especially strong partisans, align their views. To be sure, what this test cannot do is tell us whether this effect is driven by negative partisanship (a gut response to reject the other party's position) or positive partisanship (a result of a favorable view of the co-partisan leader's position).

We provide a second test of the relationship between partisanship and issue attitude change in Table 3.2. Here, we present the results of an experiment we conducted in 2018. Respondents read statements about proposed policy changes: (1) changing the federal minimum wage from $7.25 to $15.00 an hour, (2) allowing school officials to carry guns in schools to combat the problem of school shootings, (3) providing a pathway to citizenship for undocumented immigrants, and (4) including a provision that requires two-thirds of legislators to support a budget before it can pass. This last policy is perhaps familiar to Californians but likely not to other residents of the United States. In each case, respondents were randomly assigned to either a control group that referred to the policy change as proposed by "elected officials" or one of two randomized treatments: "Democratic Party Leaders in Congress" or "Republican Party Leaders in Congress." To use the minimum wage as our example, respondents were presented with the following type of question, with the randomized component in bracketed italics:

As you know, the federal minimum wage is currently set at $7.25 an hour. [Random assignment: *Elected officials/Democratic Party Leaders in Congress/Republican Party Leaders in Congress*] have proposed legislation that would increase the federal minimum wage to $15 an hour. To what extent do you favor or oppose increasing the federal minimum wage to $15 an hour?

Respondents were given four choices of responses including *strongly oppose* (1), *somewhat oppose* (2), *somewhat support* (3), and *strongly support* (4).

Table 3.2 Partisan Policy Cue Experiment Results, 2018

	Treatment	All respondents	Democrats	Republicans
Minimum wage	As you know, the federal minimum wage is currently set at $7.25 an hour. [*Elected officials*] have proposed legislation that would increase the federal minimum wage to $15 an hour. To what extent do you favor or oppose increasing the federal minimum wage to $15 an hour?	2.66	3.44	1.90
	[*Democratic Party leaders in Congress*]	2.59	3.39	1.73
	[*Republican Party leaders in Congress*]	2.73	3.43	1.87
	Treatment	**All respondents**	**Democrats**	**Republicans**
Arming teachers	In response to recent school shootings, [*some elected officials*] have proposed allowing teachers and school officials to carry guns in schools. To what extent do you favor or oppose allowing teachers to carry guns in schools?	2.32	1.53	3.10
	[*Democratic Party leaders in Congress*]	2.32	1.62	3.12
	[*Republican Party leaders in Congress*]	2.33	1.51	3.17
	Treatment	**All respondents**	**Democrats**	**Republicans**
Pathway to citizenship	As you may know, many immigrants who came illegally to the U.S. when they were children now have temporary legal status that is ending. [*Elected officials*] have proposed legislation granting them permanent legal status. To what extent do you favor or oppose granting legal status to immigrants brought to the United States as children?	2.84	3.49	2.26

Table 3.2 Continued

	Treatment	All respondents	Democrats	Republicans
	[Democratic Party leaders in Congress]	2.67[†]	3.47	1.88[**]
	[Republican Party leaders in Congress]	2.80	3.37	2.33
	Treatment	All respondents	Democrats	Republicans
Two-thirds budgetary requirement	Some states have passed a law that requires two-thirds of the legislature to agree to a budget before it can pass. Elected officials in Congress have proposed legislation to make this a requirement for the US Congress. To what extent do you favor or oppose a two-thirds budget requirement at the federal level?	2.79	2.80	2.71
	[Democratic Party leaders in Congress]	2.69	3.12[**]	2.21[**]
	[Republican Party leaders in Congress]	2.69	2.54[*]	2.89[†]

Notes: Data are from the 2018 YouGov survey. See the appendix for more details. Difference of means tests are computed between the treatment group and the control group. All scales are coded: 1 = strongly oppose, 2 = somewhat oppose, 3 = somewhat favor, 4 = strongly favor.

$N = 1,000$.

[†] p < .10, [*] p < .05, [**] p < .01, two-tailed tests reported..

This experiment was designed to provide respondents the ability to respond to "easier" issues that they likely had heard of, such as gun control, the minimum wage, and immigration reform, and "harder" issues that they had not heard debated before, like the two-thirds budget requirement. In each instance, there is also a set of respondents who receive "misinformation" cues. Congressional Republicans have not argued we should increase the minimum wage; however, this category exists.

Not surprisingly, given the nature of our previous work on "easy issues" (Dyck and Pearson-Merkowitz 2019; Evans and Pearson-Merkowitz 2012), on the minimum wage and gun control, which are perhaps the two "easiest" issues and those most ingrained in the political environment, the provided partisan cues are unconvincing to survey respondents. As one would expect with an issue long on the political agenda, we observe large differences between Democrats and Republicans in how they respond to the policy issue at hand for all three categories, regardless of the cue provided/treatment group assigned. Republicans are more opposed to gun control and the minimum wage regardless of the cue presented, and Democrats are more in favor of these things regardless of the cue.

However, on immigration reform we find evidence of cue-taking behavior and negative partisanship. Republicans are less likely to favor a pathway to citizenship than Democrats, not surprisingly, but, when Republicans are told that Congressional Democrats have proposed the plan, they become significantly more opposed to it. We will return to this point about "Republican-only" effects in the following section, but for now, this provides some evidence of negative partisanship framing issue debates.

An important fact to note here is that on the minimum wage and gun control the Republican Party has been very consistent for decades. While there have been a few elite defectors in each party over the last few decades, it is plainly evident that Republicans are overwhelmingly opposed to minimum wage increases and are supportive of increasing the number of guns in civilian hands used for security, while Democrats are those who support gun control and support minimum wage increases. However, on immigration, the Republican Party has experienced a sea change which makes their position less stable. In the 1990s, Republicans supported a very open immigration system because it supported business and economic growth. However, as immigration and racial resentment have become tied together, Republicans have become adamantly anti-immigration even though businesses, particularly farms and other agrobusinesses but also construction and many factories, are reliant on the labor. However, while many observers have pointed to racial resentment as the sole reason for Republican opposition to immigration, our results show significant differences among Republicans who were told Democrats supported the path to citizenship and the control. In short, our results suggest that the Democratic Party's embrace of undocumented immigrants may be further driving Republican opposition, a finding that strongly supports an expansion of negative partisanship.

On the final experimental issue, however, the two-thirds budget requirement, we see the most dramatic effects. Keep in mind that this is an issue where Americans likely know the least about where the parties stand. For a time in the 1990s, Republicans had staked out ground as the party of fiscal discipline as part of the Contract with America. However, both parties have run deficits. Furthermore, the issue pushes compromise as much as it does fiscal discipline and so might be seen by some respondents as a non-partisan reform issue like term limits. On this issue, all four of the treatments produce significant effects from the control group. That is, telling Democrats that the budget requirement is a Democratic bill increases their support for the bill, but telling them that it is a Republican bill decreases their support for the bill. Similarly, telling Republicans that it is a Republican bill increases their support, while telling them it's a Democratic bill drastically decreases their support. Interestingly, for Democrats, the size of the relative increase and decrease are about the same (+.32, –.26), but for Republicans, learning that it is a Democratic bill produces the single largest effect in the experiment (a change in the mean of about half a point on a 4-point scale).

Might we learn more if we did this exercise with 40 issues instead of four? Certainly. However, the experimental evidence reveals important insights. First, on some issues, it is likely that issue association with party is so strong that it is difficult to change it; we certainly cannot simulate a long-term change with a simple cue in a survey experiment. However, we have seen the ability of vocal leaders to move their parties on issues. We have mentioned this already, but it bears repeating the mental gymnastics involved in understanding how the Democratic Party became the party of free trade and the Republican Party became the party of protectionism by 2019. Second, we also see that on issues that fall into the "hard" issue typology, learning where the parties stand matters greatly, and voters follow the party cues. The two-thirds budget requirement experiment illustrates this perfectly as each treatment produced not just a significant effect but a substantive effect for Republicans that is much larger when they receive a negative cue (i.e., Democrats supported it) than a positive cue (i.e., Republicans supported it). Interestingly, Democrats showed more signs of "learning" based on cues from either side. Finally, we also see the effects of negative affect toward the out-party (e.g., negative partisanship) and the role this plays in structuring opinions. Once we know who the bad guys are, all we need to know is what "they" believe to decide that "we" do not agree. These findings are critical to understanding today's polarized partisanship in which party leaders change positions both on long- and short-term issues and strong partisans seem to fall in line and be outraged by the position of the other party even when it was something their party once endorsed.

3.3 Partisanship, Bipartisanship, and Compromise

Having examined the link between partisanship and policy attitudes, we now turn to investigating how support for legislative negotiations is affected by both relative group position and negative partisanship. Understanding the effect of partisanship on compromise is critical because it is central to the functioning of democratic institutions and is so foreign to how people have believed the American public behaved historically.

As of the 1990s, many pundits and political scientists argued that Americans preferred ideological balance in the Federal government, and intentionally (or unintentionally) voted to balance the political parties through split-ticket voting. As Jacobson (1991) noted in his article "Explaining Divided Government: Why Can't Republicans Win the House?":

> Public support for divided government has grown as divided government has persisted. An October 1990 NBC News/ Wall Street Journal survey posed this question: "In general, do you think it is better for the same political party to control both the Congress and the presidency, so they can work together more closely, or do you think it is better to have different political parties controlling Congress and the presidency to prevent either one from going too far?" [In 1990,] Only 23 percent of the respondents thought it better for a single party to control both institutions, while 67 percent preferred divided control (10 percent were not sure). (p. 642)

Central to the arguments for why Americans preferred divided government was that they wanted the parties to have to compromise—thereby protecting the system from either party taking the country too far right or too far left. Even in the face of growing partisan rancor, affective/negative partisanship, and hostility, Americans still say they generally prefer candidates who favor compromise. Gallup has regularly asked respondents about their preferences for compromise versus sticking to their beliefs. In Figure 3.1, we present the distribution of responses to this question collected at eight data points from 2010 to 2017 (Jones and Saad 2017). In general, the Gallup data confirm that Americans are much more supportive of leaders who embrace rather than eschew compromise. The percentage of respondents saying it is more important to compromise is greater than the percentage saying it is more important for leaders to stick to their beliefs (between 19 and 36 percentage points), and this range widens over time. At every data

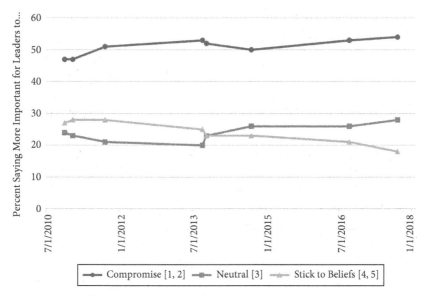

Figure 3.1 Preferences for Compromise, 2010–2017

Source: Data are from Gallup Poll Nov. 4–7, 2010; Jan. 7–9, 2011; Sep. 8–11, 2011; Sep. 5–8, 2013; Oct. 3–6, 2013; Sep. 4–7, 2014; Sep. 7–11, 2016; Sep. 6–10, 2017 (Jones and Saad 2017). The question asked respondents to rate themselves from 1 to 5, where 1 means it is more important for political leaders to compromise in order to get things done and 5 means it is more important for political leaders to stick to their beliefs even if little gets done.

point collected after September 2011, the majority of respondents prefer compromise. Quite interestingly, these data were collected over a period when the politics of brinksmanship over previously routine procedures, like raising the debt ceiling, became common and regularly threatened government shutdowns. They were also collected over the same period as the rise of the assaults against RINOs and DINOs (Republicans/Democrats in name only) that was applied to government officials willing to compromise with the other party, and the rise of "pledges," such as Grover Norquist's "Taxpayer Protection Pledge" (Americans for Tax Reform 2022) and the Republican Party's "Pledge to America" (Montopoli and Jackson 2010).

However, the fact that American institutions use supermajority veto points and separation of powers among coequal branches of government, including a bicameral legislature, also creates a system that favors gridlock. Compromise will not always be produced by such a system; more often than not, its close, and less attractive, cousin gridlock rears its ugly head instead. Part of what Americans find especially distasteful about American democracy, and about Congress in particular, is precisely the fact that there are seemingly endless arguments, protracted conflict, and gridlock. Gridlock may be, from an institutional perspective, as American as apple pie, but to most Americans it might as well be a mud pie. This is important because while Americans have an obvious knee-jerk reaction that favors compromise among legislatures, it is less clear that they favor the complicated system that makes compromise necessary. As Hibbing and Theiss-Morse (2002) wrote:

> People do not want to have to meet under Rousseau's oak tree to resolve political issues; they want someone else to meet. But they want the people who meet to be intimately in touch with the realities of the lives of ordinary people—realities they believe to be generally universal. If this is the case, disagreements among those who meet will be virtually nonexistent, and deciding what to do will be quick and painless. Governing experts will implement decisions in the most efficient manner, and the public will not have to hear about delays, debates, compromises, gridlock, egos, and agendas. (pp. 157–158)

However, there is also ample evidence that while people profess to support compromise, they do not actually like it when their legislative leaders do so. Anyone familiar with the fate of the Affordable Care Act, better known as "ObamaCare," will lament the public's stated support for compromise. Leading up to the 2008 election, a large majority of voters supported health care reform that would expand coverage for the uninsured and sick and increase access to health care (Gelman, Lee, and Ghitza 2010). However, as the legislative debate over the Affordable Care Act progressed, both Democrats and Republicans ended up unhappy with the outcome. Even more bizarre was that the blueprint for the legislation was a Heritage Foundation plan from the early 1990s. As Gelman et al. note (2010), the shift in the polls was "interpreted variously as dissatisfaction with 'Obamacare' in particular, as a more general realization that health care reform cannot be all things to all people, or as a reflection of general political polarization" (p. 1) Yet, when polled, the majority of respondents from both parties tend to support all but one of the elements that were included in the Affordable Care Act (Bialik and Geiger 2016). In addition, polls have found that what you call the program strongly determines public support. If you ask people how they feel about "Obamacare," support is much lower than if you ask them how they feel about the "Affordable Care Act," despite the fact that they are the same program: 47% opposed the program when referred to as Obamacare, whereas only 37% opposed the program when it was labeled the Affordable Care Act (CNN 2013).

In the academic literature, the most thorough treatment of compromise is given by Wolak (2020). In the book, Wolak argues that even in the age of polarization, compromise is a more common value among Americans than we might expect. This stems largely from the fact that there is a socialized aspect to valuing compromise. Yet, we also see partisan differences as out-partisans are more likely to value compromise from the other party. Perhaps one of Wolak's most optimistic findings is that because of false consensus effects, as individuals become aware of preference heterogeneity, they become more likely to value compromise.

Our question is: What happens when people find themselves in the minority (or when they find themselves in the majority, and thus compromise means giving in unnecessarily)? Does minority status make them more likely to seek out and value compromise (or candidates who promote compromise), or does it lead them to seek candidates who will hold firm to values and not compromise? Thinking about our Obamacare example, we return to this question: How do we contextualize majorities of people feeling supportive of the basic tenants of a law but opposing the law and opposing one name over another? We think negative partisanship and relative group position explain this quite well. People's perceptions of compromise, we argue, are wrapped up in their perceptions of their relative group position.

It is easy to say you value compromise in response to a survey even if you would not value it in practice; we see this as a social desirability effect. For instance, in the 2020 American National Election Study, a third of respondents indicated that they engaged in split-ticket voting at the federal level, and more than 40% of both strong Democrats and strong Republicans state a preference for divided government, even though they do not actually vote this way. The intention to *potentially* vote for the other party appears to work in much the same way that social desirability works in identifying as an independent (more on this in Chapter 7)—saying we are not beholden to the parties (even when we are) projects an air of superiority and individualism.

To attempt to address this, and to assess the effect of partisanship on attitudes about compromise causally, we designed and implemented a survey experiment to explicitly test preferences for compromise or intransigent candidates under different partisan conditions.

The experiment, part of a national survey we fielded in 2014, was designed to see whether partisans would be more likely to choose more ideologically extreme candidates when they were presented with a condition of minority status—that is, when in the minority, would people prefer a candidate who works with the other party, or sticks to their guns? This experiment builds on one by Harbridge, Malhotra, and Harrison (2014), who found that partisans rate policies lower when they are framed as having been produced through bipartisan processes than when the same policies are said to be produced by a single party, and that partisans tend to define "bipartisanship" as instances in which the other party (not their party) compromises.

Respondents in our experiment were randomly assigned to one of two categories:

Randomization 1: *Assume that the Republican Party currently holds 40% of the seats in your State Legislature; the Democrats hold 60% of seats and therefore the Democrats control which bills come up for a vote. Which type of candidate would you be most likely to support in the next election?*

Randomization 2: *Assume that the Democratic Party currently holds 40% of the seats in your State Legislature; the Republicans hold 60% of seats and therefore the Republicans control which bills come up for a vote. Which type of candidate would you be most likely to support in the next election?*

The response options were as follows:

- a Republican candidate who holds conservative views and who has vowed not to compromise any of his/her positions. (1)
- a Republican candidate who holds moderate views and is campaigning on a bipartisan agenda. (2)
- an Independent candidate who holds no party affiliation. (3)
- a Democratic candidate who holds moderate views and is campaigning on a bipartisan agenda. (4)
- a Democratic candidate who holds liberal/progressive views and who has vowed not to compromise any of his/her positions. (5)

Looking at partisans' responses, we can assess the causal impact of minority status on an individual's candidate preference. The results of multinomial logit models estimating the effects, controlling for ideology, are presented in the appendix, in Table A3.2. The substantive effects, presented as predicted probabilities, appear in Figure 3.2.

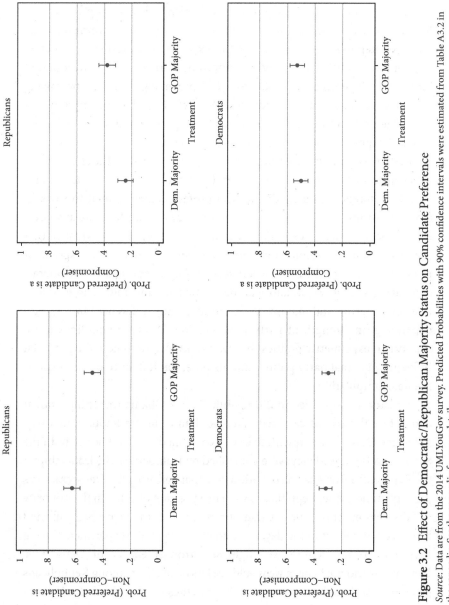

Figure 3.2 Effect of Democratic/Republican Majority Status on Candidate Preference

Source: Data are from the 2014 UMLYouGov survey. Predicted Probabilities with 90% confidence intervals were estimated from Table A3.2 in the appendix. See the appendix for more details.

In the top two panels of Figure 3.2, we observe the effect of the experimental manipulation, that the Democrats/Republicans control the state legislature. When Republicans were cued with information that their party was in the minority and did not control which bills come up for a vote, Republican voters became *more likely* to prefer an uncompromising conservative Republican candidate, at the expense of choosing a moderate Republican candidate that prefers compromise. This is a very meaningful increase of 15 percentage points, from 48% preferring the uncompromising candidate under Republican rule to 63% preferring the uncompromising candidate under Democratic rule. Democrats, presented in the bottom two panels of Figure 3.2, however, did not respond this way.

There are two important differences to note in examining the effects of the experiment on Democrats as compared to Republicans. First, Democrats' overall preference for a candidate who professed they wanted to work in a bipartisan manner was a more common answer than Republicans' preference for a moderate candidate. Furthermore, there is no evidence that the experimental manipulation had any effect on Democratic respondent preferences. We probed for differences among subgroups of Democrats comparing strong, weak, and leaning Democrats and found no evidence that the experimental manipulation produced any differences in response depending on strength of party identification. While our findings again support an asymmetric politics theory, it is important to note the potential influence of actual party politics and its potential influence on our experimental manipulation.

Our survey was fielded in 2014, while Barack Obama was still president and before the rise of candidate Donald Trump in the Republican Party. While the House of Representatives was controlled by Republicans, both the Senate and the presidency were controlled by Democrats. The leadership of the Republican Party had also made a case that defeating the Democrats was priority number one. Republicans were in a position of being in the minority in Washington. This indicates that our experiment may have been affected by the actual politics of the day, and had we repeated the experiment during President Trump's tenure, we might see stronger effects for Democrats. However, we do not believe we would see less of an effect among Republicans given the continued cues from Republican elites that the Democratic Party poses a threat to American values and the country's well-being. Thus, there are two potential ways our data may be explained: that polarization in terms of negative partisanship is larger among Republicans, or that the actual partisan landscape affects the results. However, given that the data show a large difference in preference for compromise between strong Democrats and strong Republicans, this points to Grossmann and Hopkins' (2016) "asymmetric politics" explanation.

Overall, our evidence here shows that when it comes to being on the losing end of elections, loss can lead to ideological entrenchment. In the American context, this entrenchment is especially troublesome, as compromise with the losing party is central to the design of American representative government. In recent years, as the Republican and Democratic Parties have grown more stalwart in their attempts to differentiate themselves and more likely to blame each other and play political games of power and procedure instead of working together to find compromise, we have witnessed the growing effects of negative partisanship, and of strong partisan echo chambers. Partisans can become increasingly consistent in their ability to refute the other side. The fact that we are consistently seeing an asymmetry in this behavior could reflect the underlying structure of the coalitions of the two parties; but, it may also reflect the larger media infrastructure of the right, in their ability to relay the correct behavior and the correct response to certain circumstances and the consistent rejection of bipartisanship in the right-wing media. As we explained in Chapter 2, many of our findings indicate that the Republican information environment is simply different— the cues are more direct and the transfer of information from elite to masses is more seamless.

We now turn to investigating if and to what extent partisanship can overflow to non-political issues.

3.4 Party Identification and Non-Political Preferences

Anybody gone into Whole Foods lately? See what they charge for arugula?
—Barack Obama, campaigning for President in Iowa in 2008

Who knew arugula could be political? This one comment became conservative media fodder for months to symbolize presidential contender and Senator Barack Obama as an out-of-touch elitist. Similarly, President Obama wearing a bike helmet, and the fact that he wore a tan suit to a press conference, were each irrelevant to politics or public policy yet were transformed into major issues by conservative media. The ability of the apparently non-political to become political is remarkable. A final part of our examination of the depth and breadth of partisan-motivated reasoning regards the slow drip of the political into the inane. That is, we investigate whether partisanship can make its way into non-political preferences or if this is just a ratings-driving trick that does not actually affect preferences. Here we again turn to a survey experiment, and our subject is food (hold the arugula—it's just too politically charged!).

To be sure, we are not the first to delve into the effect of partisanship and partisan-motivated reasoning on non-political preferences (see, e.g., Banda, Carsey, and Severenchuk 2020), and even on non-political issues there is strong evidence that individuals are highly motivated to avoid conversations with people who do not share their party identification (Settle and Carlson 2019). Recent research has also highlighted the loss of facts in political reasoning among Americans (e.g., Hochschild and Einstein 2015; Marietta and Barker 2019). In some situations, providing more factual information only serves to strengthen anti-fact position taking (Nyhan et al. 2014); and when issues like climate change are politicized, the development of "anti-science" attitudes can spill over to other issues where political sides do not presently exist (Dyck, Cluverius, and Gerson 2019). Part of what is occurring is that partisans openly choose to flaunt things that they know may not be true as a way to combat or troll the other party. How then could we apply this to something that is not fact based, but preference based? We argue that partisan information will affect partisans' stated preferences for something completely non-political.

Before explaining our experiment, which focuses on preferences for food, it is important to note that there are some food preferences that differ between Democrats and Republicans. According to the Pew Research Center, "Some 15% of liberal Democrats are at least mostly vegan or vegetarian, compared to 4% among conservative Republicans" while there were no differences by region of the country, education, gender, or family income (Pew Research Center 2016, p. 26). Knowing this, we intentionally stayed clear of the food preferences that are more common among Democrats and Republicans such as organics and various other food diets. We designed an experiment where individuals were assigned to a control or one of two treatment categories and asked about their positive/negative predispositions towards four generic food items, using a 4-point scale: salmon, lasagna, meatloaf, and chili. We checked to make sure there were not just food preferences between treatment groups by applying no cues for the salmon and lasagna questions. For the meatloaf and chili questions, respondents receive either the control question or a cue that tells them that the food is a favorite of President Trump or President Obama. The experiment adds the additional complexity of reality in that meatloaf, by all press accounts, is Donald Trump's favorite food (Ellison n.d.), and chili (yup, not arugula!) is Barack Obama's favorite food.[1] This, of course, also weakens the likelihood of finding evidence in favor of our hypothesis, as many people may already know these food preferences (and they are also easily searchable in the context of an online survey), so if we find evidence in favor of our hypothesis, it is still likely dampened by the information environment.

The results of the experiment, with significance tests between the controls and the treatments for all respondents, and by party, are presented in Table 3.3. The findings from this experiment reinforce two general expectations. First, partisan effects on nonpartisan preferences are driven by negative partisanship. When Democrats learn that a food is President Obama's favorite, or Republicans learn a food is President Trump's favorite, it has no effect on their underlying food preferences—they are not driven to like products more as a result of the endorsement of the leader of their preferred party. However, when Republicans hear that meatloaf or chili is "Obama's favorite," their rating of these food items decreases, and this decrease is statistically significant. For Democrats, their rating of meatloaf decreases when they hear it is Trump's favorite; their rating of chili also decreases, but the effect is not statistically significant. It is possible that this is an asymmetry similar to previous results. Or perhaps Democrats are just better at using Google to confirm that meatloaf is Trump's favorite, not chili, but we doubt this is the case. Regardless, the experiment highlights the power of negative partisanship to structure attitudes about the non-political and inane; and, perhaps most importantly, it shows that respondents are driven by negative partisanship. The change was entirely driven by increased distaste when respondents learned the food preferences of the out-party.

3.6 Conclusion

Democrats and Republicans are living different lives. Democrats are more likely to live on the coasts, close to water, and in metropolitan areas. In doing so they are more likely to encounter sexual, cultural, and racial diversity.

Table 3.3 Partisan Food Experiment Results, 2017

We want to know about some of your preferences about what you like to eat. For each of the following, please indicate if your reaction to this food is strongly positive, somewhat positive, somewhat negative, or strongly negative. (Coded from 1–4, so that higher scores reflect a more positive disposition to each food.)

Salmon	Treatment	All respondents	Democrats	Republicans
	Control group	2.93	2.93	3.02
	No treatment	2.85	2.92	2.91
	No treatment	2.82	2.99	2.73[†]
Lasagna	**Treatment**	**All respondents**	**Democrats**	**Republicans**
	Control group	3.32	3.40	3.33
	No treatment	3.37	3.40	3.35
	No treatment	3.33	3.33	3.35
Meatloaf	**Treatment**	**All respondents**	**Democrats**	**Republicans**
	Control group	3.11	2.98	3.36
	A favorite of President Trump	3.00	2.71[*]	3.37
	A favorite of President Obama	3.09	3.08	3.13[*]
Chili	**Treatment**	**All Respondents**	**Democrats**	**Republicans**
	Control group	3.16	3.06	3.35
	A favorite of President Trump	3.04[†]	2.91	3.31
	A favorite of President Obama	3.05	3.06	3.12[*]

Notes: Data are from the 2017 YouGov survey. Difference of means tests are computed between the treatment group and the control group. [†]p < .10, [*]p < .05, [**]p < .01, two-tailed tests reported. See the appendix for more details.

Democrats are also less likely to go to church, less likely to believe in God, more likely to eat organic foods, and more likely to drive smaller cars and electric vehicles. The reason why all of this is true is the sorting of the political parties into groups that overlap and add up to make an individual (Green, Palmquist, and Schickler 2008; Levendusky 2009; Mason 2018). While evangelical Christians were once evenly split between the Democratic Party and the Republican Party, as were white voters without a college degree, today all these groups are well sorted into the Republican Party, just as other groups are well sorted into the Democratic Party. This sorting means that the cultural differences between Democrats and Republicans has increased drastically to the point where many Republicans and Democrats simply cannot understand the views of the other as they have so few lifestyle similarities or shared experiences.

Well-sorted populations are more likely to experience group threat from the other group. As people's cultural experiences diverge, each group's status becomes intertwined with the status of the "other" group.

Class differences have long been observed when one class rejects something thought to be preferred by another class (e.g., members of the upper class eschew foods associated with lower classes. For example, lobster, long ago a food of the working class due to its abundance, was not eaten by the wealthy because it was considered a food for the poor.) Racial groups are also known for choosing different foods, clothing, and other staples as a way of distinguishing themselves from the group they perceive as competitors, oppressors, or a threat.

Political parties have always been considered different from racial and economic groups. They are big tents—ways to take the various groups and preferences of the public and translate those into meaningful policy in a messy representative government designed to impede change and ensure compromise. Being a Democrat, under this view of partisanship, should not change how one views a food staple, and the type of candidate one chooses should still be based on how they think the institution should function and what type of policies they wish to see enacted.

But times have changed. Those who are responsive to economic growth and who are willing to hold *both* political parties accountable for their actions now are a fraction of the electorate. As social and cultural groups have become synonymous with the political parties, people have begun to behave in ways more like historic and modern ethnic and class cleavages in which people's views are clouded by their attachment to their group. Were Jews really the reason the economy of Germany was in poor condition before the rise of the Nazis? No, but they were an out-group that was easy to identify and blame. Were African Americans the reason for the rise of the welfare state? No, but, again, they were an easy out-group to use for political purposes. People's social status was raised by blaming the other group for the economic and social changes of the country in extreme ways.

The religious groups and racial groups of the past are now one in the same with the modern American political parties. The data in this chapter show that (1) concerns over the threat of the other party controlling the

mechanisms of government influences support for democratic principles of compromise and unity, (2) policy preferences are driven by a need
for distinction from the other party, instead of true economic and social
interests, and (3) political party preferences drive people to differentiate
further outside of the political realm, from what they eat to what car they
drive.

4

Partisanship, Race, and
Intergroup Contact

Why do we want these people from all these shithole countries here?
We should have more people from places like Norway.
>   —Former President Donald Trump, January 11, 2018

The impunity of police violence is a systemic problem we must face
to save lives. Police brutality is now a leading cause of death for
young Black men in the US. The status quo is killing us.
> —Representative Alexandria Ocasio Cortez (D-NY), May 27, 2020

We have got this tailspin of culture, in our inner cities in particular,
of men not working and just generations of men not even thinking
about working or learning the value and the culture of work, and so
there is a real culture problem here that has to be dealt with.
>   —Former Speaker of the United States House of Representatives,
>   Paul Ryan (R-WI), March 12, 2014

4.1 Introduction

The preceding chapters established a dynamic story of negative partisanship and partisan-motivated reasoning. More Americans identify as strong partisans, attitudes about people who identify with the other party are incredibly hostile, and partisanship now structures more than just policy preferences. It also structures how we think about American ideals like compromise, and it can even affect preferences that are outside the realm of politics. This and the following chapters probe further into the implications of the apparent omnipresence of partisanship on social science more generally. These chapters pose a simple question: If partisanship motivates reasoning in places where it sometimes does not make sense, how does this affect theories

The Power of Partisanship. Joshua J. Dyck and Shanna Pearson-Merkowitz, Oxford University Press.
© Oxford University Press 2023. DOI: 10.1093/oso/9780197623787.003.0005

of human behavior that do not address the role of partisan elites or partisanship? Are expectations about general social or human behavior correct, or do they require asterisks regarding the level of polarization and the role of trusted elites? This chapter begins to examine these questions through a look at partisan differences in response to intergroup contact. This investigation continues in Chapters 5 and 6, which look at partisan decision making under conditions of risk (i.e., prospect theory) and the influence of the lived environment on developing preferences (i.e., contextual effects theory).

4.2 The Intergroup Contact Effect

Intergroup contact theory is the most well-researched and supported theory of how to reduce intergroup animosity and bring about positive intergroup relations and social change. The basic premise of intergroup contact theory is simple: When someone has personal interactions with people from different walks of life under reasonably favorable conditions, they engage in stereotyping less frequently (or never develop stereotypes). Moreover, people not only apply the experience to their beliefs about the individual they have contact with, but also to the group as a whole, and to social policies and rules that adversely affect that group. Hence, intergroup social contact should decrease intergroup hostility and acrimony.

While most studies attribute Allport's (1954) book *On the Nature of Prejudice* to the advent of intergroup contact theory, several studies on the theory predate its publication, including work to which Allport contributed (Allport and Kramer 1946; Brophy 1945; Deutsch and Collins 1951; and Williams 1947). Intergroup contact theory is not only thought to be a critical social mechanism for decreasing intergroup animosity; more generally, it is one of the most well-supported theories in social psychology writ large. Several meta-analyses have been conducted that show evidence that the hypothesis holds across studies and contexts (Davies et al. 2011; Lemmer and Wagner 2015; Miles and Crisp 2014; Pettigrew and Tropp 2006; White et al. 2020; Zhou et al. 2019). In full, there are over 400,000 subjects analyzed by these meta-analyses and over 900 different studies conducted in many different nations (Pettigrew 2021).

Decreasing intergroup hostility is what social psychologists refer to as the "primary transfer effect" (e.g., Boin et al. 2021). But intergroup contact has also been found to have more extensive "secondary transfer" effects, including more positive views of other minoritized groups with which the individual has not interacted (Pettigrew 2009; Schmid et al. 2012; Tausch et al. 2010). For example, Laar and colleagues (2005) researched undergraduates randomly assigned to roommates from different ethnicities. They found that white roommates with a Black or Hispanic roommate displayed less prejudice toward both groups—those with a Hispanic roommate were less prejudiced toward both the Hispanic and the Black community (and vice versa).

Intergroup contact also has been found to have "tertiary transfer effects" (Boin et al. 2021; Meleady et al. 2019). Tertiary effects are the extension of a reduction of simple prejudice. Here the evidence suggests that contact with diverse group members increases cognitive flexibility and productivity, enables better problem-solving skills, leads to more creativity, and fosters cultural openness, social competence, moral reasoning, and self-esteem. It also appears to lead to greater leadership potential (see Boin et al. 2021, as well as Hodson et al. 2018, for excellent reviews of this literature). When people have experience with a diverse set of contacts in their social network, they become more "cognitively flexible" because the contact exposes them to different ways of thinking, living, and behaving. This exposure allows people to see that there is more than one way to live, brand a product, or teach a student, and that each of these ways is legitimate and effective. Indeed, compared to homogenous groups, groups made up of culturally diverse members tend to be more likely to create higher quality and novel solutions that incorporate multiple perspectives (e.g., Antonio et al. 2004; McLeod, Lobel, and Cox 1996).

Political science work on intergroup contact has focused on how getting to know or being exposed to people from different backgrounds leads to (1) the reduction of intergroup stereotyping and animosity, (2) support for programs and policies that benefit minoritized populations, and (3) support for the government addressing injustice and inequality. For example, this area of research has shown that white respondents who have friends who are immigrants are less likely to believe that immigrants increase crime rates and cause job loss among the native-born; they are more likely to believe that immigrants have a positive impact on society and increase cultural creativity; and they are also less supportive of exclusionary (and more supportive of inclusionary) immigration policies (Berg 2020; Ellison, Shin, and Leal 2011; Escandell and Ceobanu 2009; Neumann and Moy 2018). Likewise, having contact with people who struggle to pay their bills heightens belief in class-based bias in politics and support for redistribution policies (Newman 2014).

The process by which contact affects political views is similar to the tertiary transfer effect's primary theoretical basis. Having interpersonal contact with minoritized groups allows people to understand the life experiences of people from different backgrounds. When someone has a Black or Latino coworker, they are more likely to witness subtle (or not-so-subtle) slights. For example, are Black and Latino workers scheduled for less desirable shifts than white workers? Are they made fun of by the boss and other coworkers more frequently? Are there awkward moments when coworkers make even unintentionally racist comments? These observations not only allow people to generalize that members of this group do not hold the negative traits embedded in racial stereotypes, but they also help people see how racism, classism, and ethnocentrism shape minoritized populations' experiences in society—at school, in housing, at work, or elsewhere in their daily lives.

This same process of observation and generalization happens repeatedly when people have interpersonal contact. For example, many people explain their support for a path to citizenship as grounded in their experience with an undocumented immigrant they got to know at work or in their neighborhood. They understand this individual's plight, and they generalize that understanding to a policy that may or may not help their personal contact but will definitely help those like her.

The more, and the closer, people's ties are to those unlike themselves, the more likely they will be to have experiences that challenge racial stereotypes and create common bonds. By knowing someone of another group, it is simply more likely that one will observe inequalities and understand the role government plays in exacerbating or alleviating those inequalities. As a result, those with interpersonal contact with minoritized populations are more likely to believe that discrimination exists, to see it as personally relevant, and to see the need for policies that redress inequalities (Tropp and Barlow 2018).

4.3 Why Is Polarization Important for Understanding Intergroup Affect?

Despite the well-documented effects of intergroup contact, Allport's original contact hypothesis proposed very specific conditions under which contact must occur to reduce stereotypes and intergroup hostility. While many of these conditions have been questioned over time, one that remains important is institutional support (i.e., authority, social, or cultural support).

Pettigrew (1998, 67) explains that "with explicit social sanction, intergroup contact is more readily accepted and has more positive effects. Authority support establishes norms of acceptance." Studies of intergroup contact support Allport's proposed institutional/social support condition (Landis, Hope, and Day 1983; Morrison and Herlihy 1992; Nesdale et al. 2005; Pettigrew 1998; Pettigrew and Tropp 2006; Stangor, Sechrist, and Jost, 2001a, 2001b; Tredoux and Finchilescu 2010), as does our previous work (Dyck and Pearson-Merkowitz 2014; Pearson-Merkowitz, Filindra, and Dyck 2016). The important point of these studies is that contact, in and of itself, is insufficient to increase intergroup harmony since social adherence structures how we learn from interpersonal interactions. When people perceive that their social circle will have a negative view of the out-group, they are less willing to consider new information about out-group members for fear of social sanction (De Tezanos-Pinto, Bratt, and Brown 2010). As we have pointed out elsewhere (Dyck and Pearson-Merkowitz 2014, 557), "contact is most effective if and when people perceive that it is socially acceptable to view the out-group in a positive light." However, "if the individual believes they may be punished in their social group for positive perceptions of an out-group, then intergroup contact will have little effect."

Allport (1954), in his original treatise on prejudice, was particularly clear that government support for minority rights was essential for increasing tolerance between groups because the government serves as a cue to the populous that acceptance of the minoritized population is supported by cultural and political authorities (see especially Chapter 29). However, in today's polarized political climate, it is clear to any observer that people do not take cues directly from the "government." Instead, people receive loud cues from their trusted elites about which policies are to be supported and who in the United States constitute "in-group" members, and, even more important, who is considered an "out-group" (Green, Palmquist, and Schickler 2008; Mason 2018). As we discussed in Chapter 2, in today's 24-hour news cycle and social media–intensive environment, trusted political elites deliver clear cues about in-group authority support and in-group sanctions for divergent views toward others.

In our earlier research (Dyck and Pearson-Merkowitz 2014; Pearson-Merkowitz, Filindra, and Dyck 2016), we presented evidence that the connection between intergroup contact and support for policies that benefit minoritized populations is conditional on party identification. The approach specifies that:

contact with minority groups only produces support for pro-minority public policies (or opposition to anti-minority policies) when political cues do not explicitly reject acceptance of the minoritized group. Thus, contact can only work if elites are either silent on the matter or supportive of the group. If elites profess that the outgroup is a threat to the status of the in-group, contact will fail to produce increased support for pro-minority policies. (Dyck and Pearson-Merkowitz 2014, p. 560)

Stated formally, we continue to hypothesize that contact with minoritized populations will translate into increased support for policies benefiting the group when party elites either portray the minoritized population positively or fail to provide unified and/or full-throated policy endorsements, but that contact with minoritized populations will *not* translate into increased support for policies that benefit that group when party elites send negative messages about them.

Critical to our theory is the nature of the information environment. For contact to translate to increased support for a public policy, cues *must* be present. Elites must take positions and let their co-partisans know that they support the policy; this is the link that facilitates the connection between intergroup contact and public policy beliefs. Otherwise, the connection between the personal experience of minoritized groups and the public policies that affect them may be too abstract. We previously showed that support for same-sex marriage was higher among Democrats who had contact with an LGBT community member than for Democrats without an LGBT contact, but among Republicans we found no effect from interpersonal contact. This research was conducted during the height of the fight for same-sex marriage legalization (Dyck and Pearson-Merkowitz 2014). The issue was salient and people on both the right and the left were receiving regular cues about whether their party supported the rights of the LGBT community to engage in state-recognized matrimony. Extending this research, we found similar results when studying support for the DREAM Act—a policy meant to help millions of children brought to the United States without documentation achieve a path to citizenship. Again, this research was conducted while the DREAM Act was being debated by both parties and the issue of immigration was salient to both the presidential and congressional campaigns and was hotly debated in Congress.

Here we extend our previous findings to look at Black–white relations, where the contact effect was originally tested in the literature (e.g., Allport

1954). We argue that for the contact effect to translate to support for policies benefiting minoritized communities, political elites must provide supporting cues. But, due to the long history of party elites taking opposing positions on matters of race, our ability to observe the first and secondary transfer effects that are so well established in the literature will also be limited.

More specifically, we argue that the information cues provided by Republican Party leaders prevent Republican identifiers from translating personal experiences with Black Americans (their friends, neighbors, work colleagues, etc.) into (1) their policy positions or (2) their attitudes about systemic racial discrimination. Democrats, who have a fundamentally different information infrastructure and receive cues from their party about systemic racial inequality, are far more likely to support policies addressing racial inequality in American institutions and to demonstrate greater awareness of racial disparities and discrimination when they have contact with members of the Black community.

We test this hypothesis using several new datasets. We investigate two areas of contact effects in an era of political polarization. First, we look at the effect of contact on views of systemic inequality and discrimination. Second, we look at how contact affects attitudes toward racialized policies, including government aid to Black Americans and police reform.

4.4 Racialization of the Political Parties 1960 to the Present

Before moving to our analyses, we want to interrogate our claim that the parties have sent very different cues over the last few decades about minoritized communities and racialized policies. This topic alone merits its own book (e.g., Carmines and Stimson 1989), and we are admittedly covering it very briefly. Interested readers should consider pursuing additional reading in some of the books and articles that we cite in this section to fully understand this topic.

Following Reconstruction, the two parties went through an evolution regarding race relations and racialized policy. Although the Democratic Party had been the party of slavery, and the Republicans the party of abolition during the Civil War, the post-Reconstruction period was a period of fundamental party change. By 1960, both presidential candidates and their campaigns took progressive positions on civil rights. The Democratic Party took their strongest position on civil rights in history, and Republican Vice President and Republican Party nominee for president Richard Nixon fought to ensure that the Republican platform included support for equal voting rights, a commission on equal job opportunities, prohibition of discrimination in federal housing, and a process for speeding up school desegregation orders, effectively making the Republican platform as racially liberal as the Democratic platform (Carmines and Stimson 1989, pp. 37–39).

Then came the Civil Rights Act of 1964, a comprehensive Civil Rights Bill that enabled real progress with teeth for enforcement. Like the largely watered-down Civil Rights Acts before it, the 1964 law passed with a combination of Democratic and Republican support and a large delegation of Southern Democrat opposition. However, the 1964 law was supported and led by Democratic President Lyndon Johnson and was comprehensive in coverage. As such, it revealed that the Democratic Party had "altered their historic position on this issue and become the principal defenders of [B]lack civil rights. And they had done so not only with rhetoric and proposals but also with action" (Carmines and Stimson 1989, pp. 43–44).

The racial division that then took hold between the parties did not require a Republican response. Given that both parties had pro- and anti–civil rights members, the passage of the Civil Rights Act under a Democratic president could have led to a continuation of the norm with civil rights progress requiring a coalition of both parties' liberal wings. However, a fissure began in the Republican Party. Senator Barry Goldwater led a states' rights response to the Civil Rights Act and became the Republican nominee for the 1964 presidential race largely on an anti–civil rights platform. Goldwater did not have open ties to the Ku Klux Klan, but he was endorsed by its members (Leffler 1964). Moreover, while he was overwhelmingly defeated nationally, he was the victor in what had been Democratic strongholds and have since become the most reliable "red states" in the country: Mississippi, Alabama, South Carolina, Louisiana, and Georgia. Johnson, having won the presidency, went on to champion the Voting Rights Act and other legislative priorities of the civil rights movement. In response, the Republican Party, led by Richard Nixon, followed Goldwater with calls to halt desegregation efforts and return power to the states on civil rights issues—actions that were fulfilled when Nixon became president (Murphy and Gulliver 1971).

Ronald Reagan's rhetoric and legislative actions, though, are perhaps those most clearly related to the current Republican Party and that of former President Donald Trump. From voting laws, to supporting South African apartheid, to crafting language of social policy and welfare in racialized terms, under President Reagan "whatever progress Blacks had made on a number of fronts came to a halt" (Dawson and Bobo 2004, p. 210). As Dawson and Bobo (2004) note in their opening to a special issue on the Reagan legacy and the racial divide in the *Du Bois Review*:

> Reagan himself was a racial polarizer throughout his political career. His drive for the governorship of California in the middle 1960s was significantly fueled by his opposition to the state referendum that called for open housing. He opposed the 1964 Civil Rights Act as well as the 1965 Voting Rights Act. He opened his campaign after receiving the Republican nomination in 1980 in Philadelphia, Mississippi, which was the site in 1964 of the brutal murder of civil rights activists James Chaney, Andrew Goodman, and Michael Schwerner. While remaining silent during the speech about the murder of the civil rights workers, Reagan announced his support for "states' rights"—the racist code words that had been used to justify in turn slavery, secession from the Union, Southern segregation, and the often violent opposition of Southern racists to the civil rights movement, civil rights legislation, and court decisions such as the then relatively new Brown v. Board of Education decision. While in office, he vetoed the 1988 extension of the Civil Rights Act while trying to win tax exemptions for Bob Jones University, which had openly racist policies. . . . Another of the central legacies of Reagan-era Republican electoral tactics was the use of racial code words (e.g., the "welfare queen" anecdote from the 1980 campaign) that evoked anti-Black sentiment as a means of forging a winning national electoral coalition. (pp. 209–210)

President Reagan also completely reframed government aid to the poor, particularly the Great Society programs launched by President Lyndon Johnson, as contributing and perpetuating what he saw as individual moral failures framed in racialized language, instead of a means to address societal inequalities in access to opportunity and systemic racism and sexism in housing, education, and the workforce. According to Reagan and his Republican predecessors, racism does not hold back individual or group upward mobility; any income inequality is the fault of people not "pulling up their bootstraps" and working hard enough, and the fault that lies with the government is that it had been too willing to give out "free stuff" (in the words of both former Republican presidential candidates and Governors

Mitt Romney and Jeb Bush in reference to the relationship between Black Americans and the U.S. government) that makes the U.S. poor complacent and reliant (Covert 2015). This general approach was on display when President Donald Trump blamed a lack of initiative, rather than racism, for the apparent "lack of progress" of Black Americans in the United States (Castronuovo 2020).

The fact that the federal government made racial discrimination unlawful in the 1960s has been a useful tool for the Republican Party since Reagan shifted blame for inequality from government and society to impoverished individuals as though all prior inequality had been wiped away with a law banning public segregation and discrimination and the elimination of *de jure* segregation. However, ending segregation in law did not open up housing markets to level the playing field for those who had been systematically denied access to housing opportunities, nor did it deal with predatory practices in real estate and mortgage lending industries that exacerbated racial housing segregation and inequality (Taylor 2019).

While former President Trump is notable for his openly racist comments, for many observers, Trump was simply more willing to be frank about his beliefs instead of using code words and platitudes that were clearly racist but coded. This explicitness helped, of course, crystalize the information environment for even those Republicans who pay little attention.

Democrats certainly do not have the cleanest record on policies harming or benefiting the Black community. In many cases Democrats have been the champions of policies with clear negative repercussions for Black Americans and their neighborhoods—Clinton's key legislative achievements of welfare reform and the 1994 Crime Bill are obvious examples of the Democratic Party's history of enacting policies with racist undertones that exacerbated racial inequality. Democratic Party elites also have sent mixed messages about policies that affect minoritized communities. They frequently walk a line between an attempt to reach Black voters with symbolic speech while also placating conservative white Democrats with tough talk targeting the "undeserving poor," legislation limiting social benefits, and taking hard lines on crime, particularly for drug crimes most likely to harm Black Americans, such as harsher punishments for crack than cocaine possession.

Despite this legislative record, the Democratic Party has championed the only civil rights bills passed in the last 60 years and has provided what little support there has been for policies that attempt to address systemic racism and inequality. More to the point, while failing to enact much that directly benefits the Black community or makes up for past government-imposed harms, Democrats have embraced and continue to use the pulpit to embrace cultural diversity and call for an end to racism and systemic racism. The cues sent by Democratic elites, including Bill Clinton who was affectionately called "the country's first Black president" by novelist Toni Morrison, have been far more positive toward Black people and acknowledging of the country's racist history and the continued role of racism in structuring people's lives. Their actions and symbolic speech on issues of race have also gotten both much more liberal and more progressive during times of social upheaval and public displays of racism. Democrats, perhaps most importantly, nominated and elected the country's actual first Black president, and President Barack Obama's famous speech on race, delivered during the 2008 General Election, was perhaps the clearest statement on the systemic roots of inequality in the United States made publicly by an elected official in the last 50 years. The speech explicitly laid out the connection between systemic racism historically and the present state of affairs and inequality. To quote just one section:

> We do not need to recite here the history of racial injustice in this country. But we do need to remind ourselves that so many of the disparities that exist between the African-American community and the larger American community today can be traced directly to inequalities passed on from an earlier generation that suffered under the brutal legacy of slavery and Jim Crow. Segregated schools were and are inferior schools; we still haven't fixed them, 50 years after Brown v. Board of Education. And the inferior education they provided, then and now, helps explain the pervasive achievement gap between today's black and white students. Legalized discrimination— where blacks were prevented, often through violence, from owning property, or loans were not granted to African-American business owners, or black homeowners could not access FHA mortgages, or blacks were excluded from unions or the police force or the fire department—meant that black families could not amass any meaningful wealth to bequeath to future generations. That history helps explain the wealth and income gap between blacks and whites, and the concentrated pockets of poverty that persist in so many of today's urban and rural communities.
>
> A lack of economic opportunity among black men, and the shame and frustration that came from not being able to provide for one's family contributed to the erosion of black families—a problem that welfare

policies for many years may have worsened. And the lack of basic services in so many urban black neighborhoods—parks for kids to play in, police walking the beat, regular garbage pickup, building code enforcement—all helped create a cycle of violence, blight and neglect that continues to haunt us. (Obama 2008)

As a result of this history, it is clear to co-partisans which party both supports civil rights and is inclusive of Black Americans and which party holds hostility and animosity toward Black Americans and denies the government's role in perpetuating racial inequality.

4.5   How Party Messaging and Contact Affect Views of Inequality and Civil Rights Policy

We expect partisans to equate their contact with the Black community to support for policies that are perceived as benefiting the Black community only when co-partisan elites are sending clear messages. However, we note that for at least 30 years, Democratic partisans have received cues from Democratic Party elites that racism is systemic, and that the government has a role in making up for government policies that have harmed and put barriers between the Black community and socioeconomic mobility.

We proceed by looking first at the effect of contact on beliefs about systemic inequality and racial resentment. Here, we argue, Democrats have received clear cues for some time. However, the moment in which the data were collected was a boiling point for racial inequality in the United States and led partisan elites to take uniquely clear positions on their views of the presence of racism both at an individual level and in American political institutions (e.g., systemic racism).

Originally formed in 2013 as a response to the acquittal of the murderer of Treyvon Martin, the Black Lives Matter movement erupted in May 2020, following the murder of George Floyd at the hands of a white policeman, Derek Chauvin. While the movement started with a response to the lack of weight the killing of Black people held in either the court of public opinion or the court of law in the United States, it expanded to address the wider world of systemic oppression of Black people across social arenas, including but not limited to education, jobs, and housing. President Trump publicly decried the Black Lives Matter (BLM) protesters and claimed that the movement was part of a "mob rule" that was "destroying many Black lives" (Villarreal 2020), referred to protestors as "thugs," and famously tweeted that "when the looting starts, the shooting starts," an apparent call for police brutality. He denounced the destruction of property by a small minority of protestors as "domestic acts of terror" (Beer 2021) and called on Capitol police to disperse peaceful BLM protesters in front of the White House through violent means so he could cross the street for a photo op (Pengelly 2020).

Democratic leaders, on the other hand, used the moment to highlight police brutality and systemic inequality. The Democratic National Committee devoted a significant amount of time during the national convention to police brutality, systemic racism, and the BLM movement (Linskey 2020). During his campaign for president, Joe Biden referred to the Black Lives Matter protests as a "wake up call for our nation" (Relman 2020) and regularly discussed racial inequality and the need for police reform on the campaign trail. Other central figures to the Democratic Party took very public stands in support of the BLM movement and police reform. Democratic Congresswoman Alexandria Ocasio-Cortez, often referred to as "AOC," became a public and outspoken advocate of the movement, regularly tweeting support, statistics about Black deaths at the hands of police, and defending and clarifying the call to "Defund the Police." To pick just one of many tweets by AOC: "What if activists aren't PR firms for politicians & their demands are bc police budgets are exploding, community resources are shrinking to bankroll it, & ppl brought this up for ages but it wasn't until they said 'defund' that comfortable people started paying attn to brutality" (Ocasio-Cortez 2020). The Congresswoman's tweets and public statements were widely covered in the media and amplified the voice of the protestors as endorsed by the liberal faction of the Democratic Party. Candidate and then President Joe Biden and House Speaker Nancy Pelosi's support helped clarify that it was also the position of the mainstream/"insiders" of the party. Biden even made one of his first acts as president on January 20, 2021, the same day as his swearing in, signing the "Executive Order On Advancing Racial Equity and Support for Underserved Communities Through the Federal Government." The first few paragraphs of the Order addressed the systemic inequality that continues to be pervasive in the United States and required the federal government take actions to make up for historic harms (Executive Order On Advancing Racial Equity and Support for Underserved Communities Through the Federal Government 2021).

While our data were collected in the late summer of 2020, what happened in the ensuing year only provided further evidence of partisan messaging and toxic polarization on racial inequality. Republican Party elites manufactured a new bogeyman in critical race theory (CRT), connecting discussions of systemic racism and structural inequality to Marxist ideology and arguing that children were being taught in schools that they were inherently racist and should feel personally guilty for white racism. As one op-ed put it, "Critical Race Theory is Marxist-rooted propaganda designed to divide our country and turn Blacks against whites and make white students feel guilty about alleged white superiority and alleged systemic racism" (Richardson 2021). This structured narrative was repeated by Republican elites and splayed across the airwaves of Fox News, the One America News Network, right-wing talk radio, and other conservative media, providing the counter-narrative to the calls from 2020 that instances of police brutality and systemic inequality should be connected to real policy change. In addition, in the Republican narratives responding to calls for policy reform, police have been described as victims of socialist leftists out to destroy the moral fabric of this country.

Imagine for a moment how these narratives about the role of teaching about racism in schools and calls for anti-racist policies in police departments interact with exposure to diversity. Is someone hearing messages of insidious CRT purveyors from their trusted sources likely to become less prejudiced or more likely to acknowledge the role of discrimination in fostering inequality just because they know a black person?

4.6 Research Design

We begin our examination of partisanship and intergroup contact with a simple question: How does contact affect perceptions of racism and discrimination and support for policies that are racialized among Democrats and Republicans? We are most interested in testing the difference in how partisans react to contact with minoritized community members. To do this, we make use of two observational datasets, one collected in 2014 and one collected in 2020, both explicitly designed to test these hypotheses.

For all our tests we employ a standard question to measure contact with different groups. Following the existing literature to date, we asked each survey respondent, "Thinking about the person who is Black that you know best, how would you describe your relationship with this person?" Respondents could then choose from the following answers: "I don't know anyone who is Black," "A Member of my family," "A close friend," "A co-worker," or "An acquaintance." Because this chapter focuses on contact with minoritized communities, the data only include white respondents.

Figure 4.1 presents the proportion of white respondents in each demarcation on the party identification scale with no contact with the Black community, non-familial contact with the Black community, and familial contact with the Black community. Figure 4.1 looks at type of contact by party identification. Interestingly, weak Democrats and pure independents have the lowest levels of contact, and independent-leaning Republicans and weak Republicans are the most likely to report having a family member who is Black. However, overall, we see that contact is fairly consistent across partisan categories.

In our previous research, we considered a familial contact the closest kind of contact. However, there is some reason to think that interracial familial contact may work differently among white respondents. The most common way that a white respondent is likely to gain a Black family member is through marriage by another family member. However, interracial relationships have an ugly history in the United States. They were often the foundation of violence against Black men, and the law against interracial marriage only changed in 1967 when it finally became legal in the United States for people

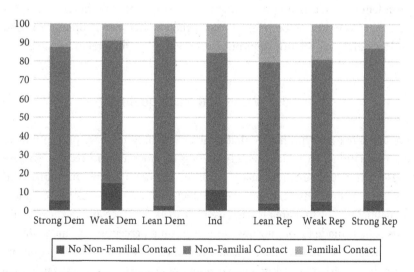

Figure 4.1 Type of Contact with the Closest Black Contact by Party Identification among Whites, 2020

Source: Data are from a 2020 YouGov survey. See the appendix for more details.

of different races to marry. However, opposition to interracial marriage took a long time to abate. In 1990, Pew (Livingston and Brown 2017) found that 63% of non-Blacks said they would be either somewhat or strongly opposed to a relative marrying a Black person. While surveys differ in their estimates, even recently up to a third of white respondents reported being "not at all comfortable" with their daughter marrying a Black person (Perry 2013). Indeed, support for interracial marriage appears to be contingent upon having another form of social contact with the Black community (Perry 2013). As a result, we do not believe that reporting that the closest Black person is a family member to the respondent will produce consistent positive contact results.

Importantly, this is because family members do not become a different race in the way a family member would reveal they are gay. In our previous work (Dyck and Pearson-Merkowitz 2014) we found that having a family member who identifies as gay produced more support for gay marriage. But we do not think that same finding will hold here, because the relationship with a gay family member is likely to be fundamentally different: When one's son, daughter, brother, or sister comes "out," the family member has a preexisting relationship with the person. They love their family member and now their family member has let them know their sexual orientation. This relationship is likely to produce a different response than when one's son, daughter, or cousin marries someone of a different race—a person the respondent has little or no preexisting relationship with. We therefore suspect that the psychological benefits of interracial contact may happen for friend and acquaintance relationships but not necessarily family relationships.

4.6.1 Views of Racial Equality

We test our first hypothesis—that contact will only increase perceptions of discrimination and racial inequity among Democrats who receive positive cues—using a poll run in August of 2020. This test uses multiple questions to investigate the link between interracial contact and awareness/acknowledgment of inequality. The first area is what we refer to as the "race and fairness" scale. This scale is made up of four questions regarding perceptions of inequality in the way people are treated. We asked respondents to say if Black people are treated less fairly than white people, white people are treated less fairly than Black people, or if both groups are treated about the same. We ask this question for each of the following areas: jobs/at work; in neighborhood shops/

business; at shopping malls and large retail chains; in entertainment venues like restaurants, bars, or movie theaters; and in interactions with the police. To create the race and fairness measure, we scale these items together using the first factor from a principal components analysis.[1] The scale represents people's views on how fairly Black people are treated compared to white people across various institutions. Indeed, few people (about 6% across each area) think Black people are treated more fairly than white people. However, between 47% and 60% of people, depending on the area, reported thinking that Black and white people are treated the same, and 28% to 51% reported they thought Black people are treated less fairly than those who are white.

Our second test employs a scale that measures the perception of discrimination. This variable was created by scaling three items together using principal components analysis.[2] Here we asked each respondent about discrimination in three areas: jobs, education, and housing. For example, we asked about housing discrimination by asking the question, "Some people think that Blacks have the same chance as whites to get any housing they can afford while others think Blacks are frequently discriminated against in the housing market, even when they are qualified renters and buyers. Where do you place yourself on this scale?" Respondents then placed themselves on a 7-point scale ranging from (1) *Blacks have the same chance as whites to get any housing they can afford* to (7) *Blacks are frequently discriminated against in the housing market, even when they are qualified renters/buyers.* We repeated this with questions regarding education and the workforce.

Our third test examines attitudes toward racial resentment (Kinder and Sanders 1996). To construct the standard racial resentment scale, we posed three agree/disagree statements to respondents. The statements included: (1) *Over the past few years, Blacks have gotten less than they deserve*; (2) *Generations of slavery and discrimination have created conditions that make it difficult for Blacks to work their way out of the lower class*; and (3) *Irish, Italians, Jewish, and many other minorities overcame prejudice and worked their way up. Blacks should do the same without any special favors.* We then scale these items together using the first factor from a principal components analysis.[3]

We employ OLS regression, incorporating the survey weights into our estimations, to model the effect of contact on attitudes toward inequality on each of our scales. For ease of interpretation, we have rescaled the measures from 0 to 1 and present only graphical depictions of the interaction effects in the main text, relegating the more complex model predictions to the book's appendix (Table A4.1). In Figure 4.2 we observe the effect of contact with

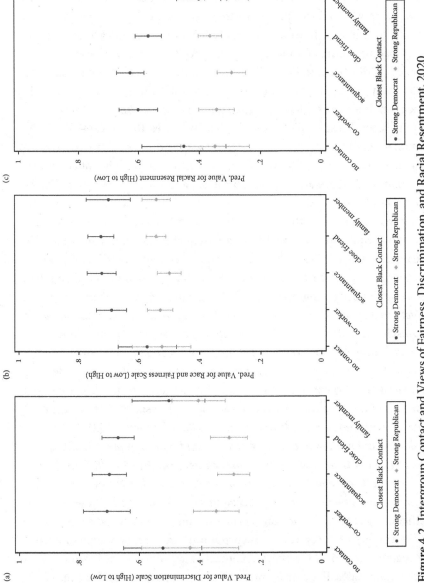

Figure 4.2 Intergroup Contact and Views of Fairness, Discrimination, and Racial Resentment, 2020

Source: Data are from the 2020 UML YouGov survey. Predicted Probabilities with 90% confidence intervals were estimated from Table A4.1. See the appendix for more details.

Black Americans for Strong Democrats and Strong Republicans. Strong Republicans are clearly no more likely to believe in discrimination, report disparities in fairness, or to have less/more racial resentment when they have a close Black contact than when they do not. The expected values for Strong Republicans remains almost identical regardless of their interracial contact. The only change is a shrinking of the confidence interval, which indicates that, if anything, contact appears to help crystalize Republican views, not move them.

On the other hand, for Democrats, the models indicate that contact with Black community members outside the family increases the likelihood of viewing the world as less fair and more discriminatory toward Black people and to be more likely to believe in societal reasons for inequality, as is evident through the racial resentment scale.

Perhaps most importantly, we see consistent evidence that contact with the Black community seems to crystalize views about discrimination and systemic racism for both groups but does not substantively change the views of individuals. Contact seems to fail to make the expected change in attitudes among partisans that the contact hypothesis has shown in the past, *except among Democrats.*

4.6.2 Attitudes toward Police Reform and Importance of Race in Discussions of Police Shootings and Government Aid for Black Americans

The core of the contact effect is that exposure to greater diversity will engender greater empathy. Third-order, or tertiary, contact effects are thought to occur when contact results in attitude change beyond empathy; this happens when policy attitudes are affected as a result of contact. In our previous work on immigration and gay marriage, we argued that those who have contact with minoritized community members should not only be more aware of injustice in society but should also be more supportive of policies that are important to equality for that community. We found that Democrats were responsive to contact on these issues, but Republicans were not. We, again, expect that Democrats, who receive cues that connect diverse experiences with Black Americans with the extant policy environment from their co-partisan leaders, are more likely to translate their interpersonal contact into policy views. But Republicans, who receive fundamentally different messaging from Republican elected officials and partisan media commentators, are provided no pathway to accept positive contact experiences in a way that would translate them into more supportive policy preferences.

We begin by investigating the connection between contact and attitudes about (1) the role of race in the politics of police-involved shootings and (2) support for redistributing financial resources from police departments to social services. Using the same original 2020 nationally representative survey, we asked respondents to tell us if their views were closer to the statement "Police -involved shootings raise important issues about race" or the statement "Race is getting more attention than it deserves in police-involved shootings" on a 7-point scale to measure the importance of discussing race in police shootings. To investigate support for the redistribution of money from police to social services, the goal of the *defund the police* campaign, we asked respondents which of two statements was closest to their views on a 7-point scale that ranged from "Police department budgets should be decreased, and funds should be reallocated into other community programs like mental health, social work, and education" or "Police budgets should be left alone." The full results of this analysis including control variables can be found in Table A4.2 in the appendix.

In Figure 4.3, we present a visualization of the models for the relationship between contact with Black friends, co-workers, and acquaintances and views of the relevance of race to police shootings. Again, our data suggest that contact has no effect on white Republican views. White Republicans are much more likely to view race as getting more attention than warranted, and that view appears to be unaffected by contact with Black community members.

On the other hand, white Democrats, on average, who have no contact with the Black community are not statistically different from white Republicans in their views on these issues. In addition, white Democratic respondents place themselves on the exact mid-point between the two options, indicating they are not sure which statement they believe in more. However, if they have a contact who is Black outside the family, white Democrats are much more likely to indicate that they believe police shootings raise important issues about race. Interestingly, the finding is strongest for those who say their closest contact is a Black acquaintance although the point estimates between Black acquaintance, friend, and coworker are not significantly different.

Figure 4.4 underscores these findings: White Republicans appear to become marginally less supportive of redistributing resources to social services

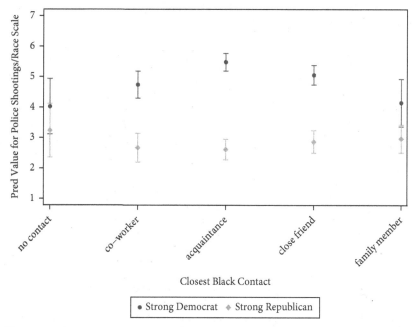

Figure 4.3 Intergroup Contact and Views on the Role of Race in Discussions of Police Shootings, 2020

Source: Data are from the UML 2020 YouGov survey. Predicted Probabilities with 90% confidence intervals were estimated from Table A4.2. See the appendix for more details.

with contact, although the effect is not statistically significant. But white Democrats appear to become more supportive as a result of contact outside the family. And again, white Democrats and white Republicans who have no contact with the Black community are indistinguishable statistically in their support for redistributing police budgets to better fund social services. Overall, these results support the same conclusion: Contact fails to alter white Republican views on this issue, but contact does alter the views of white Democrats.

4.6.3 Support for Government Role in Helping the Black Community

One critical question that has been asked of survey respondents in the past is if the government is responsible for helping address historic and current inequalities. We asked this question of our respondents to see if those with

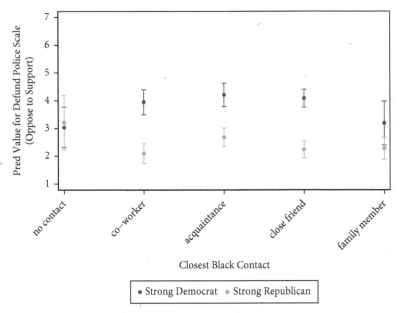

Figure 4.4 Intergroup Contact and Support for Redistributing Police Budgets to Better Fund Social Services, 2020

Source: Data are from the 2020 UML YouGov survey. Predicted Probabilities with 90% confidence intervals were estimated from Table 4.2.

contact were more likely to support government intervention in racial inequality as would be proposed by a tertiary effects hypothesis. We asked respondents to tell us if their views more closely matched the statement "Government should make every effort to improve the social and economic condition of Blacks" or the statement "Government should not help Blacks because Blacks should help themselves," again on a 7-point scale. Figure 4.5 presents the effect of contact of Republicans and Democrats on the "Role of government" scale. The models are available in Table A4.3 in the appendix. We were also able to test this question in both 2017 and 2020 surveys, which gives us additional support that our findings are replicable.

In both 2017 and 2020, white Democrats and Republicans are not statistically different in support for a government role in addressing racial inequality if they have no contact with the Black community. For white Republicans, there is no evidence of a contact effect, a finding that appears to be repeated continuously in the data. But white Republicans and Democrats do have statistically different views once contact is present. White Democrats appear to become somewhat more supportive of a government role in addressing

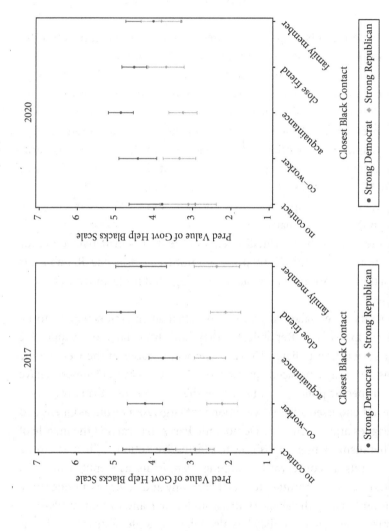

Figure 4.5 Intergroup Contact and Government Role Scale, 2017 and 2020

Source: Data are from the 2017 and 2020 UML YouGov surveys. Predicted Probabilities with 90% confidence intervals were estimated from Table A4.3. See the appendix for more details.

racial inequality, and their views become statistically different from white Republicans when they have contact with members of the Black community outside the family.

4.7 Are Partisan Cues Important?

For our last test in this chapter, we address an important potential criticism of our argument. Perhaps cues are not important. We argue that cues are critical to translating contact into beliefs about inequality and support for/opposition to racialized policies because cues in the information environment enable partisans to translate their interactions in society into their political views. However, each of our tests to this point has been about attitudes (views of fairness and discrimination) and policies (police shootings and government investment) that were politically salient at the time the survey was collected. We present here the effect of contact on support for affirmative action. If cues were not important, we would expect to see Democrats become more supportive of affirmative action simply as a result of contact. This is because the cues in the information environment on affirmative action for Democrats are mixed and do not present a unified partisan cue. Republicans present a unified anti-affirmative action message, but for Democrats, the cue is muddled.

Democrats have walked a fine line on affirmative action policy. To be sure, in comparison to Republicans, they have been far more supportive of affirmative action policies. However, no white leader of the Democratic Party has ever fully embraced affirmative action. Generally, Democrats have supported specific policies that fall under the umbrella of affirmative action but have not endorsed affirmative action writ large. As a result, as Gilens and his colleagues argue, while the Democratic Party "has carried the mantle of racial liberalism," white opposition to affirmative action is "just as strong among liberals as conservatives, among Democrats as Republicans, and among those most committed to racial harmony and equity as among those least committed to such values" (Gilens, Sniderman, and Kuklinski 1998).

Affirmative action as a policy has also taken on a life of its own. It is unclear if most of the general public understands exactly what affirmative action is. In general, it is seen as a policy that requires placing some group into jobs or schools that they are potentially unqualified for based on a quota system, instead of the actual myriad of policies that are included under the affirmative action title. Technically, affirmative action means any "positive step taken to increase the representation of women and minorities in areas of employment, education, and culture from which they have been historically excluded."[4] Most affirmative action policies are fairly mild in practice and include a requirement that search committees take a second look at, but not necessarily hire or accept, candidates of color, as is the case of many universities. Or these policies add some diversity-based points to a student's application that can help make up for other historic disadvantages. But they do not guarantee admission and are just one component of a formula for admission. In short, these policies attempt to make the institution take some "affirmative" step toward increasing representation among the historically discriminated but do not require a certain number of that group be given a job or an acceptance for admission. However, much of the public thinks of affirmative action in terms of racial quotas and zero-sum gains—for example, they or their children are seen as suffering when other children are given this second glance (Steeh and Krysan 1996). To quote Republican leader Pat Buchanan in response to the nomination of Sonia Sotomayor to the Supreme Court: white Americans "pay the price of affirmative action when their sons and daughters are pushed aside to make room for the Sonia Sotomayors."

Democrats have found themselves in an uncomfortable position as well when minoritized populations make gains. For example, in 2016, the conservative publication *The Weekly Standard*'s cover article, written by renowned conservative scholar Joseph Epstein, claimed that, if elected, Hillary Clinton would be "our second affirmative-action president" and asked readers, "How have we come to the point where we elect presidents of the United States not on their intrinsic qualities but because of the accidents of their birth: because they are black, or women, or, one day doubtless, gay, or disabled—not, in other words, for themselves but for the causes they seem to embody or represent, for their status as members of a victim group?"

What are Democrats to do with this attack? They can either say, "This is not an affirmative action election. These candidates are qualified!" thereby implying that those who benefit from affirmative action are not qualified; or they can respond with support for affirmative action, but by doing so imply that perhaps the person was not qualified but the policy worked. Instead, Democratic pundits and leaders find themselves trying to support affirmative action policies while dismissing their claims. And, as a result, Democrats have historically stayed silent on affirmative action. Left-leaning media presences have also made the case for eliminating affirmative action based on race and instead replacing it with one based on historic wealth, as Conor Friedersdorf (2011), a staff writer for *The Atlantic*, did in his essay defending Barack Obama and affirmative action before telling readers, "As it happens, I oppose race-based affirmative action, despite the fact that it may have worked out quite well in the case of Barack Obama. The country where he grew up wouldn't have elected him president. Times change. The notion of advantaged people like Sasha and Malia Obama benefiting from racial preferences is a much better argument against the policy than the experience of their father." This is a typical "I'm for it and against it" explanation that is commonly offered by Democratic leaders.

We posed a question to respondents about their support for affirmative action in both our 2014 and 2020 surveys. Support was measured on a 4-point Likert scale ranging from *Strongly oppose* to *Strongly support*. We modeled support using an ordered logit model. The full models are presented in Table A4.4 in the appendix. The substantive results are presented in Figure 4.6. In these analyses, we find no support for the contact hypothesis. We find only marginal and inconsistent differences between Republicans and Democrats, and no overall impact of contact on support for or opposition to affirmative action for either group. In short, neither Democrats nor Republicans get more supportive with contact when elite cues are absent or fuzzy. This is consistent with the theory that elites are critical to translating intergroup contact into support (or opposition) to policies more likely to benefit or harm minoritized communities.

4.8 Discussion

Writing in 1954, Gordon Allport made a passionate cry for public legislation aimed at decreasing racial inequality and argued that its effects were beyond the immediate economic impact on Black Americans. These policies, he argued, would also lead to long-term psychological changes in racist whites. In a chapter titled "Ought There Be a Law?" Allport (1954) argues that government actions send messages to the public that lead to contact, and the contact leads to less intergroup hostility:

> The establishment of a legal norm creates a public conscience and a standard for expected behavior that checks *overt* signs of prejudice. Legislation aims

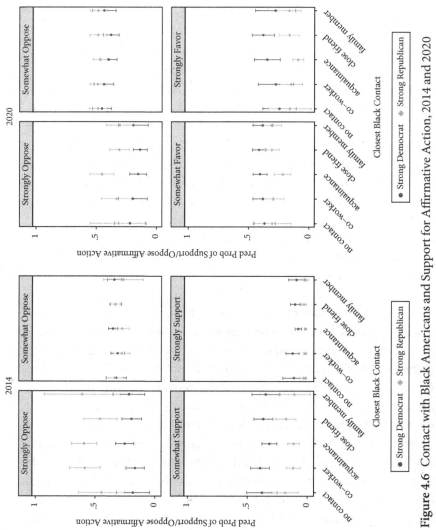

Figure 4.6 Contact with Black Americans and Support for Affirmative Action, 2014 and 2020

Source: Data are from the 2014 and 2020 UML YouGov surveys. Predicted Probabilities with 90% confidence intervals were estimated from Table A4.3. See the appendix for more details.

not at controlling prejudice, but only its open expression. But when expression changes, thoughts too, in the long run, are likely to fall into line.
(p. 470)

He goes on to take on the argument that while sometimes laws are made by
public preferences, laws also shape public preferences:

It is often said that the way must be paved for remedial legislation
through education. Up to a point this statement is undoubtedly true.
Debate, hearings, and an aroused electorate are all essential. But when
the initial work has been done, then the legislation in turn becomes ed-
ucative. The masses of people do not become converts in advance; rather
they are converted by the *fait accompli*. It is a well-known psychological fact that most people accept the results of an election or legislation
gladly enough after the furor has subsided. Even those who strenuously
favored a Democratic candidate for office accept without resentment the
Republican who is elected. And those who fought against FEPC or civil
rights legislation ordinarily abide by the majority decision if these laws
are passed. They allow themselves to be re-educated by the new norm
that prevails. (p. 471)

Reading this section of Allport's most important treatise today feels
strange. Up until 2020 this statement was true. While "he's not my president" bumper stickers sprinkled Democratic cars following the contested
elections of both George W. Bush in 2000 and Donald Trump in 2016,
Democrats responded by accepting the results of the election. The same can
be said of Bill Clinton's 1992 plurality election. Republicans also accepted
the results of Barack Obama's election and reelection, even if they were not
happy about either result. In 2020, though, Donald Trump and the conservative media created a narrative that the election had been stolen. A majority
of Republicans continue to say they believe that there was fraud in the 2020
election, and asserting this belief became a litmus test for candidates running in 2022 (Greenwood 2021). To be clear, no actual evidence of fraud
exists (Eggers, Garro, and Grimmer 2021). What is clear is that polarization
has disrupted our most basic theories of intergroup psychology.

Social scientists have largely taken for granted the fact that we should expect our social theories to work even in the face of fragmented communication networks between co-partisans. Our analysis in this chapter shows

that even as racial justice issues took center stage after the murder of George Floyd, and massive protests and public discussion began over racial inequality in the United States, any shifts in public opinion for those with interracial contact were mitigated on the right by elite cueing. The social effects of intergroup contact—of being exposed to diversity and knowing other people—work differently based on the political messaging that we hear. And this is deeply connected to our political identity.

Our data show that in the United States, interpersonal contact with Black Americans does not decrease white Republican animosity. The benefits of intergroup contact are reliant on elite support, but in the modern context, Republican leaders prevent contact from having this effect by being unsupportive. In fact, Republican elites have become openly hostile to any group they disagree with. This is apparent in the vitriol among Republicans that has manifested in death threats, physical violence, and other belligerent acts in response to the politicization of CRT, formerly an obscure social science theory. Despite decades of progress on civil rights in the United States and increased interpersonal contact between racial groups, the Republican Party has harnessed latent white racism to justify whitewashing American history and school curricula with great fanfare from their base voters (Frey 2022; People Staff 2023). As Ronald Brownstein, political analyst and lead editor at *The Atlantic*, argues, Republican states are rapidly diversifying and as a result Republican leaders are pursuing "dual goals" in their campaigns to limit discussions of racism and inequality. The movement comprises both "a defensive tool (to prevent white students from feeling guilty)" and "an equally important offensive goal" to discourage youth from "viewing systemic discrimination as a problem that public policy should address" (Brownstein 2022, para. 23). The data we present in this chapter suggest that the effort by Republican elites to limit or eliminate discussion of inequality and racism because it might make white students uncomfortable, and their rejection of all discussion of systemic inequality either in schools or in public policy, work to prevent intergroup contact theory from fulfilling its promise.

Moreover, the ability of a political party to lead voters to incivility and violence over honest discussions of American history and demographic empirical reality emphasizes how far partisan-motivated reasoning has taken us. Partisanship is changing the way people behave and respond to stimuli in their personal environments. It fundamentally changes the way people react to lived experiences to such an extent that it calls into question some of the most well-supported behavioral social science theories. This is alarming, but also provides empirical validation for our theoretical perspective of the power of partisanship. We turn to other classic social theories in the following two chapters.

5

Prospect Theory and Partisan Cues

Right now, a countless number of Trump supporters believe they are
owning the left by refusing to take a lifesaving vaccine. In a country
where elections are decided on razor-thin margins, does it not benefit one side if their opponents simply drop dead? . . . No one wants to
cave to a piece of s*** like that, or a scumbag like Fauci, or any of the
scumbags at CNNLOL, so we don't. And what's the result? They're all
vaccinated, and we're not! And when you look at the numbers, the
only numbers that matter, which is who's dying, it's overwhelmingly
the unvaccinated who are dying, and they have just manipulated
millions of their political enemies into the unvaccinated camp.

—John Nolte, *Breitbart News* (2021)

5.1 Introduction

Why do people oppose the government expanding health insurance access
even when their access to health care would improve if the government did
so (Fiscella 2016)? Why do people oppose taxing the rich to support social
services even when they are not wealthy, and they would benefit from the
expansion of social services? Why did Republicans support turning down
federal stimulus money for those on unemployment during the pandemic
despite the fact that the money was holding up the economy (Stettner 2021)?
Why do uninsured Republicans sign up for federally subsidized health insurance at lower rates than Democrats (Lerman, Sadin, and Trachtman 2017)?
And why have Republicans shunned taking public safety measures and
public health measures even when those measures will increase their personal safety and well-being? Each of these decisions increases an individual's
personal and financial risk, yet when political parties signal that increased
risk is the position of the party, the party's base appears to follow. In this
chapter, we continue our investigation of how partisan-motivated reasoning

The Power of Partisanship. Joshua J. Dyck and Shanna Pearson-Merkowitz, Oxford University Press.
© Oxford University Press 2023. DOI: 10.1093/oso/9780197623787.003.0006

has spread outside the realm of politics to personal financial and health care decisions.

As in Chapter 4, we start with one of the most well-known theories in social science to investigate how partisanship should shape the social science understanding of individual decision making. Here, we investigate prospect theory, perhaps the most well-cited and steadily replicated causal theory in economics, psychology, and political science.

In this chapter, we proceed with a relatively straightforward question: Can partisan cues alter respondents' willingness to accept risk? To determine the answer, we examine the effects of responses to partisan cues related to risk acceptance during the Covid-19 pandemic and then present the results of a survey experiment that suggests that prospect theory is sensitive to partisan cues. Our results also demonstrate that partisan cues make people more willing to take financial risks.

Throughout repeated studies of decision making across the disciplines of economics, psychology, political science, and other fields, social scientists endeavor to make generalizable claims about human behavior. But, as we have already seen from the experiments and correlative analysis in the last two chapters, many of the general claims of social science theories are subject to partisan-motivated reasoning when elite cues are introduced. In this chapter, we show that prospect theory is subject to partisan-motivated reasoning as well.

Our experiments find that partisanship makes people, particularly Republican identifiers, riskier and willing to put more on the line for partisan gains. We investigate risk aversion and acceptance through two experiments—one on support for providing free Covid-19 vaccines to all residents of the United States, conducted during the pandemic but before the release of a vaccine, and one on a tax refund proposal. We find evidence in both experiments that partisanship makes people more willing to take risks. While prospect theory was first proposed as a foil to utility maximization theory to show why people would not always choose the most financial gain, we find not only that partisanship makes people more willing to be risky for financial gain, but that people are more likely to be risky with their health due to a partisan motivation.

Our answer to the conundrum of why people support or oppose policies that seem contradictory to their self-interest when these policies are supported by their party is that risk acceptance in the political arena can include a trade-off between a personal benefit and a partisan win. Traditional rational choice logic would suggest that people are self-serving and therefore when their partisan team must lose for them to gain, they will take the avenue that is best for their self-interest: the personal benefit. But in today's highly partisan environment, we argue, people are more likely to choose the partisan win over the less risky action that could improve their financial and physical well-being.

5.2 Prospect Theory

The foundation of prospect theory was first introduced by Kahneman and Tversky in 1979. In their classic paper, they argued that people do not evaluate decisions rationally in line with expected utility theory. Instead, "prospect theory posits that individuals evaluate outcomes with respect to deviations from a reference point rather than with respect to net asset levels, that their identification of this reference point is a critical variable, that they give more weight to losses than to comparable gains, and that they are generally risk-averse with respect to gains and risk-acceptant with respect to losses" (Levy 1992, 171).

Under expected utility theory, which has formed many of the foundational assumptions in economics, people were thought to behave rationally in evaluating payoffs and risk. So, for example, take a scenario in which you can choose two paths. You can either take a gamble to flip a coin and have the chance to win $1,000, or you can simply take $400 with no coin flip. Expected utility theory predicts that a person would prefer a 50/50 chance to win $1,000 over a certain $400 because the "expected utility" (e.g., potential outcome) of the 50/50 chance at $1,000 is greater than the $400 (in mathematical terms, that would be: $0.5 \times \$1,000 = \$500$, which is more than $400). But in experimental settings, Kahneman and Tversky found that people across countries and contexts take the bird in the hand and choose the $400. In this example, because the person starts with nothing and is being offered something (a potential gain), people have a tendency to be risk averse, rather than following the mathematically driven insights of expected utility theory (Kahneman and Tversky 1979). The finding works in the opposite direction, too. A person who starts with something is more likely to gamble with what they have than take a certain loss. So, for instance, if a person is given $1,000 and is then told that they have the choice to either return $400 or take a 50/50 chance on either keeping the entire $1,000 or losing the entire $1,000 (depending on that coin flip again), the majority will gamble and try to keep the $1,000, even though the expected utility theory tells them to return $400, keep $600, and not gamble. In mathematical terms, expected utility theory says the value of the gamble is $1,000 – (0.5 ×$1,000) = $500, while the value of returning the $400 is $1,000 – $400 = $600.

The foundational elements of prospect theory have been replicated across countries, time, and scenarios (Ruggeri et al. 2020). Put simply, prospect theory suggests that people's natural behavioral instincts guide them to take the less risky option when they have something to gain (risk aversion) and the riskier option when they have something to lose (risk acceptance), even if it means that they miss out on a potentially better or more optimal outcome or strategy.

5.3 Linking Prospect Theory to Political Behavior

Perhaps one reason that prospect theory has been used less as a theoretical mechanism in the political behavior literature is that it begins with the rational actor assumption in economics as a foil (Mercer 2005). That is, under the rational actor assumption, individuals will pursue outcomes that carry higher expected utilities over those with lower expected utilities. However, prospect theory teaches us many things, and the experiments produced a number of anomalous results compared to the expectations of the rational actor model. In general, we have learned that people are bad at weighting probabilities (they underweight the certainty of high-probability events, such as catching a communicable disease, and overweight the uncertainty of low-probability events, such as being kidnapped) and that preferences come from comparisons of proposals to a reference point (for a review of the literature, see Passarelli and Del Ponte 2020).

While these anomalies have been considered to varying degrees, perhaps the strongest connection to an existing literature within the study of American political behavior is to studies of status quo bias (e.g., Bolsen, Druckman, and Cook 2014; Dyck and Pearson-Merkowitz 2019; Lang et al. 2021). This research has connected prospect theory's overweighting of negative information when in the domain of gain to people's increased likelihood of risk aversion. In voting, this means people are more likely to favor the status quo, or to vote "no" on policy proposals (e.g., referendums or the ballot initiative).

In this literature, however, the acquisition is treated monotonically. People acquire information, and risk aversion is a *ceteris parabis* part of human behavior that is probabilistically more likely. But who is and who is not risk averse and under what circumstances? There is value in studying this variation. While every individual may have an underlying predisposition to be more or less risk averse/acceptant, and overall we find that people are more risk averse when in the domain of gain, we argue that you cannot take partisan motivations out of expectations of behavior. We therefore expect that the level and degree to which a person is risk averse or acceptant can be altered by the partisan information that they acquire *if partisan gamesmanship is also an objective*. More explicitly, partisan information is acquired largely as the result of cues, and so partisan cues should be able to alter an individual's view of risk.

As in the previous chapters, we expect that our findings will be strongest among Republicans due to the nature of asymmetric political polarization and the internal dynamics of the parties (Grossmann and Hopkins 2016). As we will show, our results largely conform to this expectation. Our experimental evidence shows that Republicans are consistently more receptive to cues that make them more risk averse or risk acceptant, depending on the political situation. For Democrats, there is some evidence that they become more acceptant of risk when the political situation is in the domain of loss, but only in one of our two experiments.

5.4 Risk-Taking During the Covid-19 Pandemic

One issue that has received a great deal of attention and highlights our thesis is risky behavior surrounding the Covid-19 pandemic. This includes support for government shutdowns early in the pandemic, masking and social distancing behavior, and vaccination. A new body of work has demonstrated the strong role that partisanship played in people's public health decisions during the Covid-19 pandemic (Agranov, Elliott, and Ortoleva 2021; Allcott et al. 2020; Green et al. 2020; Rabb et al. 2021). Indeed, willingness to take on personal risk was perhaps nowhere more apparent than President Donald Trump's decision to engage in continually risky behavior at the onset of the pandemic. He held rallies where neither he nor his supporters wore masks, and openly refused to wear a mask or abide by social distancing guidelines. Republican elites, including the President, connected masking behavior and

not getting vaccinated to tropes about toughness and manliness and ultimately used arguments related to overreaction about the pandemic to oppose any and all public health policies. For example, during an interview,
Representative Marjorie Taylor Greene (R-Ga) argued on Steve Bannon's
podcast that she did not get vaccinated because of her patriotism. "You want
to know something, Steve? I'm not vaccinated. I'm not vaccinated, and I'm
not getting the vaccine because I'm an American. I can choose what I want
to do with my body. I have the freedom to decide if I want to get a vaccine
or not get a vaccine. I do not care who tells me to get one" (Gregorian 2021).
Similarly, when masks were reintroduced to the House of Representatives
after they had been lifted, Representative Jody Hice (R-Ga) tweeted, "Mask
and vaccine mandates: Bullying, Controlling, Unconstitutional, Threats to
Liberty!" (Chiacu and Cornwell 2021).

As these quotes show, while the vast majority of Republican elites in
Congress and the media were among the first to be vaccinated, many
Republicans used the pandemic as fodder to attack political opponents.
Throughout the 2020 presidential election, Donald Trump attacked Biden
for wearing a mask and continuing to abide by social distancing, and regularly played down the risk of the virus, comparing it to the flu, arguing it was
overblown, that Democrats simply wanted to take away rights, and that the
public health measures had little to do with public health.

This type of criticism, in turn, encouraged Republicans to engage in riskier
behavior and, as a result, Republicans have opposed policies that mandate
or even suggest using masks, getting vaccinated, limiting the size of social
gatherings, and other public health remediation measures. For example,
surveys conducted during the first summer of the pandemic found that fewer
than 50% of Republicans thought people should wear masks most or all of
the time compared with 86% of Democrats, and a third of Republicans said
they never wear masks themselves, compared with only 1% of Democrats
(Brenan 2020; Pew Research Center 2020).

For illustrative purposes, Figure 5.1 shows the relationship at the county
level between the Biden vote in 2020 and Covid-19 vaccine rates (Center for
Disease Control 2021; MIT Election Data and Science Lab 2018). The relationship is clear: In places with more Democrats, a larger share of the population was vaccinated. This relationship manifests in individual-level data
as well: As of October 2021, the Kaiser Family Foundation found that while
90% of Democrats reported being vaccinated, only 58% of Republicans said
they had received the shots (Hamel, Lopes, and Stokes 2021). Elite cues on

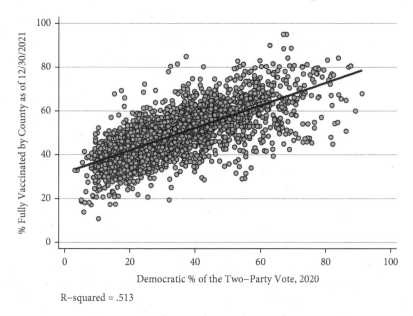

R–squared = .513

Figure 5.1 2020 County Vote Share and 2021 Year-End Vaccination Rates

Source: County vaccine data are for the 2,779 counties with data completeness of 90% or greater as of 12/30/21 (Center for Disease Control 2021). Election data are from MIT Election Data and Science Lab (2018).

the pandemic clearly had the effect of polarizing a public health issue (Green et al. 2020).

But is this finding spurious, and in which direction does the causal arrow point? Are Republican elites to blame for Republicans' risky behavior? Or are Republican elites responding to the anti-vaccine, anti-mask, and anti-social distancing desires of their voters? It certainly could be that Republican elites took an anti–public health position and that Democratic elites took a pro–public health position in response to their co-partisans' respective ideology. If this is the case, the central thesis of this book is potentially on less stable ground. Because we were working on this book during the pandemic, we foresaw the eventual place we could end up if the pandemic turned partisan. So, we ran an experiment on support for providing a Covid-19 vaccine to the public for free.[1]

We argue that prospect theory has much to contribute to understanding this policy and there is a critical role of partisan elites in this process. The probability of getting sick from Covid-19 places the policy in the domain of loss—providing everyone a vaccine for free will reduce other services or increase taxes, while individually people are likely to underestimate their own probability of getting sick. This argument is consistent with Lerman et al.'s (2017) longitudinal finding that uninsured Republicans were less likely to sign up for government-provided health insurance, and chose to instead pay a fine for not signing up in response to the partisan rancor around the Affordable Care Act. While not using the lens of prospect theory, their findings (and theory) suggest that partisans are willing to risk their health for partisan gain.[2]

Cues from trusted elites in support of the free vaccine are likely to make co-partisans more risk averse and support the policy while cues from out-partisan leaders are likely to make out-partisans more risk acceptant. Our tests in this chapter, therefore, proceed in two different ways. We first look at the effect of partisan cues in altering direct support for vaccine policies. We then apply our hypothesis to a less politically charged example (tax credits), which we modeled after one of the classic Kahneman and Tversky (1979) experiments and placed firmly in the domain of gains.[3]

5.4.1 Support for Covid-19 Vaccination Policy Experiment

Our first experiment looks specifically at cues and approval of the government providing a Covid-19 vaccine to all residents of the United States. We chose this as our experimental policy because at the time, it was well established among public health circles and policy elites that the key to ending the pandemic was both the invention of a Covid-19 vaccine and its uptake by the vast majority of Americans. Since new vaccines are very expensive and having to pay for a vaccine could prevent uninsured or underinsured Americans from receiving the shot, the government was known to be critical to funding and distributing the vaccine free of charge (Weintraub 2020).

Importantly, again, this experiment was conducted months before a vaccine was submitted for approval in the summer of 2020. Vaccinations were a distant dream at the point when we ran this study. Second, our experiment also included a willingness to pay (WTP) measure as is common in economic, business, and marketing experiments. WTP measures allow researchers to tease out the difference between respondents who object to the policy because they are concerned that they will have to pay more in taxes as a result of the policy and respondents who object to the policy due to non-financial concerns. Because Republicans are likely to be more tax-averse than

Democrats, we thought it important to control for the potential price to the respondent in our experiment. Following the literature on WTP (see, for example, Lang, Weir, and Pearson-Merkowitz 2021), we included a randomized cost to the respondent in each rendition of the experiment.

The prompts to our experiment are summarized in Table 5.1. The experiment was conducted in a survey conducted by YouGov, an internet-based market research and opinion polling company, in August 2020. The survey included a sample of 1,000 American adults, matched and weighted to be representative of the U.S. adult population. Each respondent was randomly presented with one of the cueing treatments or the control. The price was randomized within treatments following previous studies (e.g., Kotchen, Turk, and Leiserowitz 2017; Lang, Weir, and Pearson-Merkowitz 2021) and as recommended by Alberini (1995). The price of providing the policy ranged from $50 to $450 in taxes per person.

Respondents were either placed into the control group or given one of two cues (Biden or Trump). Within each group, there were nine possible values for the price of the program in taxes. The data therefore categorizes respondents into one of 27 different subgroups based on the treatment they received. To assess the effect of both the cue *and* cost, we regressed respondents' attitude toward the proposed policy (making a Covid-19 vaccine available to all residents of the United States free of charge) on the cues they received (Control/Biden/Trump) and the price point they were given

Table 5.1 Vaccine Cue Experiment with Willingness to Pay Cut Points

Control	Biden cue	Trump cue
[Public Health experts have. . . .]	*[Democratic presidential nominee and former Vice President Joe Biden, has. . . .]*	*[President Donald Trump has. . . .]*

. . . proposed making a Coronavirus vaccine available to every resident of the United States for free as soon as it becomes available. People like you would pay about [$X] more in taxes next year to pay for making a vaccine and delivering it to anyone who wanted it for free.

Do you favor or oppose [this/Trump's/Biden's] proposal to make a Coronavirus vaccine available to all residents of the United States for free?

Response options: *strongly oppose, somewhat oppose, somewhat favor, strongly favor*

Willingness to pay price points ($X): 50 (5%), 100 (5%), 150 (10%), 200 (20%), 250 (20%), 300 (20%), 350 (10%), 400 (5%), 450 (5%)

Notes: Data are from the 2020 UML YouGov survey. See the appendix for more details.

($50 to $450). We also considered the responses by party identification by interacting the cue response and willingness to pay, respectively, by 7-point party identification. The full model results are available in the appendix, in Table A5.1.

Overall, the model results demonstrate that there is some price sensitivity in overall support for the free vaccine, but that the price effect is concentrated among Democrats (see appendix Table A5.1, Model 3, and corresponding Figures A5.1 and A5.2 for more detail on this point). However, the experiment shows that the elected official advocating for the bill plays a much larger role and is the variable that has the most significant impact. Interestingly, when the experiment cued that the proposal came from President Trump, there are no statistical differences between Democrats and Republicans: On average, across-party identification groups are just shy of "somewhat" favoring the policy (3) when it was proposed by Trump. However, there are strong differences for both groups between the Trump cue and the Biden cue. Strong Democrats were 17% more likely to support free vaccines when the proposal came from Biden than when it was proposed by Trump. For strong Republicans, the difference between the Trump cue and the Biden cue is a 40% decrease in support for a free vaccine. This is demonstrated in Figure 5.2.

What do we make of this? First, we cannot separate cues from the actual political environment in which they exist. From the beginning of the pandemic, President Trump and Republicans downplayed the importance of masks, the danger of the virus, and the risk involved in exposure to Covid-19. Therefore, it is no surprise that overall, Republicans were less receptive to a free vaccine policy than Democrats. However, we also see that cueing Republicans that their president proposed the idea made them support the policy with the same enthusiasm as Democrats—that is, the in-party cue made Republicans more risk averse. But when it was Biden who proposed it, Republican support dropped to a negligible amount; indeed, in the raw data, only *two* strong Republicans expressed maximum support for the free vaccine when cued that it was a Biden policy. Democrats too were *less supportive* of the vaccine when the opposition party proposed it than when the proposal was by their own candidate; a Trump cue made Democrats more risk acceptant. Certainly, Republicans were in general less supportive of vaccines even before the pandemic (Fridman, Gershon, and Gneezy 2021) and less supportive of government intervention in the economy. However, what is critical here is that even given that starting point, partisan elite framing plays

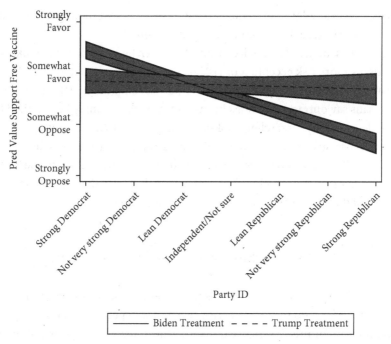

Figure 5.2 Support for a Free Vaccine by Treatment Effect and Party
Identification

Source: Data are from the 2020 UML YouGov survey. Predicted values with 90% confidence
intervals were generated from Table A5.1, Model 2 in the appendix. See the appendix for more
details.

a significant role in shaping support on these issues and in structuring how
partisans evaluate risk.

Critically, our results suggest that had Republican elites cued a pro-vaccine
message once the vaccine became available, Republican voters likely would
have been vaccinated at rates much more similar to Democrats and more
lives could have been spared in Republican communities. Co-partisan elite
cues also likely made Democrats more risk averse when it came to getting
vaccinated. These facts are borne out in real-world data. By October of 2021,
Americans in heavily Trump-supporting counties were *more than three times
as likely* to die from the virus as those in Biden-supporting counties because
of low vaccination rates (Leonhardt 2021). Moreover, high-profile cases
such as Chad Carswell, a North Carolina man who refused a desperately
needed organ transplant because he did not want to be vaccinated for political reasons (Faherty 2022), have filled the pages of news articles and Twitter

feeds. The examples of extreme partisan responses that highlight partisans' willingness to accept risk for political gain are ample.

Elite cues mattered and will continue to matter, because elite cues make co-partisans more risk acceptant or risk averse, even when that risk has life-or-death consequences. Critics of negative partisanship often claim that when partisans say outrageous things in surveys, they have simply been baited by too-clever survey researchers looking for headlines, that their responses are often "expressive" and not real. We disagree strongly with this conclusion; the varied willingness to be vaccinated and adopt other public health measures has led many people to choose their partisanship over their health and the health of their loved ones and fellow community members.

5.4.2 Partisanship, Taxation, and Prospect Theory

It certainly is possible that Covid-19 responses are a special scenario and not the standard way to measure the risk aversion/acceptance proposed in prospect theory. For this reason, we tested our thesis using an experiment intentionally designed to engage the financial mechanism originally proposed in prospect theory: decisions regarding money. Previous studies have shown that partisanship can affect financial decision making. For example, Gerber and Huber (2009) employed data on county-level taxable sales over a 16-year period and found that following elections, Democrats and Republicans spend differently. In response to their party winning, people spend more; when their party loses, they spend less. However, spending and risky behavior are different animals, so we designed a second experiment to test prospect theory and financial decisions.

In this experiment, we asked respondents to choose between two tax proposals debated by a legislature. Under one tax plan, we explained, there would be a 50% chance they would receive a $1,000 tax credit and a 50% chance they would receive no tax credit at all. Under the other plan, they were informed that they would definitely receive a $450 tax credit. Respondents were asked which of the two plans they would prefer. Prospect theory suggests that respondents should be more likely to choose the lower benefit and lower risk choice of a certain $450 tax credit. We tested our hypothesis of partisan motivation through two treatments compared with a control. Respondents to the survey were randomly assigned to one of the three treatment groups. Members of the control group were told only that the legislature was debating the proposals and were asked which they preferred. Members of the first treatment were told that the 50/50 $1,000 tax credit plan was proposed by *Republican* leadership and the guaranteed $450 plan was proposed by a bipartisan committee. Members of the second treatment were told that the 50/50 $1,000 tax credit plan was proposed by *Democratic* leadership and the guaranteed $450 plan was proposed by a bipartisan committee.

The expectation under prospect theory is that while the expected utility of the 50/50 plan is larger, respondents will be more likely to be risk averse and choose the certain $450 tax credit. However, our hypothesis is that partisanship should make people more risk acceptant than would be predicted with a classic prospect theory hypothesis. The experimental language for the control and treatments are detailed in Table 5.2.

To be sure, we are especially interested in the results of this experiment by party identification. We therefore display the result for all respondents and then separately for Democrats, Republicans, and independents. The experimental results, and significance tests between the control and treatment groups, are presented in Figure 5.3.

To begin, for all respondents in the control group, the insight of prospect theory—risk aversion—replicates well under the conditions of the experiment. Without partisan cues, 71% of respondents chose the risk-averse

Table 5.2 Prospect Theory Experiment with Partisan Cues

Control	Republican leadership cue	Democratic leadership cue
Consider the following two tax proposals being debated by your state legislature. Under the first plan, there is a 50% chance you will receive a $1,000 tax credit and a 50% chance you will receive no ($0) tax credit. Under the second plan, you are certain to receive a $450 tax credit. Do you prefer the first or second plan?	*Consider the following two tax proposals being debated by your state legislature. Under the first plan,* **proposed by the Republican leadership**, *there is a 50% chance you will receive a $1,000 tax credit and a 50% chance you will receive no ($0) tax credit. Under the second plan,* **proposed by a Bipartisan committee**, *you are certain to receive a $450 tax credit. Do you prefer the first or second plan?*	*Consider the following two tax proposals being debated by your state legislature. Under the first plan,* **proposed by the Democratic leadership**, *there is a 50% chance you will receive a $1,000 tax credit and a 50% chance you will receive no ($0) tax credit. Under the second plan,* **proposed by a Bipartisan committee**, *you are certain to receive a $450 tax credit. Do you prefer the first or second plan?*

Notes: Data are from the 2019 UML YouGov survey. See the appendix for more details.

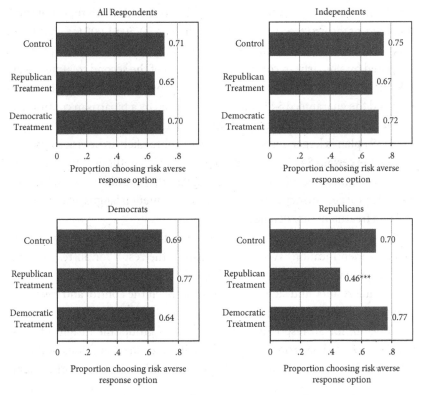

Figure 5.3 Results of the Prospect Theory Experiment with Partisan Cues

Source: Data are from the 2019 UML YouGov survey. Difference-of-means tests were computed between the treatment group and the control group. $^{**}p < .05$, $^{***}p < .01$, two-tailed tests reported. See the appendix for more details.

option ($450 guaranteed) over the risk-acceptant option (50% chance at $1,000). This confirms the longstanding and stable result going back multiple decades from Kahneman and Tversky (1979).

However, when Republicans were told that the 50/50 alternative was proposed by Republican leadership, they became considerably more risk acceptant. Compared with the control condition, where 70% of Republicans chose "risk aversion," under the Republican cue condition, Republicans chose risk aversion ($450) only 46% of the time and the riskier choice (with a higher expected utility value) 54% of the time—a decrease in risk aversion of 24 percentage points. Not only is this statistically significant, but it is also substantively meaningful. When cued that Republicans had proposed this plan, the *majority* of Republicans chose the risk-acceptant over the risk-averse position, in contrast to the well-established and stable finding from prospect theory. Interestingly, this is the only significant effect; we do not see a symmetric effect for Democrats, who remained, on par, as risk averse when cued that their party supports the riskier position with a higher expected utility value as when they were given no party information. Independents were equally (and expectedly) unmoved by the partisan cues, indicating that independents were behaving as classic prospect theory would predict.

5.5 Discussion

We began this chapter asking why it appears that partisans behave in ways that are counterintuitive to the hierarchy of needs. Partisans appear to put their financial and personal well-being below partisan gamesmanship. The data in this chapter contribute to our overarching thesis—that partisanship has begun to spread from the political sphere to the nonpolitical, to our social networks and to our decisions about how best to ensure our financial and personal health and well-being. The scope of partisan-motivated reasoning has upended our expectations about decision making based on personal experience and social and personal values.

Specifically, our analyses in this chapter show that people are more (and sometimes less) likely to choose a riskier outcome when the decision aligns with their political party's stance. While we show this with survey experiments, we also find evidence that political operatives understand this quite well and are putting this psychological mechanism to use to attempt to change the risky behavior of their voters.

Take the op-ed written on the conservative-Republican website *Breitbart News* that began this chapter. In it, regular Breitbart contributor John Nolte (2021) argued that Republicans should get vaccinated because otherwise "the left has us right where they want us." The article goes on to explain that statement: What does the left want? For Republicans to die. How are they going to do that? By mandating a vaccine because they know that Republicans will balk at anything the Democrats say someone should do.

While this argument reads like a conspiracy theory, Nolte is addressing a real phenomenon: Republicans put their lives at risk because Democrats "own" the vaccine issue. But partisanship makes Americans take on risk every day, whether it is through refusing to get a vaccine that the other party champions, choosing to pay a fine instead of signing up for health insurance, or rejecting background checks and controls on military-style weapons.

And there is no reason to believe that this is a Republican-only finding. While Republicans are right now the more extreme of the two parties, if Republicans introduced a life-saving policy, the data we show above indicate that Democrats would resist it. And while our results suggest that Democrats would be less affected by the policy being introduced by a Republican, the fact that a Republican introduced it would meaningfully reduce Democrat support. And if Democratic leaders saw the issue as one on which they could "win by losing," there is no reason to think co-partisans would not fall in line.

A 2020 poll from the right-leaning American Enterprise Institute found that 64% of Democrats and 75% of Republicans see policies introduced by the other party as so misguided that they pose a serious threat to the country (Enten 2021). When this is the case, little about the policy specifics or its impact on people's lives matters; voters take shortcuts (or use heuristics) to decide what they should and should not support. Our evidence suggests that just as Republicans became more risk acceptant in the face of Covid-19, if a Republican president were to suggest a policy that could save lives and Democratic elites objected to it for partisan gain, Democrats in the electorate would follow suit, putting their own health at risk in the process.

This chapter also ultimately continues the story from Chapter 4 about partisans, cues, and motivated reasoning. The definition of social behavior in most theories relies on some form of a shared understanding of some social idea, like risk, that can derive its meaning from the partisan information process. So, if we say that, in a general way, individuals are risk averse, the reality is that partisan information can change our definition of what something like "risk" means. Risk becomes what the party says it means. Therefore, a longstanding stable finding like *individuals are risk averse in the domain of gains* can be altered when a respondent understands the source of the proposals. It is not the theory that changes, per se. Rather, it is that a Republican who is comparing 50/50 to get $1,000 versus a certain $450 now has an additional piece of information: A cue-giver they trust proposed the first option. This, to the individual, presumably makes that outcome less risky psychologically, even if the payout or the level of certainty[uncertainty] never changes. What shifts is the perception that *this policy is one proposed by my team*—and that is enough to change. The implication of the findings of the last two chapters—that intergroup contact and prospect theory responses can be dramatically altered by a simple cue—raises the question: Are there truths about social behavior that are not constrained by our partisan identities?

6

Political Responsiveness to the Lived Experience

6.1 Introduction

For decades, the common wisdom among political scientists about American voters has been that the average person does not know much about politics, and the least informed among us are political "independents." Political independents are generally considered to be disinterested, disengaged, uninformed, and lack political sophistication. As a recent Pew study noted, "the small share of Americans who are truly independent—less than 10% of the public has no partisan leaning—stand out for their low level of interest in politics" (Pew Research Center 2019, 3). Because of this disengagement, political scientists argue, independents are the ones targeted by political advertising, the main reason for the dumbing down of American political discourse, and they do not ultimately hold leaders accountable for their shirking. In short, positive political science has passed a great deal of normative judgment on uninformed independents.

The premise of this chapter is not to argue what independents know or do not know; we save that for Chapter 7. Here, we contend that being engaged and interested in politics in the fashion of the highly partisan electorate is not a panacea toward creating better democratic citizenship. Political scientists have long argued that information helps individuals make choices more aligned with their interests. As the previous chapters show, long-understood conceptions of human behavior are upended by individuals using partisan-motivated reasoning. In this chapter, we turn to specific areas to test the notion of whether partisanship impedes or facilitates the use of information from the lived environment and personal experience in the development of political attitudes, specifically policy attitudes.

Political scientists largely agree that despite the widely accepted role of partisanship in political reasoning, one's personal or lived experience—be it where one lives and the context of our neighborhoods or personal financial

The Power of Partisanship. Joshua J. Dyck and Shanna Pearson-Merkowitz, Oxford University Press.
© Oxford University Press 2023. DOI: 10.1093/oso/9780197623787.003.0007

circumstances—informs the development of beliefs about what is relevant in politics and opinions on key policies.

Although party identification has been hailed for its ability to help voters cut the time and resources needed to make decisions generally in line with their preferences, party identification in the modern era serves as a *misinformation shortcut* more than an information shortcut. Partisans are very likely to be resistant to their lived experience in crafting policy opinions and instead are more likely to accept the narrative proposed by their party's elites. As a result, we argue that despite their low levels of general political knowledge, independents come to policy positions in response to their lived experience—again, the way political scientists have long thought people come to policy decisions.

Our evidence comes from surveys about issues related to gun violence and gun control, open space and land use, affordable housing policy, and the minimum wage. All of these share a similar thread in that a person may apply some experience from their life and their experiences to a policy attitude. The evidence is surprising, but consistent and supportive of our theory that partisans are derailed by a hyper-partisan information context and that uninformed independents act as the reasonable idiot-savants of American politics. Partisans use partisan cues in decision making. This can often distract them from important elements of the information environment, including their own observations about things like how much crime or open space there is in their own environment. Further, and perhaps more surprising, partisans are also likely to come to policy positions that exacerbate their personal economic circumstances. Instead, independents are those whose policy attitudes are responsive to their personal experience.

As our book so far has shown, partisanship tends to upend other theories of political decision making. What we show here is that partisanship as an information shortcut may lead individuals to reject the relevant information in front of them. The underlying assumption of voter responsiveness is that voters will select candidates and policies that are closer to their own positions and that will benefit their self-interest (either personally or socially understood). Instead, we find, in these instances, that when information is available in a non-partisan way—either through one's neighborhood or one's own personal situation—independents are the most likely to be responsive. In short, independents behave in the way that appears rational—they respond to the circumstances in which they live, and partisans do not.

To be clear, voter responsiveness to the lived experience is the crux of the argument for federalism's division of powers between the federal, state, and local governments and, critically, for a smaller role for the federal government in domestic affairs—people know what policies they need at the local level, and not all places need the same policies. Former presidential candidate and Senator Bernie Sanders (D-VT) once noted that gun control is a "local issue" because what is sensible in rural Vermont may not be sensible in urban New York City. This argument for a smaller role for the federal government is that voters and elected officials will be responsive to the circumstances in which they live. The potential of the federal government mandating the building of housing in a place flush with affordable housing, or preserving land in an area flush with land but no affordable housing is one of the reasons the founders wanted a "compound republic." Federalism was supposed to provide opportunities for citizens to be more involved in the government process, encourage local areas to deal with their unique conditions and needs quickly and responsively, and encourage innovation and creativity when citizens applied themselves to self-governance.

The lack of responsiveness among partisans we find in this chapter upends the theory of federalism for the majority of voters. Perhaps federalism is for independents.

6.2 Political Independents and Political Behavior

Journalists often treat independents as the lynchpin of the political campaign. If you win the independent vote (i.e., the "swing" vote), then you win the election, the logic goes. To be sure, political scientists have thrown a healthy dose of cold water on this proposition. While in any given survey, more than 40% of Americans might identify as independents, many of these Americans vote consistently for one party or the other and firmly lean toward one of the two major parties. The true number of purely independent voters is likely closer to between 10% and 15% of the American public (Keith et al. 1992; Pew Research Center 2019). When examining the swings in elections, political scientist and noted election forecaster James E. Campbell estimated that "swing voters" (the types of undecided independents journalists love to talk about) were only needed to provide a majority to the winning presidential candidate once between 1972 and 2004 (J. E. Campbell 2008).

Most elections turn on increased mobilization of partisans, not the whims of independent voters. Why? Independents do not pay attention to politics or participate at the same rate as partisans. They are simply more likely to be disengaged. Independents' level of detachment is not very surprising to some extent. Mutz's (2002) research shows that cross-cutting cues (e.g., information from both sides of a political debate) make people uncomfortable to such an extent that they tend to remove themselves from being in a position in which they have to act to support one side. Having (or believing) information from only one side, which partisanship provides, is a much more comfortable space to occupy. There is no conflict to deal with and no feelings of guilt. Thus, independents, who are not predisposed to trust one side or the other, in a polarized environment in which every issue is one in which the two dominant voices will disagree, will find it much easier to disengage and hold ambivalent views.

6.3 Why Don't Independents Know More about Politics?

When voters lack complete information about an issue, candidate, or other political question, they often use heuristics, or information shortcuts, to make sense of a complicated political environment (Lupia 1994). The most powerful and prominent of these heuristics is party identification. As the authors of *The American Voter* (A. Campbell et al. 1960) surmised, an individual may know very little about politics, but their attachments to social groups, and ultimately to their party, guides their voting behavior. The attachment then becomes the guidepost for all kinds of behavior (Popkin 1991). During elections, party cues provide an easy way for a voter to pick between candidates about whom they have little to no information. Having an "R" or a "D" next to a candidate's name helps voters know that even though on some issues the candidate may diverge from their preferences, they are likely to support at least the most basic of the party's position—or at least be more likely to support those positions than the candidate affiliated with the other party. For example, a Republican candidate may be pro-choice, but is far more likely to be pro-life than the Democratic candidate. Thus, party identification helps voters cast ballots while gathering very little information, and nine times out of ten this information will enable the voter to cast a ballot for a candidate on which they agree on at least the major issues. Furthermore, much recent research has shown that party identification can have little to do with policy positions and much to do with affect: Our side is good, their side is bad (e.g., Mason 2018). Party identification keeps the tally sheet on the good and the bad.

But partisanship provides other cueing mechanisms as well. Parties also can use partisan information networks to share position-taking with co-partisans. Important here is how we understand what makes up high and low information behaviors. Since most Americans do not appear to behave ideologically, as we discuss in Chapter 3, even "high information" behavior may be more reflective of top-down, elite-to-masses messaging, where an individual is given information on what and how to think about politics. An individual need not know intricate details of policy debates; simply knowing where the party stands is sufficient.

One critical finding from recent literature is that *having more* information does not make Americans more likely to actually *use* that information. Instead, it makes them more likely to filter out information that does not reinforce their pre-existing predispositions—what scholars call a "partisan screen." Put another way, Americans are susceptible to *rationalizing* information instead of acting *rationally* in response to information (Lodge and Taber 2013). For example, Federico and Sidanius (2002) find that having a higher level of political knowledge is related to a greater ability to apply racial stereotypes to policy attitudes. Miller, Saunders, and Farhart (2016) find that, among conservatives, political knowledge acts as a motivator rather than a salve to one's willingness to accept conspiracy theories.

The core of the motivated reasoning argument is that Americans are starting from the endpoint (a specific policy position) and backing their way to the start (an ideology). Theories and empirical research on partisan-motivated reasoning often treat independents, at least true independents, as if they do not exist. Absent the structuring partisan cue, there is nothing to motivate the reasoning, and therefore independents are left to the information that they do have, which is assumed to be lower than that of partisans but is also certainly not no information. There are circumstances under which the information conditions for independents are likely quite good and the effects of motivated reasoning obfuscate more than they illuminate.

Independents are no less likely than partisans to know when houses are being foreclosed around them, when people are being laid off, when opioid overdoses are crippling families, or when land or affordable housing are disappearing from their communities. This is information gained not from partisan news networks, mass email blasts from campaigns, or other kinds of elite signaling. This is information gathered from daily life while going to work and school, living in a family and among a group of friends, and living among neighbors and in communities. In short, there should be very little difference between independents, Democrats, and Republicans in their ability to observe what is happening in their communities and whether those happenings are positive or problematic.

6.4 The Lived Environment as a Test Case of Voter Responsiveness

Howard Dean, the former governor of Vermont, presidential candidate, and chairman of the Democratic National Committee, like Bernie Sanders referenced before, is now quite famous for saying that "it is unreasonable to apply laws that may be necessary in California to rural states like Montana or Vermont." What Governor Dean meant is a classic understanding of how policy should be made; policies should be context specific. Although a liberal Democrat who supported universal health care and drastically increasing the minimum wage, these two Vermont Democrats were informed by the place in which they lived. Vermont is a rural state with little presence of homicides or violent crime and no high-profile mass shootings. It was also a state in which the average person was likely to own a gun for hunting, not for protection or malicious actions. They could see that those who lived in areas with high gun crime might favor (and be responsive in doing so) gun restrictions, but Vermont? Why would one who lived *there* favor gun control? Just as why would someone who lived in an area in which gun crime was high *not* favor gun control that had even the potential of keeping guns out of the hands of those intent on malicious activity? This is not a "Democratic" or "Republican" idea—it is one espoused by both Richard Nixon and Bill Clinton in their presidencies and is the normative principle of federalism.

Dean and Sanders have, of course, changed their positions. In the face of gun control becoming a salient national issue, it is now an issue on which the parties do not tolerate dissension. In the Democratic Party, being pro-gun is unpalatable, just as being pro-gun control is unacceptable in the Republican Party.

Uniformity among elected officials (particularly senators and presidential candidates) makes sense. They have a party platform and party agenda to consider and have a "brand" that is tied up in their electoral and policy success (Aldrich 2011). But the electorate should be informed by their lived experience and environment, just as Dean argued. People from rural Vermont are responding to their lived experience when they apply what is salient in their community to their policy preferences. Are the schools in one's district falling apart? If so, people respond by calling on elected officials to improve them. Similarly, if one lives in an area in which the nearest police station is an hour away and the biggest threat is the presence of mountain lions, one might respond by wanting to protect their right to own a gun. While people rightfully argue over what is the "best" policy approach to a societal problem, at the very least, regardless of the party with which one identifies, every American should be able to accurately identify the issues in their community.

The contextual effects literature dating back as far as Key (1949) and Berelson, Lazarsfeld, and McPhee (1954) posits just this—that a person's social surroundings and physical location are the primary influence on political beliefs and opinion formation. In the geography literature, this is often referred to as Tobler's first law of geography—that "everything is related to everything, but near things are more related than distant things" (Tobler 1970). The importance of geographic context in determining political perceptions has been well documented in many studies (e.g., Eagles 1995; Huckfeldt and Sprague 1995). Burbank (1995) suggests that "contextual effects do not come about as the result of social composition alone but result from individuals learning and acting in an environment with an informational bias" (p. 169); as a result, "individual cognition is a product of social experience" (p. 172), and "different environments will stimulate different political content" (p. 173).

The psychological mechanism of contextual theories is well established: Exposure to environmental cues changes how people perceive the importance of issues and how to solve problems (Huckfeldt 1986; Huckfeldt and Sprague 1995). The term "contextual effects" is meant to describe the process through which interpersonal interactions, observations, and experiences (both socially and in the natural world) affect the political beliefs and voting choices of the people living within a geographic space (Gimpel and Schuknecht 2009).

While some contextual effects theories have come under fire due to the causal inference problem (e.g., Oakes 2004), recent research has found that assumptions about the "treatment" people receive in their environment is well-grounded in reality (Newman et al. 2015). What is critical here is that most political decisions require (and a healthy democracy requires of its citizens) an understanding of (1) the rules by which politics are governed; (2) a knowledge of the major domestic and international issues of the day including current social and economic conditions and key policy initiatives, and (3) the major players in government and the political parties (Delli Carpini and Keeter 1996). But this should not be the case when issues are at the root of the context in which a person lives—either socially or environmentally. In these environments, people will make informed decisions when they forego what is "salient" nationally and what the primary players have defined as consistent with one political party or another and instead respond to what is happening in their local context. For example, Republicans may not want a strong national presence in Washington, D.C., taxing individuals and making decisions to ensure educational quality, yet Republicans regularly vote to tax themselves to increase the quality of their local schools. This is a logical, if politically inconsistent, response to context.

The challenge, of course, is that while it may be logical to be responsive to where you live, political polarization and the easy access to partisan frames produced in the modern media-saturated environment, means that issues beyond the political core have become "easy." Partisans, because their ideology and partisanship are so well sorted, and the parties are so clear about their positions across such a wide variety of issues, may be resistant to information gained from their daily lives and instead be almost solely informed by partisan views. Carmines and Stimson (1980) argued that there was a distinction between what they referred to as "easy" and "hard" issues. However, it is also possible to think of this delineation less as "easy" and more as "partisan." Carmines and Stimson defined an "easy" issue as one in which most people would have a consistent response on surveys because the issues are "understood by the public at an emotional 'gut level,'" "symbolic rather than technical," "more likely to deal with policy ends than means," and they have been "long on the political agenda" (Carmines and Stimson 1980, p. 80). "Hard issues" are those that require relatively high levels of political sophistication, education, and/or effort to understand (Carmines and Stimson 1980). Historically, issues such as taxation, labor and employment, financial regulation, and natural resource and land use are all "hard" in nature and the debates surrounding these issues rarely make it into the information environment (Evans and Pearson-Merkowitz 2012). However, today, partisans are privy to a level of framing they had not been—that had not been possible—just a decade ago. Cues from the political parties, their friendly news networks, and social media reach far beyond issues that have histori-cally been able to fit this category. Instead, any issue that enters the political sphere becomes symbolic and "easy" quite quickly as partisan elites frame every issue as a moral issue that taps into one likely to produce a gut opinion and abandon the complexities that policy discussions require. As a result, the parties and issues have been nationalized (Hopkins 2018) and anything discussed by party elites becomes "easy."

As we argued in previous work (Dyck and Pearson-Merkowitz 2019, p. 184), "the unfortunate consequence of the 'easy/hard' dichotomy is that people tend to interpret 'hard' as meaning 'difficult.' While 'easy' issues do require very little thought, it is not because the issues are actually simple. Instead, it is because the voter has received so many cues on the issue and the issue is so well positioned in the political sphere that voters can locate where they are in an ideological space by just looking at a single word." And, as we have shown (Dyck and Pearson-Merkowitz 2019), when the parties give clear ideological cues, partisans are strongly resistant to arguments made in favor of or in opposition to the issue if the arguments do not conform to the public position of the party.

Thus, as more and more issues have become "easy" because party leaders have expanded the scope of political conflict to encompass an innumer-able number of issues and because partisan news is now so easy to access, we argue that party cues make knowledge gained from an individual's so-cial and geographic context less relevant. Partisans, we argue, will be more likely to forego applying their lived experience to either political perceptions or policy positions, and instead will apply a policy position consistent with their preferred political party. Independents, on the other hand, will be more likely to use the contextual information at their disposal and behave as re-sponsive decision makers—taking what is available from their lived experi-ence and applying it to both their perceptions of politics and, ultimately, their policy preferences.

6.5 Designing Two Types of Tests

We test this theory in two settings. The basis of the social context theory is that individuals gain information from their lived experience. But the lived experience includes both their personal context, which no one outside their social circle would know, and the physical and social context of the neighborhood or city in which they live. We proceed by taking on two different versions of an individual's context.

First, we investigate the limits by which political perceptions and policy positions among partisan identifiers and independents are informed by the *geographic context* in which they live. We investigate this through two very different policy areas—gun crime/gun control and development/land preservation. While gun control is a fairly straightforward test in that it has become a clearly "easy" issue as defined by the extant literature (long on the political agenda, etc., and is likely to produce a gut response, although why is a bit unclear), land conservation, on the other hand, is not one on which the parties have taken clear positions, nor has it been long on the political agenda. This test allows us to see the extent to which partisans are resisting information from their geographic context. Importantly, we look not just at policy positions but also at the level of concern people say they have over issues. We would suspect that regardless of the policy mechanism a person thinks best to deal with gun crime, people should report that gun crime is a problem in neighborhoods that have high rates of gun crime and that those who live in areas with low rates of gun crime should be less likely to report this.

Second, because there is a solid argument to be made that people self-sort into geographic areas, we move to looking at people's self-reported economic positions. A long line of literature argues that people's personal financial situation will be at the top of their mind when making policy decisions (Bartels 2005; Downs 1957). Thus, here we investigate if people who self-report being in economic peril are more/less likely to support polices that stand to help their personal economic situation. This test helps us really tap into whether partisans or independents are more likely to make responsive policy decisions based on their lived experience. And, because we are looking at preferences on specific polices and not voting for candidates, this allows us to look at issue position development outside of situations in which one *must* make a trade-off if they have competing policy preferences. For example, in voting, an evangelical Christian minimum-wage worker must make a choice: Do they choose to support the candidate more likely to support restricting abortion rights or the candidate more likely to support increasing the minimum wage? Voters could choose either candidate because it is a decision about which issue to prioritize. But both positions—being pro-life and being pro-increase in the minimum wage—are responsive policy positions given their personal lived experience. Thomas Frank (2007) asks, *What's the Matter with Kansas?*

because he believed conservative Kansas voters who would benefit from a raise in the minimum wage and other polices more likely to be supported by Democrats are being duped by voting for Republicans based on social issues such as abortion. But voting "against" one's self-interest, as Frank posits that Republican voters do when they vote for candidates who do not support economic benefits for the working poor, requires voters *to hold competing positions* and make a choice to prioritize one over the other—specifically to prioritize economic self-interest over religiously informed social issues. We see no reason why one would always choose economics over moral values or vice versa. This is an individual choice. But in policy positions, voters need not prioritize one policy over the other: A person can be both pro-life and in favor of increasing the minimum wage.

What we argue is that we should not be asking, "What's the matter with Kansas?" but should be asking, "What's the matter with partisans?" If partisans fail to be responsive to their lived experience on specific policy proposals, then neither Democrats nor Republicans are using information other than that provided to them by party cue givers (and, by extension, our measures of political knowledge are endogenous to that information exchange). Instead, they are acting only as partisans. Independents, then, for all their faults, may be those most likely to behave in a manner informed by their context. We proceed now by laying out how we research partisans and independents in the different ways in which context could affect political perceptions and policy position development.

6.5.1   Research Design I—Context and Gun Violence/Gun Control

The data to test our theory come from two sources. The first is a nationally representative survey of American Adults conducted in April of 2014 by YouGov on behalf of the UMass Lowell Center for Public Opinion. We matched the data at the county level to the FBI's 2013 uniform crime reporting database (see Pearson-Merkowitz and Dyck 2017). This allows us to measure the actual amount of crime in an individual's local environment and test (1) if higher/lower levels of crime affects the manner in which individuals perceive crime and violence in their local neighborhoods and (2) whether the level of crime in their social context has an effect on their attitudes about policies surrounding guns and gun control. The context measure used in all models is violent crime at the county level, with a per-capita adjustment to account for varying population sizes.[1]

We group seven different plausible dependent variables into two categories: (1) perceptions of crime and violence, and (2) policy attitudes. Our three measures of perceptions about crime and violence come from questions about individuals' concern about gun violence in the United States, concern about gun violence in the respondent's local community, and beliefs about whether school shootings have gotten better or worse in the past 10 years. Our four measures of policy attitudes about guns and gun control policy are 4-point Likert scales asking respondents to indicate the strength of their support for or opposition to policies to (1) ban assault weapons, (2) make background checks to purchase firearms harder, (3) close the so-called gun show loophole, and (4) train and arm teachers in school classrooms.

The basic estimation strategy is to model each dependent variable using ordered logit as a function of an interaction of context (crime per capita) and a series of dummy variables representing party identification, with *strong Democrat* as the excluded category. Here we collapse party identification into a 5-point scale with weak partisans and leaning independents in a single category, as these categories tend to behave in a consistent manner (Kaufmann, Petrocik, and Shaw 2008; Keith et al. 1992). The model contains controls for gender, age, education, political awareness, ideology, and gun ownership, as well as a contextual control for the urbanicity of the county.

We present two versions of each model. One version includes the full sample of respondents; the second version restricts the model to only non-Hispanic white respondents.[2] The logic behind this is threefold. First, the geographic distribution of non-white populations is considerably less varied in the data than it is for white respondents. Because non-white respondents, particularly Black and Latino respondents, tend to be clustered in urban areas due to decades of segregationist policies, and since there is a high degree of correlation between urbanicity, poverty, and violence, respondents from minoritized backgrounds included in our data are more likely reside in areas with higher levels of violent crime than the white respondents. Second, there is also considerable evidence suggesting that non-partisan identification for non-white respondents, especially in immigrant communities, reflects a sense of "otherness" that includes being outside the two-party system; this distinguishes them from white independents, who are often thought to be more moderate (Hajnal and Rivera 2014). Finally, gun policy has become a race-coded policy because pro-gun interest groups have used race-coded language and tropes in pursuit of their policy aims (Filindra and Kaplan 2016). As we have discussed, the Republican elite messages regarding gun control have been consistent for a long time making guns a classic "easy issue" because of the depth and length of the party's stable and vociferous position on gun rights and its overlap with the National Rifle Association. Democrats, on the other hand, have experienced an "issue evolution" on gun rights and control; until very recently, Democratic elites have presented a mixed message on guns and gun control. Admittedly, now there is little space for dissent on gun control in the Democratic Party, but that ideological rigor is relatively new. Thus, due to the uneven distribution of polarization and motivated reasoning in the United States, we expect the link between experiences in the lived environment and the acquisition of policy attitudes to be even less likely for white Republicans than for white Democrats (e.g. Pearson-Merkowitz and Dyck 2017). Furthermore, we expect that observed effects among independents may be more pronounced among white independents.

6.5.2 Results I—Context and Gun Violence/Gun Control

The results of the models are presented in the appendix, in Tables A6.1 through A6.3. In Table A6.1, we present the models for perceptions of crime and violence. To be clear, if voters are acting rationally, we would expect all voters, regardless of partisan affiliation, to acknowledge gun crime as a problem as a function of actual high gun crime (e.g., saying gun crime is a problem should be more likely as actual gun crime increases). The coefficient on "Crime per capita" represents the logit coefficient for the category "Strong Democrat." The subsequent interactions represent the alterations in that effect. The significance tests here are helpful for interpreting what is happening in the model. For instance, in each model, for "All respondents" or the restricted models with only white respondents, the pure independent interaction returns a positive, statistically significant coefficient in each and every case. None of the other partisan categories are consistently significant across the models.

We present the predicted probability for independents of being "very concerned" about gun violence and gun-related crimes in the United States, the amount of gun violence in a respondent's local community, including the places that the respondent lives and works, and perceptions that school shootings are "getting worse" in Figure 6.1 to help visualize the effect. In each

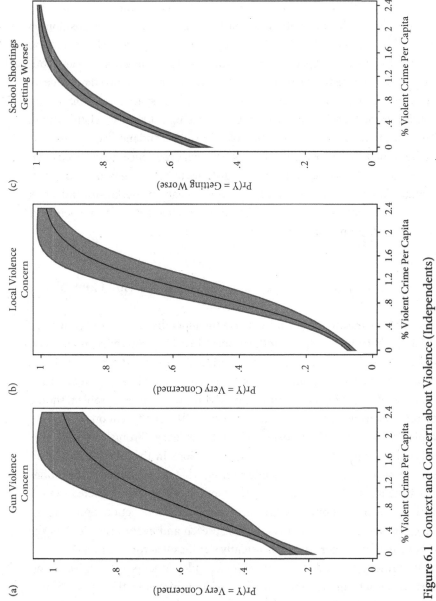

Figure 6.1 Context and Concern about Violence (Independents)

Source: Data are from the 2014 UML YouGov survey. Predicted Probabilities with 90% confidence intervals were generated from Table A6.1. See the appendix for more details.

case, an increase in the percent of per capita violent crime across the plausible range of the scale leads to large increases in the predicted probability of being concerned. For local gun violence, for instance, at the lowest levels of violent crime per capita in the local environment, the model predicts a less than 10% probability of an independent saying they are very concerned, but at the highest levels of violent crime per capita, the model predicts nearly a 100% probability of saying one is very concerned. Simply put, for independents, living in a place with more violence means greater perceptions of violence at the local level, at the national level, and greater perception that school shootings have gotten worse—we see this as evidence of responsiveness. Independents apply their lived environment to political concerns.

The same cannot be said of partisans. In Figure 6.2, we graph the predicted probability for strong partisans for the three models of perceptions of crime and violence, in the restricted models with white respondents, although the substance of the effect is the same regardless of whether we include non-white respondents in the models. In all three of the models presented, neither strong Democrats nor strong Republicans demonstrate an apparent responsiveness to the contextual environment. In Panel 6.2a, there is some evidence that Republicans respond to violent crime, but the effect is in the opposite direction than one would expect. Republicans say they are less concerned about gun violence as violence in their county increases. This finding highlights the gap between Republicans and Democrats on the question of gun violence in the United States, in particular, and how politically charged this issue has become. The results make it clear that partisan-motivated reasoning plays a role in structuring the attitudes of partisan responses to the local environment by stopping the transmission of relevant contextual information and substituting partisan reasoning to questions that are not about policy.

A very clear and similar pattern emerges on questions that ask about gun policy. In Tables A6.2 and A6.3 in the appendix, we present the models with all respondents and, again, with only white respondents, for each of the four policy areas identified. For three of those models—banning assault weapons, closing the gun show loophole, and training and arming teachers—we see the largest significant interactions among pure independents, with partisans once again often failing to reach statistical significance. Substantively, this means that partisans do not change their policy attitudes based on their lived experience but independents do change their attitudes in a manner consistent with responding to the lived environment. Again, we turn to figures of predicted probabilities with 90% confidence intervals to help elucidate the effects.

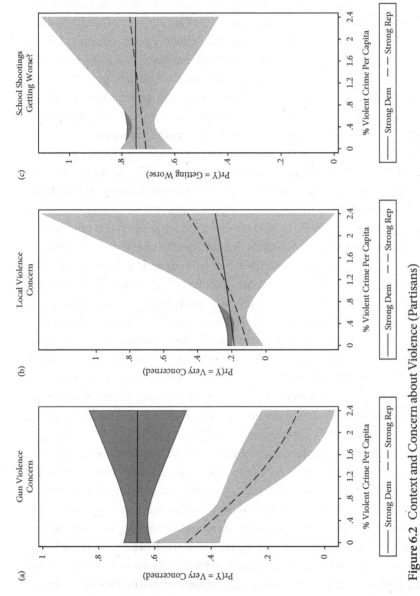

Figure 6.2 Context and Concern about Violence (Partisans)

Source: Data are from the 2014 UML YouGov survey. Predicted Probabilities with 90% confidence intervals were generated from Table A6.1. See the appendix for more details.

In Figure 6.3, we present the effect of crime per capita on attitudes about four policy areas for political independents. As we can see in Figure 6.3a, individuals who reside in counties with higher crime rates are more much more likely to support a ban on assault weapons—the probability of strongly supporting the ban increases from 27% to 91% moving across the range of context. In Figure 6.3b, we see that the effect for political independents is actually not significant on the question of background checks.[3] However, on the question of "closing the gun-show loophole," as crime per capita increases over its entire range, the predicted probability of "strongly support" goes up by more than 50 percentage points. When it comes to training and arming teachers, context has a significant effect. Independents who live in a context with more crime per capita are less likely to support a policy of arming teachers than those who live in a context with less violence.

For partisans, as demonstrated in Figure 6.4, we again see notable differences between Democrats and Republicans in how they respond to these policy questions. The effects of context, however, are inconsistent. We observe a positive effect of crime context for Strong Democrats in their support for banning assault weapons and making background checks harder. Democrats appear to become more pro–gun control as violence increases, consistent with the arguments of Howard Dean and Bernie Sanders that we quoted near the beginning of the chapter. However, for Republicans there is no effect one way or the other. When it comes to closing the gun show loophole, there appears to be no effect of context on Democrats, and a negative effect of violent crime context for Republicans; that is, *Republicans who reside in counties with more crime per capita are less likely to support closing the gun show loophole.* We see no discernible context effects when it comes to training and arming teachers in the classroom. Taken altogether, we find relatively consistent context effects for independents, whose attitudes across three measures of perceptions of crime and violence and four measures tapping policy attitudes seem to respond to the level of crime at the local level. Partisans, however, show no similar pattern. Here, it is independents who respond to information in the lived environment by adjusting their policy positions in a way that could help alleviate said crime.

Figure 6.4d is particularly illustrative here. We began this chapter acknowledging that there are different policy approaches that partisans may prefer given their worldview, but we argue that if partisans are responsive to their lived environment, they should still have different policy views. As a result, we included traditional gun violence policies that have typically

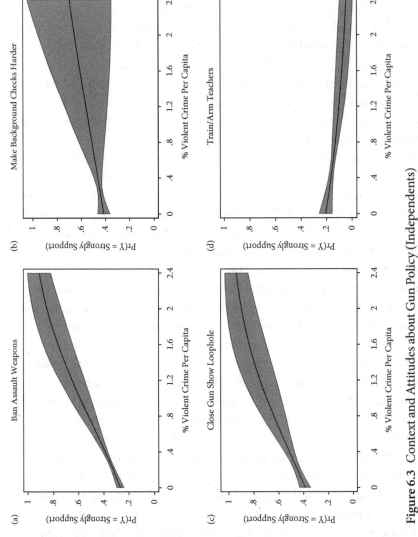

Figure 6.3 Context and Attitudes about Gun Policy (Independents)

Source: Data are from the 2014 UML YouGov survey. Predicted Probabilities with 90% confidence intervals were generated from Table A6.1. See the appendix for more details.

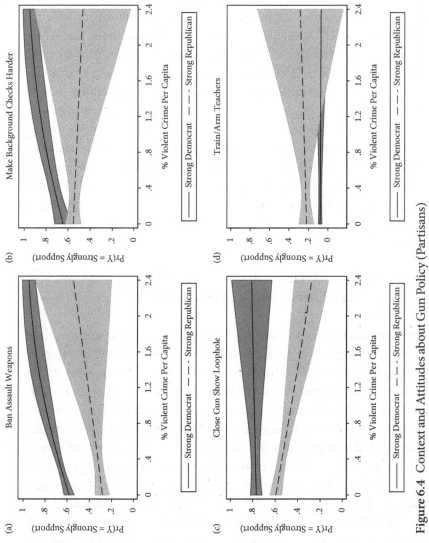

Figure 6.4 Context and Attitudes about Gun Policy (Partisans)

Source: Data are from the 2014 UML YouGov survey. Predicted Probabilities with 90% confidence intervals were generated from Tables A6.2 and A6.3. See the appendix for more details.

been supported by Democrats (background checks, assault weapons ban, and closing of gun show loopholes) and a gun violence policy proposed by Republicans (training and arming teachers). But while we see evidence that Democrats are somewhat more supportive of typical left-wing policies to control gun violence when they live in high-violence areas, we do not see that Republicans are more supportive of Republican-proposed gun violence policies. As a result, we believe that if we had other questions that measured support for other potential ways to control violent crime that are more likely to be supported by Republicans, such as increasing funding for police, or increasing mandatory minimums or three-strikes policies, independents would be more likely to support those programs as violence increases. However, we see no reason to think we would find increased support among Republicans as crime in their area increases, even though these are more common policy proposals among Republicans to address violent crime. While these policies would likely be more popular among Republicans, our evidence suggests that they would not be more popular among Republicans in higher-crime areas than among Republicans in lower-crime areas.

6.5.3 Research Design II—Context and Attitudes about Land Availability and Land Preservation

There is the chance that our findings on gun policy and gun violence can be attributed to the fact that the issues have been so well debated by partisans that guns are simply an "easy issue" for which no information matters. So, for our second test we move to a much "harder" policy area—that of land preservation. Support for land and "open space" preservation have been extensively studied. In general, this literature investigates the link between the changing nature of local land use, such as rapid development and the loss of natural landscapes, and support for or opposition to conservation (e.g., Howell-Moroney 2004b, 2004a; Kline and Wichelns 1994; Kotchen and Powers 2006; Lang and Pearson-Merkowitz 2022; Lowry 2018; Pearson-Merkowitz and Lang 2020; Prendergast, Pearson-Merkowitz, and Lang 2019; and others). The takeaway from this large environmental economics and political science literature is that land preservation is adopted by citizens when there is a threat to open space in the community due to rapid growth. Our theory would suggest that this is not quite the case for partisans.

The data for this test come from a 2016 representative survey of American adults conducted by YouGov as part of a study on land use preservation (see Prendergast, et al. 2019). The survey first asked respondents to evaluate the amount of open space in their own community using a 5-point Likert scale consisting of: *none, almost none, a little, some,* or *a lot*. The survey then asked respondents' likelihood of supporting a community bond referendum that would allocate funds to protect open space in their community. We look to connect each of these measures to a measure of context, interacting that variable with party identification. We propose that if respondents gain information from their environment, then they should acknowledge the availability of land in their community when there is such and note its absence when there is not.

For the model that accounts for individuals' perception of open space in their local community, we measure open space at the community level as the amount of physical open space in the zip code where the respondent resides. For the open-space bond models, we constructed two measures of community open space to account for changes in context that the literature suggests should be connected with land preservation bond support. Each of these was calculated by the authors of and used in Prendergast et al. (2019). The first is the amount of open space available at the zip code in which the respondent lives as of 2011. The second is the *change in development* in the state between 2001 and 2011. The third, *open space loss*, is a measure of the reduction in open space in the state from 2001 to 2011. Each was created using data from the National Land Cover Database (Homer et al. 2015).

There is less clarity for the bond support models as to the correct geographic unit to measure change in development and open space loss. The issue is that if we choose too small of a geographic area, we may be far too precise for the concept. Open space is not simply experienced at the neighborhood level; a person can experience open land in their vicinity by living in a state or a region. We like to think of this as the *fall in New England* effect. Fall in New England is remarkably beautiful, and people often will make trips to visit to enjoy its beauty. But, for local residents, just because one lives in a city like Boston or Providence does not preclude a person from enjoying the fall in New England given the greenery that exists as one drives or takes the train within an hour from their urban home into New Hampshire, western Massachusetts, or southern Rhode Island. Indeed, the residents of any New England state can nearly universally enjoy the open space afforded throughout their state. Even in larger states, regional plans usually prioritize preserving open space outside of cities but making them publicly available so that all the state's residents, regardless of their neighborhoods, can enjoy getting out for a hike or bike ride or going to the beach. California is a great example here. While Los Angeles has very little land available to preserve, California has led the nation in preserving land across the state in ways that the residents of Los Angeles or San Francisco can still access. At the same time, some states may also be too large for residents to reasonably enjoy and consider all the aspects of the landmass when considering what open space means to them. So, at what geographic level should we measure open space? Since we lack a better alternative, and we cannot individually geocode respondents and look at their personal open space constraints within, say, a 100-mile radius, states are likely the best, if bluntest way to construct these measures. Further, we would expect that making the geographic area this large should bias us away from finding any evidence at all in favor of our hypotheses.

Our modeling strategy mirrors the gun control models—we model open space perceptions (a 5-point Likert scale) first, and then support for a bond measure expanding open space (a 4-point Likert scale) using ordered logit as a function of an interaction of context and a series of dummy variables representing party identification, with "strong Democrat" as the excluded category. For the open space perception model, the measure of context is the proportion of the zip code (the smallest geographic identifier available in our data) that is deemed to be open space, from 0 to 1. The two measures of context for open space for the bond models are "Change in development from 2001–2011" and "Open space loss from 2001–2011." In each case, we expect the measures of context to matter more for pure independents than for partisans, who will be resistant to information from their own lived experience. Like the crime context models, these models contain controls for gender, race, age, education, income, political interest, and ideology. We also include a variable regarding home ownership, as land planning decisions affect the values of home investments (Fischel 2005, 2017; Lang 2018).

6.5.4 Results II—Context and Attitudes about Land Preservation

The results for all three models are presented in Table A6.4 in the appendix. In the first model, context is measured as the percent of open space at the zip code level of the respondent. A positive and significant coefficient on

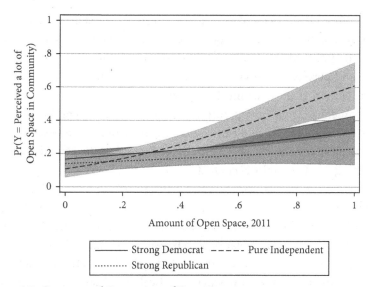

Figure 6.5 Context and Perception of Open Space

Source: Data are from the 2016 URI YouGov survey. Predicted Probabilities with 90% confidence intervals were generated from Table A6.4, Model 1. See the appendix for more details.

the variable "Total open space, 2011" indicates that when strong Democrats live in places with more open space, they are moderately more likely to indicate that their local community has higher levels of open space. Among the interactions, the only significant interaction is that for independents, indicating that the relationship is much stronger for independents.

How much stronger? We present the substantive effects as probability changes in Figure 6.5. The figure highlights the differences in open space perceptions for both independents and partisans. As the amount of open space in the community increases, we see that this predicts as much as a 48-percentage-point increase in an independent saying that their community has "a lot" of open space. In fact, the effect of the change for independents is exactly what one would expect—when there is objectively more open space available in their community, independents are more likely to say their community has a "lot" of open space. Interestingly, we see considerably more muted effects for strong partisans. For strong Democrats, the effect is still positive and significant, but it is less than half the size of the effect for independents (the maximum increase is 20 percentage points). And, as one can see from the graph, the slope of the line is very slight; even in areas with a lot of objective open space, Democrats have less than a 40% chance of saying their community has a lot of open space. For strong Republicans, we observe a relationship between actual open space and perceived open space that fails to reach statistical significance. Mirroring the results from actual violent crime and perceived gun violence, we see that pure independents are considerably more likely to connect their experiences with land use in the lived environment to their own perceptions of that environment. This suggests that Democrats and Republicans are taking the national conversation about conservation and the disappearance of open space in the United States and projecting it onto their local context.

A related question is, does this also translate into policy opinions? In the second set of models context is measured as the increase in development over a 10-year period. The negative coefficient on the development variable indicates a negative relationship between context and support for an open space bond proposal for the excluded category, strong Democrats. Only one interaction term reaches statistical significance in the model—that for independents. A very similar pattern between the measure of open space loss (a negative coefficient for strong Democrats and a positive and statistically significant coefficient for independents) emerges in the second model. The key, of course, is to see what these effects look like once we plot them.

In Figure 6.6, we plot the effect of open space context measured as development (Panels 6.6a and 6.6c) and open space loss (Panels 6.6b and 6.6d) for both independents and partisans. In both cases, we see that the predicted probability of an independent saying that they are "very likely to support" the proposed open space bond increases from about 20% to 60% as the context measure reflects greater open space constraint. That is, in states with more development and more open space loss, reflected as a 10-year change, independents are more likely to support a bond to preserve open space. Interestingly, the effect predicted by the models is negative for Democrats and null for Republicans. In places where there has been less development and less open space loss, there are clearer partisan divides between Republicans and Democrats regarding open space. But in places with more development/ more open space loss, we see less difference in support for open space bonds between Democrats and Republicans. It is difficult to surmise what exactly is happening with partisans here, particularly Democrats given that the context effects are in the opposite direction of what we would predict if they were responding to the local environment. Regardless, the effects are clear for

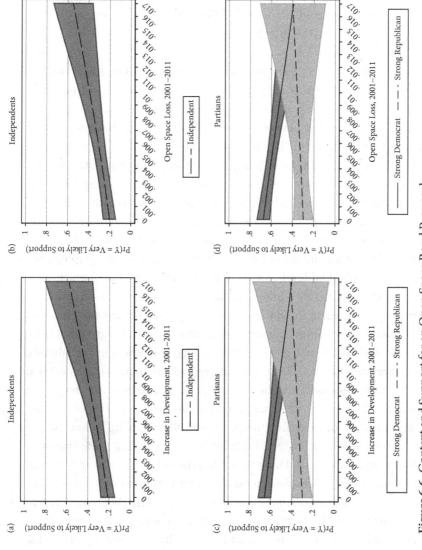

Figure 6.6 Context and Support for an Open Space Bond Proposal

Source: Data are from the 2016 URI YouGov survey. Predicted Probabilities with 90% confidence intervals were generated from Table A6.4, Models 2 and 3. See the appendix for more details.

independents. The only group behaving in a way that appears to demonstrate a response to the lived environment are political independents.

6.5.5   Research Design III—Personal Financial Context and Attitudes toward Affordable Housing Development and Raising the Minimum Wage

For our final set of tests, we employ the same national survey utilized to look at attitudes toward open space preservation above. However, in this set we move away from looking at how people respond to their geographic context and look instead at how partisans and independents respond to their personal financial context. This is an important distinction for a couple of reasons. First, it is possible that a skeptical reader might think that the contextual geographic areas in the previous tests are too large to account for variation within the areas in which Republicans and Democrats actually live. But more importantly, when we measure context, we assume that individuals use local-level knowledge of their contextual environment as the basis of their behavior. If we measure something that is not a social or geographic context, but an individual-level context, then we can assess the interaction of that context and partisanship on policy attitudes without this assumption.

Personal economics should lead one to support different policies. This link is the basis of historic partisan differences between groups. Under the New Deal coalition, Catholics, immigrants, and others in the laboring classes gravitated to the Democratic Party and the upper class gravitated toward the Republican Party because these parties served their respective economic interests. But personal economics and voting for candidates are weakly linked. To be sure, the concept of "pocketbook voting" is not without some controversy (Bartels 2005; Feldman 1982; Lewis-Beck 1985; Sigelman, Sigelman, and Bullock 1991). Importantly, however, we are not arguing that economics will influence *who* one votes for. Our very premise is that it is partisanship, not policy opinions or economics, that ultimately drives voters to decide who to vote for. Instead, we argue that in the face of economic hardship, it makes sense that voters should respond by supporting policies that will directly benefit them. Those making the minimum wage should be more likely to want the minimum wage increased. Those struggling to make ends meet due to rising housing costs should be more likely to support the building of affordable housing even if they hold, as Feldman (1982) argues, a belief in personal responsibility and economic individualism. Indeed, one of the strongest predictors of most social welfare policy attitudes is one's personal financial situation.

Thus, here we look at how personal financial context affects the likelihood of supporting policies that stand to help one's personal situation. We choose an "easy" issue, the minimum wage, and a "hard" issue, affordable housing. To avoid confusion, each survey respondent was offered a definition of affordable housing as follows: "'Affordable housing' is a general term used to describe housing that is purposely made available at or below the median household value of the community to ensure that people of all incomes can afford housing." Importantly, this definition did not provide for government subsidies or "public" housing, both of which are significantly less popular than affordable housing development. The question then asked respondents, "If you were given the opportunity to vote on a bond measure that would create or preserve affordable housing in your local community, how likely would you be to support it?" Respondents then had the choice of answering on a 4-point Likert scale ranging from (1) *Very unlikely* to (4) *Very likely*. For the minimum wage, respondents were asked how likely they would be to support a policy to raise the minimum wage to $15; this was also measured using the same 4-point Likert scale.

To measure personal economic situations, we utilized a question that asked respondents how often their housing costs affect their ability to afford other basic necessities; this is a 4-point scale that ranges from (1) *Never* to (4) *Every month*. The model then includes all the same controls as the open space models presented previously. Notably, both models also include a control for income. We utilize both variables to account for the fact that there are broad differences in the value of incomes between geographic locales in the United States and because economic hardship may be affected by a number of factors, including whether an individual has family support, if they have dependents, and if they receive government assistance.

6.5.6 Results III—Personal Financial Context and Attitudes toward Affordable Housing Development and Raising the Minimum Wage

The results for the Affordable Housing and Minimum Wage models are presented in Table A6.5 in the appendix. The results for the two models are remarkably similar. The effect for "Strong Democrat," the excluded category, is the effect of the variable "Personal financial struggles" on the support for the affordable housing bond proposal or minimum wage increase. In both models, the coefficient fails to reach statistical significance. Also, in both models, among the interactions, we see that only the interaction term for "pure independent" is statistically significant and it carries a positive sign, indicating that for independents, the effect is significantly different than for Democrats, and in a positive direction. We graph the effects with confidence intervals of personal financial struggles, a measure of individual financial context, on support for a proposed affordable housing bond proposal and support for an increase in the minimum wage to $15 for partisans and independents in Figure 6.7.

In Figure 6.7a we see that independents respond to their personal context. An independent who indicates that they struggle to afford basic necessities every month is 16 percentage points more likely to be "very likely to support" a proposed affordable housing bond than an independent who says they never struggle to afford basic necessities. This effect is statistically significant. However, in 6.7c, we see that there is a clear partisan dimension to this issue. Strong Democrats are much more likely than strong Republicans to support an affordable housing bond but, importantly, this is true at each and every level of the measure that taps respondents' personal financial struggles. Strong Democrats and Republicans are no more or less likely to support affordable housing bonds if they struggle or don't struggle financially—for strong Republicans *and* Democrats, there is no variation in their response due to personal context. The model does not predict that a struggling Republican is more likely to support affordable housing than a not-struggling Republican, nor does it predict that a Democrat whose personal financial situation is comfortable is less likely to support affordable housing programs than a struggling Democrat.

The result is nearly identical for the minimum wage model. An independent who struggles to afford basic necessities (6.7b) is 20 percentage points more likely to be strongly in favor of raising the minimum wage to $15 an hour than an independent who never struggles financially. Strong Democrats and Republicans (6.7d) are, once again, very different from one another, but neither responds to personal financial circumstances in developing their opinions about the minimum wage. In both the case of affordable housing and the minimum wage, partisanship determines these attitudes for partisans, whereas personal circumstance determines

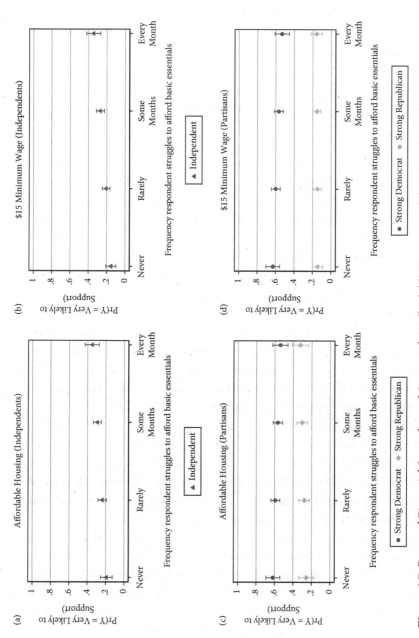

Figure 6.7 Personal Financial Struggles and Support for Affordable Housing and the Minimum Wage

Source: Data are from the 2016 URI YouGov survey. Predicted Probabilities with 90% confidence intervals were generated from Table A6.5, Models 1 and 2. See the appendix for more details.

them for independents. All of these models point to a relatively consistent finding: Independents use information from their immediate environment—their local, geographic, contextual, and personal environments—in the formation of political attitudes. Once an individual has acquired partisanship, an attitude inertia to context emerges.

6.6 Discussion

MIT economist Jonathan Gruber, the man once dubbed the "Obamacare architect," became a viral YouTube sensation after he was caught on tape repeatedly calling American voters "too stupid to understand" the Affordable Care Act and its implications (Walshe 2014). While many in the news media attacked Gruber for his comments, many political scientists shrugged their shoulders. While it was a poor choice of words on Gruber's part, political scientists have long documented the extent to which Americans fail to know who holds office, correctly assign policy positions to the political party that holds them, or understand how the most fundamental elements of American government work.

But generations of political scientists, particularly since Lupia (1994) wrote his seminal work on the ability of voters to use cues to make decisions that look informed, even if they are not, have also believed that voters are able to behave as though they are informed because they have the helpful information provided by party elites. Since party cue givers help communicate what voters should and should not support, and since it was assumed that their interests and policy positions would align with their preferred party, simply being able to identify and listen to elites was sufficient. As the story goes, with just a little information, party identification allows the voter to evaluate a complicated scenario with an information shortcut in a way that leads to the voter casting votes that align with their self-interest.

We disagree with this proposition. Certainly, knowing who the parties are enables one to repeat and vote in the way one is told one should. But is that consistent with what voters want or what is in their self-interest? And, shouldn't there be a limit? Even if they do not change their policy views, shouldn't voters at least interpret their environment correctly instead of being resistant to information gained from their lives?

When people have shortcuts, partisan-motivated reasoning can overwhelm the information environment and render new information useless to such an extent that cues serve as disinformation. So, the only people who respond to their lived context/environment are those who do not have the weight of partisanship to structure their views.

The irony of this situation is that political independents—those long bemoaned by political scientists for their lack of political knowledge and interest, respond to their lived context in more rational and informed ways than partisans. They observe their lives and their neighborhoods and make reasoned political judgments and support policies that are, at least on their faces, likely to help them.

Partisans, on the other hand, seem unwilling to take in new information, and instead simply answer in ways that will reinforce and justify the political positions of their parties. Independents, while far from the idealized democratic citizen, are able to make use of information without constraint because of the absence of cues and heuristics, rather than with them.

7

Independents, Political Knowledge, and Alienation

7.1 Independents and Information

In the preceding chapter, we showed that when information is contextual, it is independents who are most likely to react to that information by developing or changing their view of the world and their policy attitudes. In contrast, the partisan structure of the information environment appears to act as a counterbalance to the lived experience. Partisans rely on the partisan view of the world as presented by partisan elites. Whether this view is real or imagined is worthy of additional scrutiny.

As an epilogue to chapter six, we revisit the literature on partisanship and political knowledge and ask the question: What do independents know about politics, and does it matter? Part of the built-in assumption to the previous chapter is that local or contextual information is something everyone can access. It might be a high bar of political knowledge to read a newspaper and learn facts about state or national politics regularly, but everyone can have a sense of how much crime or open space there is in one's community simply by living in an area. Here we seek to revisit the longstanding way that independents have been characterized, and often dispensed with, in the political behavior literature. First, scholars have long argued that the level of political knowledge that voters have is consequential to democracy (Delli Carpini and Keeter 1996). Second, it has also been established that political independents, especially pure independents, tend to have the lowest levels of political awareness and are also the least engaged in the political process (Zaller 1992). If we start with the assumption that participation is a normative "good" in democracy, then information has routinely been posited as the salve to low rates of political involvement.

In this chapter, we wish to make three broad points, drawing on both the extant literature and trends in data. First, as political information has become more intwined with partisanship, the supposition that more information

The Power of Partisanship. Joshua J. Dyck and Shanna Pearson-Merkowitz, Oxford University Press.
© Oxford University Press 2023. DOI: 10.1093/oso/9780197623787.003.0008

is a tonic for what ails democracy is problematic; those with political information use it to bolster their own political predispositions. Second, we must distinguish between *pure independents*, who truly do not have partisan attachments, and "PINOs" (partisan independents in name only)— who obfuscate their partisan identity for reasons of social desirability (Klar and Krupnikov 2016). This distinction is important, particularly as it involves negative partisanship, cue-taking, and political knowledge. Finally, we conclude with a challenge to the general characterization of independents as generally uninformed. This is an overstatement of the variation in how political independents score on a political knowledge scale. While pure independents are the least informed partisan subgroup, more than half score 50% or better on a standard political knowledge scale. But, as we point out, the traditional scale favors partisans because two questions in the traditional scale regard which party holds power. Furthermore, there are strong signs that pure independents are unique in both their level of dissatisfaction with the political process in the United States and their external political efficacy, a finding that stands in contrast to some previous literature. We conclude with some thoughts about what traditional political knowledge scales measure in a polarized two-party system.

7.2 What Is Political Knowledge?

It has long been assumed that if the input of democracy is a better-informed public, the output will be measurably better. Lippmann (1925) wrote about the potential ills to society when people do not know or understand the basic functioning of their government. The authors of *The American Voter* found shockingly low levels of conceptualization among average Americans. Economists have argued that information asymmetries lead to increases in shirking (Buchanan and Tullock 1962). And, in perhaps the most thorough treatment of this topic, Delli Carpini and Keeter (1996) note that political awareness is key to participation, self-awareness, and self-advocacy in American democracy. When Americans know more, they participate more and can better understand their own needs, as well as the needs of their communities, and they are more likely to be capable of doing something about it. This is consistent with longstanding research in political participation that situates the decision to participate as reliant on resources, most notably education (Verba, Schlozman, and Brady 1995).

However, there is an implicit assumption that political knowledge acquisition acts as a freeing mechanism, allowing an individual to be better able to find and realize their own interest. The paradox is that those with high levels of political awareness tend to be the most partisan and exhibit the least response instability (Zaller 1992). As we noted in Chapter 6, the expression of interest does not make people more open or less racist. For instance, Federico and Sidanius (2002) find that political knowledge amplifies the link between having racist attitudes and adopting racist policy positions. This tells us something interesting and potentially troubling about the role of information in connecting racial attitudes/predispositions to racial policy positions—they are connected through the information environment. The gathering of political knowledge is partisan learning, and it leans heavily on identity and predispositions. Politically knowledgeable individuals learn where the parties stand, and what they stand for.

In such an environment, individuals tend to be highly skeptical of information that challenges their existing predispositions (Lodge and Taber 2013). This creates both confirmation bias and disconfirmation bias—and this behavior tends to be strongest among Americans, once again, who have higher, not lower, levels of political awareness (Lodge and Taber 2013). The role of information in promoting motivated reasoning and bolstering polarization creates a paradox in the way we view information and knowledge acquisition. Information is seen as necessary to promote participation and self-actualization, but in practice, political knowledge leads to a great deal of confirmation bias and rejection of challenging information, which ultimately promotes polarization.

We know that, generally, independents tend to have less information than partisans, but is this lack of information acquisition a signal of a lower ability to complete basic democratic functions, or is it simply endogenous to being less partisan? The literature here has tended to focus on partisans and information, without thinking as critically about independents. As we discussed in previous chapters, partisanship provides the anchor to help partisans sort through a complicated information environment. But if that environment is filled with biased information, and if its chief purpose is to motivate skepticism and reasoning, is it reasonable to expect independents to be motivated to consume information about who controls Congress, or which Democrats and Republicans are in control of the government? These are the exact sorts of questions that are usually contained in knowledge indices. Our assertion is that this information is less valuable for independents.

7.3 What Do We Mean When We Say "Independent?"

As should be clear, for our purposes, an independent is a person who does not affiliate with either party and does not consistently vote for candidates of either party. On a 7-point scale, these are "pure independents," as those who are independent but lean toward one of the two major parties are at least as partisan (if not more) than weak party identifiers. To be sure, this definition differs a bit from the definition that classifies an independent as anyone who labels themselves as such, regardless of their voting behavior. Political scientists and members of the media have not always agreed on who is an independent and who is not.

The most thorough treatment of independents in political science is by Klar and Krupnikov (2016). The authors argue that *both* media and academic conceptualizations of independents are generally incorrect. Media tend to characterize elections in terms of a hopeful (and false) view of independents that characterizes undecided voters as carefully weighing differences between parties and candidates when, in reality, most voters who identify as independent exhibit partisan behavior. On the other hand, academics tend to characterize independents and partisans as behaviorally indistinct, therefore leading to the conclusion (also to the title of the most famous work in this literature) that independent voters are largely a myth in American politics (see Keith et al. 1992). However, Klar and Krupnikov (2016) argue that there is a *paradox* among independents, especially independent leaners, because leaners are not observably distinct from partisans in how they vote. Instead, they argue, the act of hiding one's partisan inclinations is especially meaningful to how we understand social communication and political participation: Being partisan but claiming one is not signals that the individual may be trying to make a better impression on others and not give off the undesirable attribute of partisanship. As a result, independent leaners do not engage in the kind of social communication thought to be so central to information dissemination in between elections. In other words, while most of us know that it is undesirable to be partisan, the vast majority of Americans are partisan and "covert partisans" are those for whom keeping up social appearances of impartiality matters the most (even if they are, in fact, still partisan).

In one of their experiments, Klar and Krupnikov argue specifically that those who care more about what others think about their opinions—what they term "high self-monitoring"—are more likely to identify as independent, *even if they exhibit consistent and highly structured partisan behaviors.* Identifying as an independent does not stop these behaviors; rather, it is a signal that it is important to conceal their partisan behavior. Klar and Krupnikov find that this is most common among those who are both high self-monitoring *and* have high levels of political awareness. This finding is particularly interesting because it departs from most characterizations of what it means to be independent, which focus on the implications of independents being poorly informed: politically disinterested, disaffected, and distanced from candidates running for office.

Indeed, if we think of "independent" as a behavior rather than an identity, those who are more likely to exhibit response instability in survey responses are those with moderate levels of political awareness (Zaller 1992). In contrast, high awareness reinforces response stability. Therefore, strong partisanship and strong ideological coherence are thought to be high-awareness behaviors. This is because highly aware individuals have a more well-developed cognitive map; they are easily able to reject new information that conflicts with existing predispositions and accept information that confirms those predispositions. This makes the perceptual screen of partisanship both dependent on political information and yet also susceptible to a skewed interpretation of political events. This is why we see repeated examples of partisanship motivating perceptions in how individuals evaluate policies like the economy (Duch, Palmer, and Anderson 2000).

But what is the theory motivating pure independent behavior? Historically, the literature has engaged in negative theory building on this topic; it is based on the absence of the synergy of partisanship, knowledge, and bias. Our view is that political knowledge ultimately serves as a proxy for acceptance of the two-party regime. Rejection of that regime is likely to be motivated by political disaffection, low levels of external efficacy, political distrust, and dislike of the political parties. In the section that follows, we examine political knowledge and political independence empirically, using both longitudinal data from the American National Election Studies (ANES), as well as some analyses from the most recent (2020) ANES. Furthermore, we look at the connection between knowledge and political disaffection and find a strong link. Independents have the highest rates of political disaffection generally, and political disaffection leads to a lower motivation to garner knowledge about the political process. This helps us explain the problem with independents and the traditional questions used to capture civic competence and political awareness.

7.4 Data

7.4.1 How Much Do Independents Know?

So, just how uninformed are independents? In the early work on political knowledge (e.g., Luskin 1990; Zaller 1992), the scales for political knowledge included 20 or more questions on policy knowledge, civic knowledge, and partisan knowledge such as the names of political leadership and which party controls the House and Senate. However, since then the standard measurement of political knowledge has relied on questions that are only about name recall of political leaders and who controls political institutions. This latter measure is biased toward respondents who have a partisan identity, so we constructed a scale of political knowledge from the 2020 ANES that includes four questions. The questions measure respondent knowledge of four partisan and nonpartisan facts: which party controls each chamber of the US Congress (two questions), the length of the term of a US Senator, and an ability to identity which category makes up the smallest portion of the US budget from a list of four possible spending areas. Overall, political knowledge is normally distributed: 16% of respondents scored a perfect four out of four, 27% correctly answered three, 29% correctly answered two, 20% correctly answered one, and 8% answered no question correctly. Knowledge by party identification is presented in Table 7.1.

What can be surmised from the table? At first glance, it is clear that pure independents are, in fact, the least knowledgeable group. Forty-four percent of pure independents scored a 0 or 1 on this political knowledge scale, while partisans did better. For example, 28% of strong Democrats and 28% of strong Republicans answered fewer than two questions correctly. Similarly, only 27% of independents answered three or four questions correctly, compared to 45% of strong Democrats and 40% of strong Republicans. Interestingly, weak partisans and covert partisans/partisan leaners appear to be *more knowledgeable* than pure independents and just as knowledgeable as strong Democrats and Republicans.

These patterns replicate over time as well. In Figure 7.1, we present the average political knowledge scale by partisanship, rescaled from 0 to 1 in every year that the scale was available in the ANES Cumulative Data File. Importantly, the measure here is somewhat different. We rely on a scale constructed from the three questions that were asked consistently over time—ability to identify the House Speaker, the Vice President, and the

Table 7.1 Political Knowledge by Party Identification, 2020

Number of Correct Responses	Strong Democrat	Weak Democrat	Lean Democrat	Pure independent	Lean Republican	Weak Republican	Strong Republican
Zero	7	9	8	11	6	11	8
One	21	23	16	33	20	22	20
Two	27	32	29	30	29	30	32
Three	28	23	27	19	28	24	25
Four	17	13	18	8	17	14	15

Notes: Data are from the 2020 ANES. See the appendix for more details. Cell entries are column percentages.

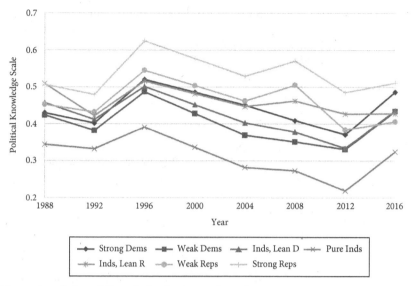

Figure 7.1 Political Knowledge by Party Identification, 1988–2016

Source: Data are from the ANES Cumulative Data file. Knowledge is measured using a three-question political knowledge index that ranges from 0 to 1.

Chief Justice of the Supreme Court. We rescaled them into a single index that ranges from 0 to 1. Missing data are excluded from the 0–1 mean calculations.[1] Again, the data show that pure independents are clearly the least informed Americans on these traditional measures (i.e., the ones most commonly used over time in the ANES and thus included in the Cumulative Data File).

Importantly, though, most of the traditional questions used in measuring political knowledge regard *politics*—who or which party is in control, and the names of political figures, and the frequency by which these individuals can be reelected. These questions are a bit odd in terms of measuring knowledge, as they are about the game of politics, not the substance of policy or the actions of those figures. And only one question, regarding participants' knowledge of federal spending, measures information on something relevant to policy.

Interestingly, focusing on the federal spending question reveals a slightly different pattern. We present this in Table 7.2. In the 2020 ANES data, the question asked respondents which policy the federal government spent the least on: foreign aid (the correct answer), Medicare, national defense, or Social Security. Overall, a majority of respondents answered this question

Table 7.2 Federal Spending Knowledge by Party Identification, 2020

On which program does the federal government spend the least?
1. *Foreign aid (correct)*
2. *Medicare*
3. *National defense*
4. *Social Security*

			% Correct			
Strong Democrat	Weak Democrat	Lean Democrat	Pure independent	Lean Republican	Weak Republican	Strong Republican
40%	36%	37%	33%	43%	39%	31%

Notes: Data are from the 2020 ANES. See the appendix for more details. Cell entries are column percentages.

incorrectly: 36% picked foreign aid; 30% picked Social Security, 23% picked Medicare, and 8% picked national defense. Here, we see much more evenly distributed *wrongness* among partisans. The least knowledgeable group is actually strong Republicans (31% correct), followed by pure independents (33%), weak Democrats (36%), leaning "independent" Democrats (37%), weak Republicans (39%), strong Democrats (40%), and leaning "independent" Republicans (43%).

On this question, we may be observing some partisan-motivated reasoning in how strong Republicans pick answers other than foreign aid, given that the Trump administration was quite verbose in its criticism that the United States spent too much money externally, like funding NATO peacekeeping operations (Browne 2019). But putting that aside, most importantly, we do not observe the gap in knowledge that is present on the factual questions about the names of partisan officials elected to office. This highlights Lupia's (2016) argument that evaluations of political knowledge/awareness should be related to the tasks necessary to perform the democratic function. The major driver of the differences in political knowledge appears to be associated with measures that are endogenous to the partisan order—which party controls the legislative body and whether respondents can identify major political figures. These questions are not dissimilar to asking someone if they can name the quarterback for the Dallas Cowboys or the New England Patriots—Cowboys and Patriots fans (and their rivals) will be more likely to answer correctly because they have a built-in motivation to know the answer. But those who don't care about those two teams may have little incentive to learn who the players are, even if they are paying taxes to support a stadium and follow football more generally.

As we will show in the subsequent section, (1) there is a link between higher rates of political disaffection and lower levels of political knowledge, and (2) independents experience higher rates of political disaffection than partisans.

7.4.2 Independents and Political Disaffection

One of the central contentions of the dealignment literature was that growing independent identification was related to political disaffection. This idea was briefly considered and dismissed by Keith et al. (1992) in Chapter 8 of their now classic treatment on the subject, *The Myth of the Independent Voter*. Not only did they argue that independents who leaned to one of the major parties were behaviorally indistinct from partisans, they also found that independents—both pure independents and leaners—were not any more or less likely to distrust government. The political world, however, has changed considerably since the early 1990s when Keith and his colleagues conducted their research.

In this section we investigate if political polarization has affected pure independents. And if so, how? While one possibility is that independents are just as likely as partisans to express political alienation, it is also possible that they have lower levels of political efficacy, political trust, and general political alienation as a result of polarization. While we presented detailed evidence of negative affective polarization—the way Democrats and Republicans view each other—there has also been a recent decline in how pure independents view the parties. Independents' ratings of both political parties, using the party "feeling thermometer" we utilized in Chapter 2, are presented in Figure 7.2.

A rating of 50 on this figure represents the break-even or neutral point on the 100-point feeling thermometer scale. From 1978 to 2008, these ratings were relatively stable, just at or slightly above the mid-point. But after 2008, we see a sharp decline of about 10 points, consistent with the acrimony of an era of hyper-negative partisanship that culminated with the 2008 election. Independents now share a collectively negative view of both major political parties, whereas they once viewed the parties on the positive side of neutral. Whereas partisans view their own party very highly and the other party

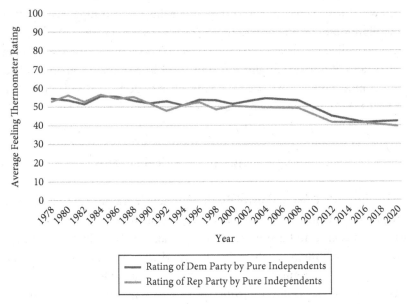

Figure 7.2 Average Feeling Thermometer Ratings of the Two Parties by Pure Independents, 1978–2020
Source: Data are from the ANES Cumulative Data file.

extremely negatively, as we presented in Chapter 2, independent voters view both parties cynically.

Little attention has been paid to the effect of polarization and negative partisanship on Americans who truly do not have an attachment to either party. Why is this change in independents from neutral to negative important? Using 1972 data, Keith et al. (1992) observed few differences between partisans of all sorts and independents in terms of their political alienation, particularly trust in government. Today, however, pure independents are twice as likely as leaners and about three times as likely as strong partisans to say they never trust the government to do what's right. This is demonstrated in Table 7.3. Similarly, Table 7.4 shows that when asked how many people in government are corrupt, pure independents are the most likely to say most/all (47%). Independents' responses of "most are corrupt" or "all are corrupt" are 18 percentage points higher than those of either strong Democrats or strong Republicans and considerably higher than those with weak and/or leaning partisanship.

Table 7.3 Trust in Government by Party Identification, 2020

	Strong Democrat	Weak Democrat	Lean Democrat	Pure independent	Lean Republican	Weak Republican	Strong Republican
Never	8	10	11	21	10	8	6
Some of the time	42	48	51	42	49	49	35
About half of the time	35	29	28	26	27	29	35
Most of the time	13	11	9	9	13	14	21
Always	1	2	*	2	*	1	2

Notes: Data are from the 2020 ANES. See the appendix for more details. Cell entries are column percentages.

Table 7.4 Views of Government Corruption by Party Identification, 2020

	Strong Democrat	Weak Democrat	Lean Democrat	Pure independent	Lean Republican	Weak Republican	Strong Republican
	How many in government are corrupt?						
None	1	1	1	3	1	*	1
A few	32	27	28	24	26	32	29
About half	39	33	29	26	33	33	41
Most	25	35	38	35	38	32	27
All	4	3	4	12	3	3	2

Notes: Data are from the 2020 ANES. See the appendix for more details. Cell entries are column percentages.

The corruption question has not been asked regularly, and there has been some contention over how to best measure trust in government that has led to a break in the time series. However, we can measure over-time external political efficacy, a question battery which captures the perceived responsiveness of government to the public (e.g., Craig, Niemi, and Silver 1990; Gamson 1968). Using the two-question external efficacy index from the ANES from 1952 to 2020, we observe in Figure 7.3 that not only has external efficacy declined, but over the course of the time series, pure independents have retained their status as the *least efficacious* partisan subgroup.[2]

Taken together, these findings on efficacy, trust, and corruption—all dimensions of political alienation—point to an important reality and identify a trend. Measures of political discontent, as measured by political efficacy, have grown more negative in the last 20 years, but independents are the least externally efficacious group. The remaining question is if alienation is related to the motivation to acquire political knowledge.

7.4.3 Disaffection and Knowledge

Does knowledge covary with political disaffection? To test this hypothesis, we model political knowledge in the 2020 ANES as a function of political efficacy and views of government corruption.[3] We include well-known correlates of political knowledge as controls, including age, race, gender, education, and political interest. We also include a folded 4-point measure of partisanship ranging from pure independent (1) to strong partisan (4).

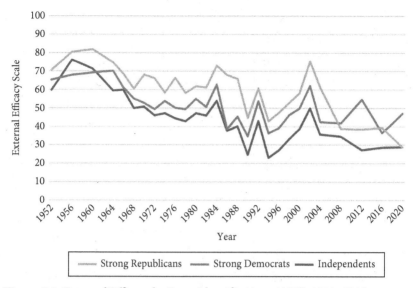

Figure 7.3 External Efficacy by Party Identification, ANES, 1952–2020

Source: Data are from the ANES Cumulative Data file. The external efficacy scale is composed of two items and has been rescaled from 0 to 100.

Finally, we include both the measures of political efficacy and government corruption presented earlier in the chapter.[4]

The results of the model are presented graphically in Figure 7.4. Overall, we find that the model's controls perform to expectations. Political knowledge is predicted by age, gender, race, education, political interest, and strength of partisanship. Additionally, we also see that political alienation covaries with low political knowledge. Those with lower levels of external efficacy—that is, those who see government as less responsive to people—are less knowledgeable about politics. Additionally, those more likely to view the government as corrupt are also less likely to exhibit high levels of political knowledge. Both effects are significant at the $p < .01$ level. Comparing the most to least efficacious person, the model predicts the most efficacious person scores about 3 percentage points higher on the political scale. The effect for the government corruption scale is almost three times this size (an 8-percentage-point difference). Overall, then, the models point to support for our hypothesis—political alienation is associated with lower general political knowledge acquisition. We discuss the implications of this finding in the final section.

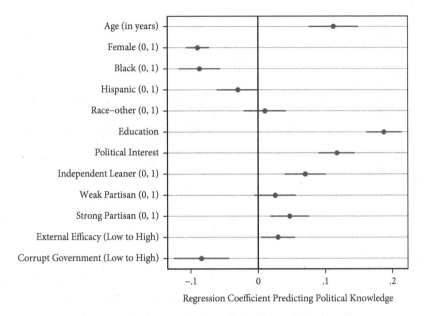

Figure 7.4 Regression Predicting Political Knowledge, 2020 ANES

Source: Data are from the 2020 ANES. This is a graphical representation of Model 3 from Table A7.1, with all variables recoded from 0 to 1. See the appendix for more details.

7.5 Conclusion

A skewering 2012 *Saturday Night Live* sketch captures the prevailing academic view of independent voters. Scrolling through a variety of purported undecided voters in the 2012 Presidential election, the cast quips:

> Before you get our vote, you're going to have to answer some questions . . . questions like: When is the election? How soon do we have to decide? What are the names of the two people running, and be specific? Who is the president right now? Is he or she running? Because if so, experience is maybe something we should consider. How long is a President's term of office? One year? Two years? Three years? Or Life? Because if it's for life, we're not comfortable with that. We don't need to be electing a dictator.

Generally, independents are characterized by their inattention to politics, lack of political knowledge, and lack of political participation. The notion of a thoughtful or careful independent voter has largely been considered a myth. Despite this fact, large numbers of partisans still view appearing non-partisan and labeling themselves as independents to be socially desirable, even when their behavior is very partisan. Pure independents, however, do not have firm partisan attachments, but fall well short of the democratic ideal given their informational limitations.

Throughout this book, we have sought to reconsider the role of information in American democracy. Flows of information so routinely happen through partisan channels and are processed in a partisan manner that following partisan cues can lead to disinformation. As we demonstrate in this chapter, partisans have higher knowledge of facts like the names of government leaders, but on questions of important policy knowledge like the basics of the federal budget, there is far less of a difference between partisans and pure independents.

While much of this book focuses expressly on partisan behavior, the purpose of Chapters 6 and 7 has been to contrast that behavior with that of the much-maligned pure independent. In these chapters, the data paint a collectively rosier view of political independents than the one usually offered by studies of American political behavior. To be sure, pure independents have lower levels of political awareness than partisans, but there are many pure independents who are politically aware—more than a quarter are highly informed and more than half score 50% or better on a typical political knowledge battery. At the same time, pure independents are less trusting and less efficacious than partisans, and they are more likely to believe that all politicians are corrupt. Their views of the two political parties have also grown more negative in the last decade, moving from an average neutral to a net negative evaluation. A final point offered in the chapter is that political alienation and knowledge are connected. While we do not have causal data to demonstrate that independents are more alienated and are *therefore* less knowledgeable politically, we offer a plausible story as to why independents can so ably use local or contextual political knowledge in a manner consistent with high levels of political sophistication in Chapter 6, but they score considerably lower on general political knowledge tests available in national surveys. Lupia (2016) argued that political knowledge should focus on what is required for the democratic task associated with that knowledge. Is knowing the name of the Chief Justice of the Supreme Court or the name of the Majority Leader important to the task of meaningfully participating in democracy? We argue it is not. But is knowing what the federal government spends money on and acknowledging if crime is an issue in one's neighborhood important? We argue it is. In the modern context, measuring political knowledge must contend not only with information but with the bias contained in partisan-motivated behavior. Pure independents may come to this arena with fewer political resources, but it is also apparent that they come with less bias.

8

An Elite Problem Calls for an Elite Solution

In March 2010, former Governor and vice-presidential candidate Sarah Palin released a map highlighting 20 Congressional districts that she and John McCain had won in 2008 but whose members of Congress had voted in favor of the Affordable Care Act (i.e., Obamacare). The map, released amid a rise in violent attacks against Democratic lawmakers, marked each of these districts with a set of target crosshairs. Palin promoted the map, tweeting "Don't Retreat, Instead—RELOAD" (Fisher 2011). In November of 2021, Rep. Paul Gosar (R-AZ) shared a video on Twitter showing him killing Rep. Alexandria Ocasio-Cortez (D-NY) and swinging swords at President Biden. In December 2021, Congresswoman Alexandria Ocasio Cortez (D-NY) went to Twitter to share a video round-up of her accomplishments for the year. But her Tweet simply said, "Instead of clickbait with guns in front of Christmas trees, we decided to actually tell you what we accomplished for the community and country this year." This tweet was an attack on Congressman Thomas Massie's (R-KY) sharing a picture of himself and six of his family members posing with military-grade rifles, including the Congressman himself holding an M60 machine gun, in front of their Christmas tree with the note "P.S.: Santa, please bring more ammo!" (Everson 2021). These are very different Tweets, but all are representative of the last decade of American politics. The Twitterverse, the airwaves, and the newspapers are filled with attacks from one party's leaders on the other's—often direct, sometimes violent, usually insulting, and always one-upping. When debates do pertain to policy, they are filled with hyperbole. Given how Democrats and Republicans categorize the policies enacted by the other party, it is remarkable that any legislation makes it out of Congress.

There are, to be sure, meaningful differences on policy to be debated. The environment, the economy, the health and welfare of citizens, individual freedoms, and the stability of democracy do hang in the balance. Which party is in power will make a fundamental difference in the lives of people

The Power of Partisanship. Joshua J. Dyck and Shanna Pearson-Merkowitz, Oxford University Press.
© Oxford University Press 2023. DOI: 10.1093/oso/9780197623787.003.0009

around the world in each of these areas. However, the parties are not ideo-logically consistent: Both parties pursue large government intervention in some areas and a hands-off approach in others. Both parties are hawks at times and doves at others. Both parties believe the government has the right to "be in your bedroom" and in the boardroom when the policies suit their political fortunes. There is no broad ideology guiding the modern manifesta-tion of the two parties. There is not even internal consistency when it comes to the division of powers between the federal and state governments. Which policies are "conservative" and which policies are "liberal" is completely de-termined by which party proposed them. As a result, policy attitudes are en-dogenous to partisanship.

This is a natural outgrowth of well-sorted parties. If a voter knows they be-lieve and support one party, it is not a stretch to imagine that the party shares the voter's values on all other policy issues as well (e.g., Levendusky 2009). Policies are hard to understand—when is the right time to get involved in the politics of another country? Does public health or the economy justify gov-ernment intervention? Does the need for a program warrant a tax increase, or does the economy need a boost via a tax cut? When is the right time to increase taxes and spending and when is the right time to decrease taxes and reduce the size of government? These are hard questions that call for study, theory development, data collection, and hypothesis testing, and it is not crazy to think that even with prolonged attention to details, and weighing the benefits and drawbacks of each decision, elected officials will, at times, get it wrong.

But in a politically polarized two-party system marked by strong par-tisan attachments in the electorate, parties do not weigh arguments for and against, and admit wrong decisions, and neither do the partisan members of the public who support them. The era of accountability, if the U.S. ever had one, is over. What one party believes is always what the other party does not. Any problems or negative externalities are always the other party's fault. As a result, much of U.S. politics has become simple negativity. While we like to believe that co-partisans are persuaded to adopt policy beliefs in line with their party based on structured, sound arguments grounded in po-litical ideology, today's negativity leads people to have knee-jerk reactions against the policies of the other party, leaving no room for bipartisanship or accountability.

In this book, we have argued that partisan sorting and the partisan infor-mation environment have brought bigger issues to the fore. The bounds of politics have come undone. Today, people bring their partisanship to their community gatherings, their dinner tables, their pharmacies, and their grocery stores. The power of partisanship to influence the nonpolitical means the decision making of partisans is no longer as influenced by important social and lived experiences. The partisan perceptual screen is an opaque wall that keeps meaningful and important information from informing behavior. Partisanship makes us less likely to compromise with our opponents, stops us from getting to know and empathize with people from different walks of life, and changes the way we weigh risk.

The power of partisanship calls into question the importance of information in politics. If information is mostly used to reinforce and stabilize partisan positions, it serves no greater good. The normative essential of information is no longer warranted. This has some profound consequences for how we think about politics, social science theories of human behavior, and the future of the United States. To conclude this volume, we will use this space to discuss some of these implications.

8.1 Expressive Responding Is Indicative of Instrumental Behavior

Much of the work on political polarization, particularly negative partisanship, has been criticized for being just responsive or what some people call partisan-motivated survey responses. The criticism suggests that survey responses like those presented in this book are simply expressive and are not reflective of actual behavior. It is psychologically pleasing for Democrats to report that the economy is doing poorly when there is a Republican in power even if, on objective measures, the economy is doing quite well (Gerber and Huber 2009). So, does partisan-motivated reasoning really extend to real-world behavior? Or are partisan respondents just answering surveys in a manner consistent with political "cheerleading" for their team? It is certainly true that survey responses are sometimes unstable and inaccurate, and response acquiescence and priming offer good reasons for skepticism when interpreting partisan survey responses (Gerber and Huber 2009). But we join a small chorus of scholars and argue that "cheerleading" responses correspond to real-world actions.

In our view, we have some fairly clear evidence that expressive responding is (1) prompted by the negative environment created by elites, and

(2) indicative of how people behave outside the survey context. The willingness to polarize on anything and everything is a window into deepening divides in our public conscience that center on who is "good" and who is "evil." The rhetoric that goes into backing these positions up has spilled over in fundamentally troubling ways. Certainly, Democrats may go on to eat meatloaf after finding out about Trump's affinity for it, and Republicans may get a vaccine despite a negative reaction to a Democratic endorsement: Partisans might balk but not change their behavior. However, we see events over the last several years as substantial evidence that partisanship manifests in real behaviors, behaviors that are troubling for individuals and the community, not just perfunctory survey responses.

The most obvious example of this is the Capitol insurrection on January 6, 2021. Former President Trump, high-profile Republican members of Congress, and Republican media programs all touted the narrative that the election had been "stolen" and that Trump was the legitimate president. Elites sent the message and voters responded. Several thousand U.S. residents from across the country got in their cars, boarded planes, and made a journey, sometimes thousands of miles long, to attempt to overturn a fair election (Dreisbach, Anderson, and Woerkom 2022).

In a similar vein, Republican opposition to public health measures during the Covid-19 pandemic, including the vaccine but also masking, social distancing, and refraining from attending social gatherings, is not expressive in nature; it carries real consequences. As detailed in Chapter 5, Republicans took on considerably greater risk and were more likely to get sick and to die from Covid-19. Anti-precaution, anti-vaccine, and anti-mask messaging came directly from their trusted partisan elites. Several stories emerged of outspoken opponents of vaccine and mask mandates contracting and dying from Covid-19, including Orange County Deputy District Attorney Kelly Ernby (age 46) and Washington State Senator Doug Erickson (age 52). Matters of life and death are not superficial matters of partisan-motivated survey expression; they represent consequential partisan-motivated behavior.

As we discuss in the introduction to this book, there has also been increased violence and intimidation against school board members over concerns broadcast by Republican elites about "critical race theory," a theory that is not even taught in the districts in which the violence and intimidation has occurred (Anderson 2021). There was an unprecedented number of gun sales after President Biden was elected and altered videos were released by

Republican elites insinuating that the president and Democratic members of Congress were going to make all guns illegal and take them away. But the public health misinformation has perhaps been the most spectacular. After President Trump publicly contemplated in April 2020 that injections of disinfectant could help defeat the coronavirus, there was an increase in calls to poison control from ingestions of bleach and other disinfectants (Kluger 2020). In 2021, pet and animal feed stores were unable to stock the antiparasitic drug Ivermectin, which is commonly used as a dewormer for horses and dogs, after Fox News host Laura Ingraham and podcaster Joe Rogan started pushing it as an alternative treatment for Covid-19 (Dickson 2021).

None of these are expressive responses without consequence. These are real acts taken in response to elite messaging. If even a few thousand people are willing to go to these extreme measures, certainly many more are willing to take small steps, choosing to forgo arugula or, more importantly health insurance.

We are, to be sure, not the only scholars to make note of the heightened temperature in American democracy. Webster (2020) argues that there has been an increase in anger motivating the political behavior of Americans, and notably, that rage weakens the public's commitment to democratic norms. Kalmoe and Mason (2022) connect partisan extremism to the justification of violence through a series of well-constructed surveys and experiments.

When seen through these lenses, the stakes of toxic affective partisanship are very high. They have damaged our ability to have civil, level-headed debates about public policy; and in a democracy, debate and compromise are required. These are extremely troubling consequences of the power of partisanship, and they signal something that is far beyond "expressive partisanship."

8.2 American Democracy Requires Compromise, and Compromise Is Becoming Less Tenable

In designing the Constitution, James Madison and the Framers of the Constitution made several value judgments that have come to define the American ethos. Central among them is that broad consensus would be needed to adopt policies and laws. By creating a system where power checks power, elites elected and appointed in different ways need to agree, often in groups constituting greater than a majority, to pass new laws. A premium here was also placed on the concept of dual sovereignty, recognizing the constitutional authority of both the nation and its states.

In practice, such a system places a large emphasis on and deference to the status quo. The normal practice of American politics is stasis. Political science theories of policymaking, change, legislative gridlock, and compromise all emphasize the importance of the status quo in the American ethos. Mayhew (1991) noted that major pieces of legislation were as likely to pass during divided as during unified government, highlighting inaction during unified government and the necessity of bipartisan compromise. As Krehbiel (1998) and others have argued, the normal outcome of the legislative process is gridlock, but our political institutions and their rules (e.g., the filibuster and presidential veto) help us understand under which circumstances gridlock will be broken.

A system built on party compromise and cross-partisan coalitions had defined most of the twentieth century. But in today's party system we see something very different. Our legislative politics is characterized by a high degree of party discipline within the chambers and rampant gridlock. The gridlock has become so pervasive that government shutdowns have become regular business, and the threat of shutdown looms every few months. More dangerously, Congress has slowly been chipping away at legislative rules adopted in the 1700s to protect the rights of the minority party to influence legislation so that they can do away with compromise and make policy without any accommodations for the other party. A system of institutionalized gridlock without cross-partisan compromisers can turn to one of partisan atrophy, a system that lives in a perpetual state of inaction. When members of the parties despise each other, a system of checks and balances intended to lead to incrementalism and moderation, instead leads to stalemate. To be sure, the Framers of the U.S. Constitution wanted stability for people, for the markets, and for foreign affairs. By enshrining gridlock and compromise as essential elements to pass policies, they also ensured that markets, foreign powers, and the citizens of the country would know what to expect and how to plan, and would be reassured that whoever was in power, they would have some say and they could be sure that things would function as they always have.

The failure of our co-equal institutions to advance policy and combat extremism during this time is part of what Drutman (2019) has identified as the "Doom Loop" of failure. Writing before the 2020 election, Drutman argued that a Democratic victory in the 2020 presidential race would result

in the Republican Party doing everything it could to undermine, delegiti-
mize, and obstruct policy making. With the Congress divided after the 2022
election, the normal expectation is inaction. If Republicans win back the
presidency in 2024, it will likely evoke the same obstructive response from
Democrats, leading to more and continued decline in Americans' faith in
their government. The problem is a well-sorted two-party system defined
by negativity. In a two-party system where toxic affective party identification is high, Americans will forgive any sin, even criminality, from their own
party and criticize anything promoted by the other party, because the goal is
solely to keep and preserve power. Frances Lee (2009) explains this concept
well—when elections hang in the balance, parties do not have an interest in
legislating through compromise, they have an interest in making the party in
power look bad.

   While Drutman and Lee expect gridlock, that is but one possible outcome.
The other is instability. The weakening of rules to protect the influence of the
minority party, the strengthening of the presidency, and other changes that
parties use to overcome the gridlock endemic to the system also bring instability, as public policy can be drastically changed each time partisan control
changes hands. Changes to protections to partisan minority rights will not
just come back to haunt the majority party when they become the minority
party (e.g., Binder 1997); they will also wreak havoc on the stability of the
nation. Businesses and individuals will have no means of predicting what
regulations, taxes, or rules will be in place two years out, and U.S. allies will
no longer count on American support in international affairs. The United
States' status as a world leader and its power in the international market is a
product of its stability and consistency. This has been imperiled by political
polarization as wide swings in policy have made the U.S. an unstable market
and international partner.

   The compromise experiment presented in Chapter 3 reveals that while
Americans give lip-service support to party compromise, Republicans find
compromise especially distasteful when they are in the minority. It is easy
to say you are for compromise when in the majority, as compromise usually requires the minority party to bend further toward to your will than
your majority bends toward theirs. When there is no supermajority party,
U.S. institutions require compromise, but our political allegiances are built
on a strategy of never compromising. This is a problematic stasis, a mismatch
of preferences and institutions. Our concern is that such a stalemate is likely
to lead to greater dissatisfaction with government more generally, and this is

what leads people to turn to authoritarian populist leaders who will *just get things done*, often at great expense to democracy.

8.3 The Critical Importance of the GOP

We pursued this research agenda with a general theory about the power of partisanship to structure political behavior in the United States. Theoretically, our argument works for both Democrats and Republicans, and we present *some* evidence that conflict extension into the nonpolitical is a two-party phenomenon.

However, the empirical results suggest that our theory is more applicable, at least currently, to Republicans than to Democrats. It is Republicans, but not Democrats, who are sensitive to their majority/minority status in their willingness to compromise (Chapter 3). It is Republicans whose elite cues stop the transmission of the intergroup contact effect on issues of discrimination (Chapter 4). And it is Republicans who are sensitive to the cue giver in the prospect theory experiment and who therefore become risk acceptant when theory would expect them to be risk averse (Chapter 5). Democrats, to be sure, are sensitive to cues about Donald Trump in the food experiments (Chapter 3), and in the Covid-19 vaccine experiments (Chapter 5). Data also show that *both* Republicans and Democrats have increased negative partisanship (Chapter 2), and both are resistant to information gained from their lived experience and social environment (Chapter 6); but the transmission of elite-to-mass behavior appears to be more consistent among Republicans.

The asymmetry of many of our results certainly may be due to the nature of some of our tests and potentially to when they were conducted. For example, it was a political decision made by Richard Nixon to pursue the "southern strategy" and to cultivate a Republican Party that opposed progress on civil rights, and it was Republican elites who, following Nixon, continued to play on white fears and stereotypes of Black, Hispanic, and Asian people in political appeals. As we discuss in Chapter 4, Democrats were certainly not blameless in this regard; there are plenty of examples of Democratic Party leaders stoking white racism through implicit appeals before changing their policy approaches and language to be more racially liberal in the last decade. But Democrats have also been the face of civil rights and are the home to the vast majority of non-white elected officials and women. Democrats effectively "own" the issue of civil rights and, therefore, we would expect intergroup contact effects to be disrupted among Republicans, not Democrats. But that does not mean we do not expect that it could run the other way. Indeed, a good test for future research would be to look at how contact *with Republicans or white evangelical Christians* among Democrats affects attitudes toward Republicans or evangelical Christians (e.g., Castle et al. 2017).

However, we see an important takeaway in our tax-cut experiment (Chapter 5) and our compromise experiment (Chapter 3). In both of these instances, we utilize proposals not derived from real-world events or things "long on the political agenda" (e.g., Carmines and Stimson 1989) on which partisans should have gut responses based on cues already received in the information environment. These were developed based on our previous work on the importance of avoiding "easy issues" (Dyck and Pearson-Merkowitz 2019). In the experiments we presented in this book we see evidence that it is Republicans, not Democrats, that are most affected by partisan elite cues. These results lead us to think that the elite- to mass-polarization connection (or, to use Layman and Carsey's [2002a] term, "conflict extension") is stronger in the Republican Party.

There are several reasons for greater elite–mass transmission for Republicans. We believe the most important explanation is the asymmetry of political polarization. Although political polarization is usually discussed as two-sided—both parties moving toward the ideological poles—the data suggest that polarization is driven by the Republican Party's four decades–long trek to the right (Hacker and Pierson 2005, 2015; Mann and Ornstein 2016) and the tactics they used to get there (Theriault 2013).

For one, as we discuss in Chapter 2, the Republican Party has a much larger and more well-developed partisan news infrastructure with personalities Republican voters have come to know over a generation. MSNBC simply does not have the viewership, reach, or reputation of Fox News, and Democrats do not have a corollary to conservative talk radio, which dominates the political AM/FM and now satellite dial (Hacker and Pierson 2015). Certainly, this media infrastructure is a large reason for the elite–mass transfer. But if there was considerable diversity in the Republican Party, this transfer would not be as easy. The Democratic Party is a conglomeration of various interests, each with its own agenda and little agreement as to a central mission (Grossmann and Hopkins 2016). The Republican Party, on the other hand, is a product of elite actions to bring the party together and create a unified front that would be able to challenge Democrats for power following the one-party dominance the Democratic Party sealed in Congress after the 1954 election (Lee 2016).[1] The GOP cultivated a racially, religiously, and ethnically homogenous party that has presented a unified message of politics driven by a dedication to a Christian God and policy that is informed by faith, patriotism, and "traditional family values" (Layman 2001).

The Republican Party achieved this through masterful political strategy. As we discuss in Chapter 2, high-profile Republican elected officials, starting in the 1970s, used mass mail and media strategies to reach well outside their Congressional districts and states to appeal to voters across the country using well-crafted political appeals that drew on people's Christian faith and their fears of a diversifying nation. And in the 1980s, Congressman Newt Gingrich began producing audiotapes to "give Republican candidates strategies and talking points to run for office" (Theriault 2013, 23–24). The Republican talking points first developed by Gingrich became a foundation for the Republican Party to facilitate Republican Party operatives, elected officials, and co-partisan media personalities to communicate a consistent message to voters. This message had little to do with policy specifics; Gingrich and his colleagues revived the anti-intellectual politics of the 1950s that questioned experts and facts, treated skepticism of science and policy experts as a weapon instead of a tool, and cultivated a hatred and distrust of government and particularly the Democratic Party. As Dionne, Ornstein, and Mann (2017) explain in their book documenting the transformation of the Republican Party and Congressional politics:

> Although he had a deep interest in science, Gingrich also launched an attack on the use of science and facts in public policy that would be picked up by other Republican politicians in the years to come. . . . As Speaker, Gingrich abolished the Office of Technology Assessment, a blue-ribbon congressional agency that had been established for scientists to offer objective analysis on issues ranging from defense and space to climate and energy. The new majority defended shuttering the Office's doors as a cost-saving measure, and it was part of Gingrich's larger (and more successful) effort to centralize power in the Speaker's office. But the move also sent a message that ideological commitments would trump evidence. (p. 76)

It was also Republican Speaker of the House Dennis Hastert who crafted the "Hastert rule," the doctrine under which the speaker will not allow a floor vote on a bill unless the majority of the Republican Party supports it. Finally, there is the diversity of the parties; the Republican Party, as represented by its elected officials, is a party primarily of straight, Christian, white men, a contrast to the more racially, ethnically, religiously, and sexually diverse Democratic Party. This was not always true, but it is today (e.g., McTague and Pearson-Merkowitz 2013).

Democrats, though, have fought fire with fire. The tactics used by Republicans to hold their members accountable and stoke fear and resentment in their voters is easy to observe in today's Democratic Party. While Republicans started using these tactics first, Democrats have certainly learned how to play by the new rule book. Russell (2018) analyzed the Twitter messages of members of the U.S. Senate in 2013 and 2015 and found that while Democrats sent more Tweets, Republicans were far more likely to send out negative partisan Tweets. But when Russell (2021) reanalyzed the data with Tweets from 2017 she found that, in response to the election of Donald Trump, Democrats had eclipsed Republican negativity on Twitter. Importantly, in both analyses, the leadership of both parties—those with the loudest voices and the most followers—were the most negative of all members. This is consistent with more research analyzing Tweets of Congressional candidates that finds that while Republicans are more likely to post uncivil Tweets about their opponents, "incivility begets incivility" (Heseltine and Dorsey 2022, p. 1). As the number of uncivil Tweets increases by one candidate, so do the chances that the other candidate will respond with uncivil Tweets. And critically, uncivil Tweets are more likely to be "liked" and retweeted than civil communication.

Finally, we also see growing evidence that the Democratic Party is moving left, lending support to primary challengers, to remove more moderate members from office who failed to toe the party line. There is good reason for the Democratic Party to do so: When one party can hold their coalition together, and the balance is held by only a few votes, the other party relies on all their members voting together. If they lose a single member, they can get nothing accomplished. As a result, polarization on one side drives polarization on the other.

While the Democratic Party is still a more diverse "big tent" of a party, the Democratic Party's embrace of the tactics employed by Republicans that drove polarization, may result in an increased mass-elite transfer effect for the Democratic Party. On this, only time will tell.

8.4 A Reckoning for Political Science Theory and U.S. Democracy

In their 1950 report, the American Political Science Association (APSA) Committee on Political Parties (1950) argued that the United States needed a stronger two-party system; one with more intraparty cohesion, real and effective opposition, and party loyalty. Part of the need for a "responsible party" system at the elite level was based on assumptions of what it would do for voters. A clearer party system, they argued, would create stark choices, and stark choices were more commensurate with democracy and breaking one-partyism. It would give voters clear choices and allow them to hold parties and elected officials accountable. While a careful/close read of the APSA report suggests that not all of their suggestions have transpired, to be sure, today we observe a considerably stronger party system. There is far greater party discipline in Congress, and the parties offer stark choices to voters. Voters, in turn, are better sorted into parties, and partisanship and policy positions are highly correlated.

Levendusky (2009, 140–-141) sees this as the "positive side of elite polarization." He argues, as the APSA report suggested, that elite polarization helps voters "participate more effectively" and vote "correctly." On this we think there is some sliding of conceptual definitions. Voting "correctly" and "effectively" assumes that people develop policy positions and then choose the party that best aligns with those positions. But is it a "correct vote" if policy preferences and vote choice are endogenous to party identification? If policy positions are knee-jerk reactions against the opposition party, it is empirically impossible to decipher if the vote was "correct."

The data presented in Chapter 6 provides little evidence that personal experience or community context informs policy positions for partisans. Democratic and Republican policy preferences are unaffected by their pocketbooks. Democrats' and Republicans' concerns about gun violence are generally not affected by the level of violence in their neighborhoods, and their support for land preservation is not informed by growth and development in their communities. Instead, even Democrats' and Republicans' ratings of how much land is in their community appears unaffected by reality. Both Democrats and Republicans rate the amount of open space in their community the same, regardless of how much actually exists or how much has disappeared. Only independents seem to have their perceptions of their community informed by the reality within their community and allow their policy positions to change in response to their lived experience and their environment.

To be clear, we do not argue that people are incorrectly choosing one party over another, as Thomas Frank does in *What's the Matter With Kansas?* We do not take a position on whether it is more "logical" or "correct" for any individual to be a Republican or a Democrat. People could have real reasons for gravitating toward either side, and when voters are "cross-pressured"—that is, they hold values that do not neatly align with the two-party system—there is not a "correct" way to prioritize one issue over another. People can be pro-life and pro–social welfare. People can be in favor of environmental preservation and against raising the minimum wage. Since these do not neatly line up with the current manifestation of the political parties, voters have to choose one policy to prioritize and sacrifice the other to cast their ballot. But either choice would be a "correct" vote. Our takeaway here is that determining the "correct" vote relies on voters gaining nonpartisan information and weighing it against their personal value system. In a system in which the parties do not align with value systems, and partisanship is driven by toxic negativity, we cannot judge if people are making "correct" choices.

We find no evidence of learning or abstracting relevant information to political decision making. Instead, we find that polarization and partisan negativity are simply creating an easy mechanism for Americans to adopt positions that align with their party and skills to resist dissonant information. Affective polarization is increasing, both for individuals over the course of their life span, and in the aggregate, as each generation is more polarized than the one before (Phillips 2022). One of the great paradoxes we have grappled with in this book is that partisans consume a great deal of political information, and offer the most stable opinions, but those opinions are just as much products of elite messages as they are antecedent to the choice of parties. Partisanship stops learning and the reception of new information. What then, is the benefit to democracy of increased *meaningful* choice between two different parties if the primary outcome of that choice is to ground voters into camps unwilling to listen to, compromise with, or learn from each other? What type of democratic ideal is polarization that drives disgust, hatred, and fear of the opposition party? As we have moved toward a responsible two-party government at the elite level, the public has followed and is irresponsibly polarized.

In Federalist No. 10, James Madison argued that the element that deserved the most attention in the design of the new republic was its ability to control factions.

> The friend of popular governments never finds himself so much alarmed for their character and fate, as when he contemplates their propensity to this dangerous vice. He will not fail, therefore, to set a due value on any plan which, without violating the principles to which he is attached, provides a proper cure for it. The instability, injustice, and confusion introduced into the public councils, have, in truth, been the mortal diseases under which popular governments have everywhere perished. (Madison 1787, p. 42)

Madison argued that factions could not be eliminated from society, because to eliminate factions would require the denial of liberty, a remedy worse than the problem. He therefore surmised that in order to manage the existence of factions, the solution was to have many factions enveloped in a system built on checks and balances and separation of powers. Madison believed that this arrangement gave society the best opportunity to avoid a ruler who would govern with autocratic impulses. Moreover, the size and diversity of the country would ensure that when factious leaders were elected and managed to "kindle a flame within their particular States," they would be "unable to spread a general conflagration through the other States," (Madison 1787, p. 48). Madison's message: Responsible, sorted, polarized parties are bad for democracy *and* the citizens of the republic.

Today we live in a society that is everything Madison feared. Factions, better known as the Republican and Democratic Parties, have spread their "general conflagration" across each and every state (e.g., Hopkins 2018).

Support for democracy in the United States is in peril. While there is general agreement on the principle of democracy, what democracy means in practice is in the eye of the beholder. For example, Hurwitz and Mondak (2002) found that support for core tenets of democracy, like the right to peaceful protest, falls off sharply when those holding the protest is a group they disagree with. And the more threatened people feel toward the group, the less likely they are to agree that the group should have core civil rights and liberties. Recent World Values Surveys (Haerpfer et al. 2020) have found that only about half of Americans said it was absolutely necessary that "People choose their leaders in free elections," almost 60% said they had very little or no confidence in elections, 20% said that in U.S. elections votes are counted fairly either "not often" or "not at all often," over 30% say voters are frequently bribed, and over a fifth of Americans said it would be either "very good" or "fairly good" if the military were to rule the country. Additionally, over 35% of Americans reported it would be either "very good" or "fairly good" to have a strong leader who does not have to bother with a legislature and elections as a way of "governing this country." If people are willing to compromise on the basic tenets of democracy, what keeps democracy going?

Elites play a central role in preserving the democratic creed (Prothro and Grigg 1960). Without elite support and agreement from both political parties on some fundamental system values and democratic norms, it is easy to see how the Capitol insurrection occurred, and how a majority of Republican voters continue to defend and justify it. The cues they received from the loudest elite in the Republican Party was and is that the election was stolen and that there was widespread voter fraud. This information has flowed from the top down, and no level of greater education or information among Republicans will act as a salve to the messages they receive from their trusted elites. This will only change if Republican elites change their messaging.

The parties are now locked into a competition for power that has led them down a very dangerous path. There is no motivation for the political parties to work together. They benefit when the ruling party (and the country along with them) fails. Decades of polarization have created a situation where the parties no longer tolerate anyone in their party working with the other side. We are on the path to a constitutional crisis. When voters do not trust elections won by the opposition party, democracy is in peril. At the time of this writing, it is the Republican Party that no longer has faith in election processes and calls for the firing of election workers and throwing out legitimate votes. Indeed, the Republican Party's willingness to do whatever it takes to win continues to back Democrats into a corner. We do not expect that Democrats will suddenly match Republican efforts to disenfranchise voters (see, e.g., Piven, Minnite, and Groarke 2009), but the calls are growing louder within Democratic circles to pass aggressive reforms to match Republican power-grabbing strategies, all with the goal of expanding Democratic Party power, such as the immediate expansion of the number of seats on the Supreme Court. Suddenly, policy proposals that have long sat dormant because they would greatly expand Democratic power in Congress and yet were not even supported by most of the Democratic Party because of their possible effects on the system, such as statehood for Washington, D.C., and Puerto Rico, and a reorganization of the Senate to match the underlying population of states, are on the table. Polarization accompanied by affective and negative partisanship will send us down a spiral where any reform, well intentioned or not, enacted by one party, is rejected and feared by the other. Would it be normatively good for Washington, D.C., residents to have full voting representation? Yes. Would it further polarize the country and be seen by Republicans as an attempt to quell Republican influence in government? Most definitely. Consideration and passage of such policies, well intentioned or not, from either party will further instability.

8.5 Is There a Path Forward?

Unfortunately, we are not optimistic that there is a path forward. Several scholars have argued that the toxic animosity between voters from different political parties could potentially be dampened or even solved through intergroup contact or meaningful deliberation (e.g., Fishkin et al. 2021; Mason 2018; Whitt et al. 2021). Unfortunately, as Chapter 4 shows, while we cannot completely discount the potential of intergroup contact to decrease the animosity between partisans from different camps, the evidence throughout this book, and the research we conducted on immigration and gay marriage over the last decade, lead us to think that it is unlikely that contact between the parties will improve the situation without the support of party leaders. Allport's (1954) original text discusses the likelihood that individuals will take contact with outgroups as isolated incidents when they are not backed up by social or authority support. Without a change in the messaging of partisan elites, co-partisans who have positive contact with a member of the opposition party are unlikely to generalize to the larger population. In effect, a Democrat may come to like their neighbor who is a Republican, but they are unlikely to think of that person as representative of other Republicans—they will be thought of as the exception, not the rule. Scholars have also suggested that intergroup contact could be achieved through the media, with television, radio, and other outlets featuring more nuanced and sympathetic presentations of members of both parties. Given our review of the current state of the media in Chapter 2, we also think this is unlikely given that balanced news coverage appears to *reduce* news consumption compared to one-sided coverage (Wojcieszak et al. 2016).

Frances Lee (2016) suggests that it is the fact that either party could win in each election that drives the majority of the conflict between the parties.

In this case, one-party domination would break the polarization and encourage the minority party to work with the majority party. If there is no chance the minority party will take control of the institution in the next election, then the minority party is more likely to work with the majority so that they can have any effect on policy outcomes. While several pundits and political scientists have pointed to demographic changes that could lead to a one-party wave, given the uneven distribution of the two party's voters across states and districts (Gimpel and Hui 2015; Lang and Pearson-Merkowitz 2015; Tam Cho, Gimpel, and Hui 2013) and the gerrymandering of House districts into one-party monopolies, it is hard to see how national changes in partisan preferences will manifest in a change in the political predispositions and partisan identities of who is elected to office, at least in the near term.

We argued in this book that the problem of partisanship starts with political elites—political elites putting politics above the stability of the country. Partisan elites need to take that power seriously and realize that partisanship is a tool. It can be used to give voters choices and understand meaningful differences in policy approaches. It can help overcome the problem of collective action both in legislatures and in the public (Aldrich 1995). But, just as a hammer can be used to build or to destroy, the power of partisanship can also be wielded in both productive and destructive ways. There is no easy solution here, and we must admit we are overcome by skepticism that things will get better anytime soon. But if they do, it will start with a concerted effort on the part of partisan elites to change their messaging and rhetoric.

Appendix

Data appendix

There are two main sources of data used throughout the book. The first is the American National Election Studies (ANES). Specifically, we use information from the Cumulative Data File from 1948 to 2020, as well as the 2020 Time Series Study. In addition, we use original data from a series of nationally representative surveys designed by the authors and conducted with YouGov in 2014 (two), 2016, 2017, 2019, and 2020. Details on the surveys appear below.

American National Election Studies

Analyses in Chapters 2 and 7 examine data from the American National Election Studies (www.electionstudies.org). These materials are based on work supported by the National Science Foundation under grant number SES 1444721, 2014–2017, the University of Michigan, and Stanford University. We specifically use the Time Series Cumulative Data File and the 2020 Time Series Study.

YouGov Data

2014 UML YouGov Survey

The survey was conducted between April 21 and 28, 2014. YouGov interviewed 1,172 respondents who were then matched down to a sample of 1,000 to produce the final dataset. The respondents were matched to a sampling frame on gender, age, race, and education, party identification, ideology, and political interest. The frame was constructed by stratified sampling from the full 2010 American Community Survey (ACS) sample with selection within strata by weighted sampling with replacements (using the person weights on the public use file). The matched cases were weighted to the sampling frame using propensity scores. The matched cases and the frame were combined and a logistic regression was estimated for inclusion in the frame. The propensity score function included age, gender, race/ethnicity, years of education, and ideology. The propensity scores were grouped into deciles of the estimated propensity score in the frame and post-stratified according to these deciles. This survey is used in Chapters 3, 4, and 6. In Chapter 6, these data are merged with contextual data from the Federal Bureau of Investigation's 2013 Uniform Crime Reporting database. The measure *Crime per Capita* is matched at the county level with data in the survey.

2014 UML CCES Module

This survey is a 1,000-respondent module that was conducted as part of the 2014 Cooperative Congressional Election Study (CCES). The 2014 CCES survey was conducted by YouGov in October 2014 (pre-election data) and November 2014 (post-election data). For the full CCES, YouGov interviewed 87,389 who were then matched down to a sample of 56,2000 to produce the final dataset. YouGov constructed a sampling frame of U.S. Citizens from the 2010 American Community Survey, including data on age, race, gender, education, marital status, number of children under 18, family income, employment status, citizenship, state, and metropolitan area. The frame was constructed by stratified sampling from the full 2010 American Community Survey (ACS) sample with selection within strata by weighted sampling with replacements (using the person weights on the public use file). The matched cases were weighted to the sampling frame using propensity scores. The matched cases and the frame were combined and a logistic regression was estimated for inclusion in the frame. The propensity score function included age, gender, race/ethnicity, years of education, and voter registration. The propensity scores were grouped into deciles of the estimated propensity score in the frame and post-stratified according to these deciles. For the team data, the matched cases were then weighted to the sampling frame using entropy balancing by age, gender, education, race, voter registration, ideology, baseline party identity, born-again status, political interest, and their interactions. The weights were trimmed at 7. This survey is used in Chapter 3.

2016 URI YouGov Survey

The survey was conducted between October 7 and November 7, 2016. YouGov interviewed 937 respondents who were then matched down to a sample of 850 to produce the final dataset. The respondents were matched to a sampling frame on gender, age, race, and education, party identification, ideology, and political interest. The frame was constructed by stratified sampling from the full 2010 American Community Survey (ACS) sample with selection within strata by weighted sampling with replacements (using the person weights on the public use file). Data on voter registration status and turnout were matched to this frame using the November 2010 Current Population Survey. The matched cases were weighted to the sampling frame using propensity scores. The matched cases and the frame were combined and a logistic regression was estimated for inclusion in the frame. The propensity score function included age, gender, race/ethnicity, years of education, voter registration status, political interest, non-identification with a major party, ideology, and census region. The propensity scores were grouped into deciles of the estimated propensity score in the frame and post-stratified according to these deciles. This survey is used in Chapter 6. To estimate the models in that chapter, these data were merged with land use data from the National Land Cover Database (NLCD) (Homer et al. 2015). The NLCD created a pixelated map of the United States, for years 1992, 2001, 2006, and 2011. Each pixel was assigned a category based on land use type. Prendergast et al. (2019) define open space as NLCD pixels that are coded as forest, shrubland, herbaceous, planted/cultivated, and wetlands to correspond to the definition of "open space" that was provided to respondents at the beginning of the survey. The respondents were first given the definition of open space in the following way before they were asked about their attitudes toward preservation. "'Open space' is a general term used to describe forests, farms, wetlands, recreation areas, parks and other land that is not developed with buildings or industry." ArcGIS was then used to calculate the percentage of total area that is "open space" in the respondents' state/zip-code/county. For the objective measurement of open space change, ArcGIS was used to calculate the percent change in open space pixels in the respondents' zip-code and county from 2001 to 2011 to proxy for the change in the amount of open space in the respondents' community in the past 10 years. This survey was supported by the USDA National Institute of Food and Agriculture, Agricultural and Food Research Initiative Competitive Program, Agriculture Economics and Rural Communities, grant number: 2015-67024-22937.

2017 UML YouGov Survey

The survey was conducted between June 27 and July 6, 2017. YouGov interviewed 1,057 respondents who were then matched down to a sample of 1,000 to produce the final dataset. The respondents were matched to a sampling frame on gender, age, race, and education, census region, ideology, and political interest. The frame was constructed by stratified sampling from the full 2010 American Community Survey (ACS) sample with selection within strata by weighted sampling with replacements (using the person weights on the public use file). The matched cases were weighted to the sampling frame using propensity scores. The matched cases and the frame were combined and a logistic regression was estimated for inclusion in the frame. The propensity score function included age, gender, race/ethnicity, years of education, voter registration, non-identification with a major party, ideology, and census region. The propensity scores were grouped into deciles of the estimated propensity score in the frame and post-stratified according to these deciles. This survey is used in Chapters 3 and 4.

2019 UML YouGov Survey

The survey was conducted between July 22 and August 12, 2019. YouGov interviewed 2,229 respondents who were then matched down to a sample of 1,800 to produce the final dataset. The respondents were matched to a sampling frame on gender, age, race, and education. The frame was constructed by stratified sampling from the full 2016 American Community Survey (ACS) 1-year sample with selection within strata by weighted sampling with replacements (using the person weights on the public use file). The matched cases were weighted to the sampling frame using propensity scores. The matched cases and the frame were combined and a logistic regression was estimated for inclusion in the frame. The propensity score function included age, gender, race/ethnicity, years of education, and region. The propensity scores were grouped into deciles of the estimated propensity score in the frame and post-stratified according to these deciles. The weights were then post-stratified on 2016 Presidential vote choice, and a four-way stratification of gender, age (4-categories), race (4-categories), and education (4-categories), to produce the final weight. This survey is used in Chapter 5.

2020 UML YouGov Survey

The survey was conducted between August 20 and 25, 2020. YouGov interviewed 1,154 respondents who were then matched down to a sample of 1,000 to produce the final dataset. The respondents were matched to a sampling frame on gender, age, race, and education. The frame was constructed by stratified sampling from the full 2017 American Community Survey (ACS) 1-year sample with selection within strata by weighted sampling with replacements (using the person weights on the public use file). The matched cases were weighted to the sampling frame using propensity scores. The matched cases and the frame were combined and a logistic regression was estimated for inclusion in the frame. The propensity score function included age, gender, race/ethnicity, years of education, and region. The propensity scores were grouped into deciles of the estimated propensity score in the frame and post-stratified according to these deciles. The weights were then post-stratified on 2016 Presidential vote choice, and a four-way stratification of gender, age (4-categories), race (4-categories), and education (4-categories), to produce the final weight. This survey is used in Chapters 4 & 5.

Model Appendix

All of the statistical models, including replication files and datasets have been publicly archived on the following dataverse: https://dataverse.unc.edu/dataverse/jjdyck.

Table A3.1 Regression Analyses Examining Policy Position Stability Pre- and Post-Election, 2014

	Minimum wage pre	Minimum wage post	Auto bailout pre	Auto bailout post	Foreign policy pre	Foreign policy post	Free trade pre	Free trade post	Birth Control Pre	Birth Control Post
Not strong Democrat	0.177 (0.109)	0.278** (0.103)	0.387* (0.173)	0.323* (0.150)	0.0164 (0.132)	-0.0593 (0.144)	0.326** (0.0986)	0.214* (0.103)	0.00966 (0.0613)	-0.132+ (0.0715)
Democratic leaner	0.319* (0.125)	0.276* (0.125)	0.451* (0.215)	0.330 (0.217)	-0.251 (0.194)	-0.335 (0.207)	0.364** (0.116)	0.357** (0.117)	0.108+ (0.0578)	-0.00021 (0.0624)
Independent	0.661** (0.173)	0.493** (0.167)	0.920** (0.157)	0.792** (0.154)	-0.0231 (0.186)	-0.216 (0.162)	0.307** (0.117)	0.331** (0.124)	-0.132+ (0.0720)	-0.248** (0.0747)
Republican leaner	1.141** (0.190)	1.034** (0.163)	0.944** (0.209)	1.108** (0.174)	0.0504 (0.224)	-0.111 (0.215)	0.451** (0.120)	0.402** (0.125)	-0.329** (0.0966)	-0.464** (0.102)
Not strong Republican	0.896** (0.156)	0.824** (0.174)	0.798** (0.197)	0.748** (0.185)	0.0617 (0.217)	-0.102 (0.228)	0.185 (0.119)	0.189 (0.124)	-0.448** (0.0843)	-0.501** (0.0863)
Strong Republican	0.958** (0.167)	0.913** (0.178)	0.980** (0.187)	0.957** (0.182)	0.356† (0.204)	0.117 (0.225)	0.344** (0.130)	0.196 (0.131)	-0.418** (0.0852)	-0.507** (0.0847)
Age	0.000648 (0.00254)	-0.000891 (0.00248)	0.00217 (0.00304)	-0.000455 (0.00282)	0.0092** (0.0027)	0.0074** (0.0026)	0.0076** (0.0018)	0.0080** (0.0019)	-0.00144 (0.0012)	-0.00077 (0.0013)
Gender	-0.00533 (0.0844)	-0.00246 (0.0825)	0.129 (0.0927)	0.0956 (0.0918)	-0.0432 (0.0912)	-0.105 (0.0926)	-0.0735 (0.0574)	-0.0988† (0.0575)	0.122** (0.0391)	0.0929+ (0.0412)
Black	0.0834 (0.193)	0.130 (0.181)	-0.0500 (0.207)	-0.332* (0.160)	-0.112 (0.189)	-0.355* (0.158)	0.120 (0.121)	0.0657 (0.130)	0.00673 (0.0676)	-0.0558 (0.0963)
Hispanic	0.304 (0.193)	0.364† (0.209)	0.0611 (0.212)	-0.140 (0.261)	-0.144 (0.219)	0.0268 (0.232)	-0.0107 (0.127)	0.00558 (0.111)	-0.0393 (0.0895)	-0.134 (0.103)
Other race	0.265 (0.170)	0.453** (0.158)	-0.204 (0.150)	0.189 (0.134)	0.244 (0.172)	0.0831 (0.168)	-0.0355 (0.101)	-0.164† (0.0909)	-0.113 (0.0708)	-0.0657 (0.0720)

Family income	0.0407	0.0185	−0.0438	0.0260	0.0329	0.0806†	−0.0434	−0.0190	0.0117	0.0155
	(0.0424)	(0.0406)	(0.0466)	(0.0465)	(0.0478)	(0.0464)	(0.0285)	(0.0284)	(0.0189)	(0.0194)
Education	0.0987*	0.165**	0.0204	−0.0311	0.132*	0.105*	−0.0580	−0.0345	−0.0517*	−0.0304
	(0.0499)	(0.0473)	(0.0673)	(0.0623)	(0.0525)	(0.0512)	(0.0386)	(0.0388)	(0.0222)	(0.0259)
Ideology	0.358**	0.408**	0.195*	0.199*	−0.0327	−0.0306	−0.0339	−0.00784	−0.147**	−0.138**
	(0.0682)	(0.0668)	(0.0866)	(0.0850)	(0.0817)	(0.0947)	(0.0524)	(0.0529)	(0.0354)	(0.0378)
Constant	0.221	0.0494	1.685**	1.792**	1.642**	1.847**	1.259**	1.127**	2.186**	2.156**
	(0.225)	(0.201)	(0.337)	(0.314)	(0.300)	(0.313)	(0.198)	(0.196)	(0.121)	(0.130)
N	753	753	752	752	752	752	416	416	742	742

Notes: Data are from the 2014 UML CCES team module, $N = 1,000$ sample of American adults aged 18 and older. Models estimated using OLS regression.
$^{**}p < .01.$ $^*p < .05.$ $^\dagger p < .10.$

Table A3.2 Multinomial Logit Model Predicting Candidate Preference, 2014

	Model 1, Republicans (Reference category: Rep-compromise)			Model 2, Democrats (Reference category: Dem-compromise)		
	Coef	SE	$p <$		Coef	SE	$p <$
Rep—no compromise				Rep—no compromise			
ideology	1.542	0.245	0.000	ideology	1.296	0.352	0.000
Randomization (Republican majority)	−0.850	0.294	0.004	Randomization (Republican majority)	0.412	0.710	0.562
Constant	−4.239	1.006	0.000	Constant	−7.899	1.808	0.000
Independent				Rep-compromise			
ideology	−0.067	0.266	0.801	ideology	0.495	0.232	0.033
Randomization (Republican majority)	−0.315	0.411	0.444	Randomization (Republican majority)	0.365	0.437	0.403
Constant	−0.296	1.131	0.794	Constant	−4.232	1.011	0.000
Dem-compromise				Independent			
ideology	−0.532	0.576	0.355	ideology	0.373	0.166	0.025
Randomization (Republican majority)	−0.458	1.026	0.655	Randomization (Republican majority)	−0.409	0.310	0.187
Constant	−0.596	2.463	0.809	Constant	−1.941	0.665	0.004
Dem—no compromise				Dem—no compromise			
ideology	−0.184	0.903	0.839	ideology	−0.696	0.130	0.000
Randomization (Republican majority)	−0.484	1.434	0.735	Randomization (Republican majority)	−0.120	0.214	0.575
Constant	−2.428	3.778	0.520	Constant	1.208	0.440	0.006
N	295			N	487		
Pseudo R^2	.120			Pseudo R^2	.063		

Notes: Data are from the 2014 UML YouGov survey, N = 1,000 sample of American Adults aged 18 and older. Model 1 is restricted to only Republican respondents; Model 2 to only Democratic respondents. Models are estimated using multinomial logit. The dependent variable is candidate preference between a Republican candidate who will not compromise, a Republican candidate who will compromise, an independent, a Democratic candidate who will compromise, and a Democratic candidate who will not compromise.

Table A4.1 OLS Regression Models for Discrimination, Fairness, and Racial Resentment Scales, 2020

	(1)	(2)	(3)
	Discrimination scale (high to low)	Race/fairness scale	Racial resentment scale (high to low)
Party ID (7-point)	−0.0151	−0.00798	−0.0170
	(0.0244)	(0.0165)	(0.0209)
Co-worker	0.229*	0.137	0.176
	(0.107)	(0.0810)	(0.110)
Acquaintance	0.229*	0.180*	0.215*
	(0.103)	(0.0787)	(0.105)
Close friend	0.192	0.176*	0.133
	(0.102)	(0.0766)	(0.104)
Family member	−0.0194	0.146	−0.0514
	(0.127)	(0.0887)	(0.113)
PID7 × co-worker	−0.0450	−0.0188	−0.0259
	(0.0258)	(0.0177)	(0.0225)
PID7 × acquaintance	−0.0533*	−0.0293	−0.0384
	(0.0248)	(0.0172)	(0.0212)
PID7 × close friend	−0.0458	−0.0225	−0.0167
	(0.0251)	(0.0168)	(0.0210)
PID7 × family member	−0.00124	−0.0184	0.00177
	(0.0285)	(0.0186)	(0.0233)
Ideology	−0.0918**	−0.0468**	−0.115**
	(0.0142)	(0.00889)	(0.0110)
Born again (0,1)	−0.0114	−0.0599**	0.00699
	(0.0280)	(0.0179)	(0.0211)
Education	0.0293**	0.0141**	0.0235**
	(0.00766)	(0.00520)	(0.00639)
Age	−0.00584	−0.00468	−0.0121**
	(0.00377)	(0.00240)	(0.00275)
Age^2	0.0000478	0.0000401	0.0000990**
	(0.0000348)	(0.0000225)	(0.0000264)
Female (0,1)	0.0210	0.0372*	0.0459**
	(0.0220)	(0.0149)	(0.0174)
Married (0,1)	0.0156	−0.00384	−0.00179
	(0.0225)	(0.0158)	(0.0185)
Constant	0.859**	0.796**	1.039**
	(0.142)	(0.0953)	(0.125)
N	738	735	738

Notes: Data are from the UML 2020 YouGov survey of 1,000 American adults. Models include only white respondents. OLS regression coefficients with standard errors in parentheses. OLS models are estimated with survey weights.

*p < .05. **p < .01.

Table A4.2 OLS Regression Models for Attitudes toward Race and Policing, 2020

	(1)	(2)
	DV, 1–7 scale: Race getting more attention than it deserves (1)/Police involved shooting raise important issues of race(7)	DV, 1–7 scale: Keep budgets the same(1)/ Defund the police(7)
Party ID (7-point)	−0.131 (0.149)	0.0282 (0.138)
Co-worker	0.930 (0.745)	1.247* (0.625)
Acquaintance	1.798* (0.700)	1.452* (0.621)
Close friend	1.266 (0.705)	1.382* (0.585)
Family member	0.188 (0.868)	0.331 (0.777)
PID7 × co-worker	−0.214 (0.164)	−0.337* (0.148)
PID7 × acquaintance	−0.346* (0.152)	−0.283 (0.148)
PID7 × close friend	−0.233 (0.155)	−0.336* (0.144)
PID7 × family member	−0.0650 (0.177)	−0.180 (0.164)
Ideology	−0.695** (0.0803)	−0.762** (0.0799)
Born again (0,1)	−0.498** (0.178)	−0.429** (0.161)
Education	0.195** (0.0483)	0.115* (0.0487)
Age	−0.0477* (0.0230)	−0.0456* (0.0227)
Age^2	0.000443* (0.000219)	0.000242 (0.000210)
Female (0,1)	0.338* (0.141)	0.0656 (0.136)
Married (0,1)	0.0143 (0.146)	−0.0220 (0.141)
Constant	6.694** (0.925)	6.639** (0.780)
N	737	738

Notes: Data are from the 2020 YouGov survey of 1,000 American adults. Models include only white respondents. OLS regression coefficients with standard errors in parentheses. OLS models are estimated with survey weights.

*$p < .05$. **$p < .01$.

Table A4.3 OLS Regression Models for Support for Government Help to Blacks Scale, 2017 and 2020

	2017	2020
Party ID (7-point)	−0.127	−0.113
	(0.142)	(0.133)
Co-worker	0.749	0.702
	(0.867)	(0.708)
Acquaintance	0.153	1.237
	(0.833)	(0.664)
Close friend	1.502	0.755
	(0.839)	(0.661)
Family member	0.854	0.158
	(0.912)	(0.807)
PID7 × co-worker	−0.208	−0.0671
	(0.152)	(0.145)
PID7 × acquaintance	−0.0775	−0.156
	(0.148)	(0.137)
PID7 × close friend	−0.328*	−0.0245
	(0.146)	(0.143)
PID7 × family member	−0.202	0.0778
	(0.164)	(0.162)
Ideology	−0.446**	−0.757**
	(0.100)	(0.0841)
Born again (0,1)	−0.124	−0.268
	(0.152)	(0.192)
Education	0.0883	0.126**
	(0.0468)	(0.0484)
Age	−0.0403	−0.0855**
	(0.0282)	(0.0240)
Age^2	0.000403	0.000791**
	(0.000266)	(0.000220)
Female (0,1)	0.232	0.394**
	(0.153)	(0.147)
Married (0,1)	0.000379	−0.108
	(0.168)	(0.141)
Constant	5.704**	7.750**
	(1.006)	(0.925)
N	735	737

Notes: Data are from the 2017 and 2020 UML YouGov surveys, each of 1,000 American adults. Models include only white respondents. OLS regression coefficients with standard errors in parentheses. OLS models are estimated with survey weights.

*$p < .05$. **$p < .01$.

Table A4.4 Ordered Logit Models for Support for Affirmative Action, 2014 and 2020

	2014	2020
Party ID (7-point)	−0.234	−0.0953
	(0.161)	(0.189)
Co-worker	0.252	0.204
	(0.833)	(0.763)
Acquaintance	−0.410	0.707
	(0.753)	(0.671)
Close friend	−0.0944	0.747
	(0.790)	(0.654)
Family member	−0.152	0.205
	(0.962)	(0.841)
PID7 × co-worker	−0.126	−0.0429
	(0.185)	(0.204)
PID7 × acquaintance	−0.0358	−0.204
	(0.169)	(0.190)
PID7 × close friend	0.00625	−0.103
	(0.181)	(0.189)
PID7 × family member	−0.0841	−0.0222
	(0.256)	(0.212)
Ideology	−0.743**	−0.755**
	(0.115)	(0.156)
Born again (0,1)	0.0340	0.288
	(0.218)	(0.208)
Education	0.0326	0.0572
	(0.0580)	(0.0584)
Age	0.00186	−0.0766**
	(0.0305)	(0.0264)
Age^2	−0.0000159	0.000593*
	(0.000282)	(0.000255)
Female (0,1)	−0.0531	0.392*
	(0.171)	(0.164)
Married (0,1)	−0.111	0.167
	(0.171)	(0.165)
Cut 1	−4.159**	−5.532**
	(1.001)	(0.891)
Cut 2	−2.476*	−4.062**
	(1.000)	(0.876)
Cut 3	−0.229	−1.860*
	(1.023)	(0.857)
N	713	738

Notes: Data are from the 2014 and 2020 UML YouGov surveys, each of 1,000 American adults. Models include only white respondents. OLS regression coefficients with standard errors in parentheses. OLS models are estimated with survey weights.

*p < .05. **p < .01.

Table A5.1 Vaccine Cue Experiment Results, 2020

	Model 1		Model 2		Model 3	
	β	SE	β	SE	β	SE
Biden treatment	−0.651	0.112	0.437*	0.201	−0.071	0.103
Trump treatment	0.069	0.115	−0.435†	0.228	0.061	0.115
Willingness to pay amt.	−0.612	0.024**	−0.075**	0.023	−0.140**	0.047
Party ID	—	—	−0.164**	0.038	−0.266**	0.050
WTP × PID	—	—	—	—	0.020†	0.010
Party ID × Biden	—	—	−0.138**	0.044	—	—
Party ID × Trump	—	—	0.138**	0.526	—	—
Constant	3.022	0.130	3.690**	0.162	—	—
R^2	.013		.153		.113	
AIC	3030.00		2987.52		3028.13	
BIC	3054.54		3021.87		3057.58	

Notes: Data are from the 2020 UML YouGov survey of 1,000 American adults. Models are OLS regressions with coefficients and standard errors reported.

*$p < .05$, **$p < .01$, †$p < .10$.

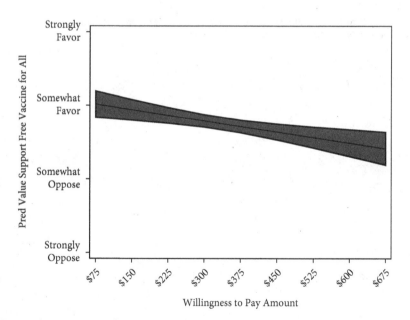

Figure A5.1 Support for a Free Vaccine by Willingness to Pay

Source: Data are from the 2020 UML YouGov survey. These are the predicted values with 90% confidence intervals generated from Table A5.1, Model 3.

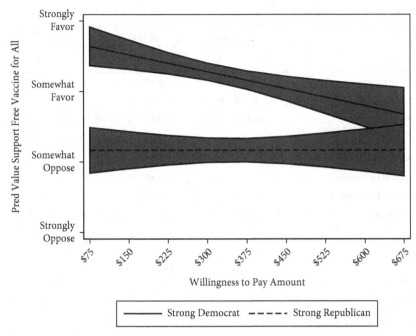

Figure A5.2 Support for a Free Vaccine by Willingness to Pay and Party Identification

Source: Data are from the 2020 UML YouGov survey. These are the predicted values with 90% confidence intervals generated from Table A5.1, Model 3.

Table A6.1 Ordered Logit Models for Concern about Gun Violence and School Shootings, 2014

Variable	Concern over gun violence[a] White respondents		Concern over local gun violence All respondents		White respondents		School shootings are getting worse All respondents		White respondents	
	β	S.E.	β	S.E.	β	S.E.	β	S.E.	β	S.E.
Crime per capita	-0.003	0.250	0.593	0.198**	0.263	0.400	-0.245	0.277	0.005	0.300
Weak/leaning Dem	-0.690	0.189**	-1.197	0.200**	-1.008	0.283**	0.736	0.131**	0.895	0.194**
Independent/unsure	-1.891	0.216**	-1.369	0.143**	-1.461	0.197**	-1.051	0.131**	-1.266	0.181**
Weak/leaning Rep	-1.371	0.196**	-1.406	0.146**	-1.453	0.245**	-0.362	0.156*	-0.437	0.223*
Strong Republican	-0.798	0.370*	-1.126	0.419**	-0.644	0.576	-0.170	0.273	-0.201	0.332
Crime PC × Weak Dem	-0.337	0.378	1.314	0.344**	0.704	0.532	-1.729	0.417**	-2.298	0.381**
Crime PC × Pure Ind	2.079	0.708**	1.953	0.319**	2.687	0.716**	1.634	0.285**	2.111	0.304**
Crime PC × Weak Rep	0.227	0.381	1.048	0.345**	1.550	0.643*	0.867	0.308**	0.613	0.436
Crime PC × Strong Rep	-1.004	0.536†	1.311	0.836	0.576	0.992	0.493	0.437	0.136	0.586
Gender (0,1)	0.409	0.084**	0.113	0.066†	0.088	0.115	0.256	0.062**	0.261	0.096**
Non-white(0,1)	—	—	0.166	0.047**	—	—	-0.017	0.060	---	—
Age	-0.041	0.015	0.033	0.018†	0.025	0.026	0.000	0.011	-0.015	0.019
Age²	0.001	0.000**	0.000	0.000	0.000	0.000	0.000	0.000*	0.000	0.000*
Education	0.024	0.028	0.078	0.019**	0.116	0.034**	0.047	0.021*	0.123	0.029**
Politicalawareness	0.012	0.048	-0.149	0.019**	-0.103	0.030**	-0.031	0.018†	-0.093	0.026**

(continued)

Table A6.1 Continued

Variable	Concern over gun violence[a] White respondents		Concern over local gun violence All respondents		White respondents		School shootings are getting worse All respondents		White respondents	
	β	S.E.	β	S.E.	β	S.E.	β	S.E.	β	S.E.
Liberal (0,1)	0.408	0.270	−0.050	0.101	0.098	0.136	−0.187	0.115	0.008	0.296
Moderate (0,1)	0.080	0.275	0.012	0.104	0.282	0.136*	−0.171	0.111	0.148	0.234
Conservative (0,1)	−0.495	0.304	−0.429	0.133**	−0.321	0.190†	−0.952	0.172**	−0.647	0.372†
Very conservative (0,1)	−0.065	0.192	−0.728	0.192**	−0.763	0.299*	−0.877	0.168**	−0.451	0.210*
Urbanicity	−0.019	0.067	−0.131	0.033**	−0.097	0.045*	−0.012	0.029	0.084	0.047*
Gun in HH, not owner	0.499	0.247	−0.017	0.096	0.313	0.148*	0.026	0.168	0.971	0.258†
No guns in HH	0.787	0.174**	0.385	0.075**	0.433	0.097**	0.399	0.158*	0.602	0.152**
Cut1	−3.988	0.353	−1.547	0.507	−1.271	0.783	−2.744	0.303	−2.878	0.394
Cut2	−2.398	0.329	0.449	0.493	0.733	0.766	−0.525	0.389	−0.152	0.426
Cut3	−0.184	0.323	2.260	0.473	2.677	0.810	—	—	—	—
N	660		900		660		900		661	
Pseudo R²	0.100		0.071		0.060		0.055		0.070	

Notes: Data are from the 2014 UML YouGov survey, $N = 1,000$ sample of American Adults aged 18 and older. Models estimated using ordered logit with clustered standard errors.

** $p < .01$. * $p < .05$. † $p < .10$.

[a]The "All respondents" version of this model appears in Pearson-Merkowitz and Dyck (2017).

Table A6.2 Ordered Logit Models for Policy Attitudes about Guns, 2014 (1)

Variable	Ban assault weapons[a] White respondents		Make background checks harder All respondents		Make background checks harder White respondents	
	β	S.E.	β	S.E.	β	S.E.
Crime per capita	1.341	0.374**	0.256	0.296	1.119	0.424**
Weak/leaning Dem	−0.410	0.151**	−0.304	0.153*	0.074	0.266
Independent/unsure	−1.465	0.166**	−1.127	0.203**	−1.083	0.323**
Weak/leaning Rep	−1.052	0.168**	−0.372	0.245	−0.124	0.352
Strong Republican	−1.597	0.319**	−0.639	0.214**	−0.446	0.264[†]
Crime PC × Weak Dem	−1.198	0.379**	−0.453	0.277	−1.935	0.464**
Crime PC × Pure Ind	0.319	0.436	0.209	0.343	−0.554	0.691
Crime PC × Weak Rep	−1.678	0.456**	−1.612	0.437**	−2.771	0.607**
Crime PC × Strong Rep	−0.753	0.726	−0.058	0.679	−1.282	0.669[†]
Gender (0,1)	0.452	0.073**	0.326	0.089**	0.483	0.126**
Non-white(0,1)	—	—	−0.234	0.121[†]	—	—
Age	−0.049	0.015**	−0.011	0.007	−0.003	0.011
Age^2	0.001	0.000**	0.000	0.000**	0.000	0.000
Education	0.069	0.051	0.032	0.024	0.092	0.030**
Political awareness	−0.116	0.036**	−0.062	0.024*	−0.102	0.051*
Liberal (0,1)	0.086	0.133	0.302	0.365	−0.040	0.314
Moderate (0,1)	−0.826	0.273**	−0.246	0.336	−0.582	0.352[†]
Conservative (0,1)	−1.583	0.347**	−0.931	0.310**	−1.262	0.346**
Very conservative (0,1)	−2.102	0.290**	−1.633	0.263**	−1.912	0.310**
Urbanicity	−0.056	0.028*	−0.088	0.033**	−0.133	0.037**
Gun in HH, not owner	1.088	0.162**	0.247	0.167	0.693	0.297*
No guns in HH	1.334	0.119**	0.920	0.085**	0.810	0.148**
Cut1	−2.630	0.328	−3.175	0.414	−3.050	0.554
Cut2	−1.326	0.314	−1.938	0.380	−1.854	0.490
Cut3	−0.310	0.312	−0.660	0.357	−0.446	0.468
N	660		895		658	
Pseudo R^2	0.185		0.092		0.113	

Notes: Data are from the 2014 UML YouGov survey, N = 1,000 sample of American adults aged 18 and older. Models estimated using ordered logit with clustered standard errors.

** $p < .01$. * $p < .05$. [†] $p < .10$.

[a] The "All respondents" version of this model appears in Pearson-Merkowitz and Dyck (2017).

Table A6.3 Ordered Logit Models for Policy Attitudes about Guns, 2014 (2)

| Variable | Close gun show loophole | | | | Train and arm teachers | | | |
| | All respondents | | White respondents | | All respondents | | White respondents | |
	β	S.E.	β	S.E.	B	S.E.	β	S.E.
Crime per capita	−1.307	0.233**	0.126	0.388	0.817	0.263**	−0.052	0.312
Weak/leaning Dem	−0.564	0.159**	−0.099	0.224	0.743	0.116**	0.519	0.143**
Independent/unsure	−1.450	0.169**	−1.560	0.247**	1.431	0.287**	1.118	0.245**
Weak/leaning Rep	−1.304	0.160**	−0.879	0.233**	1.712	0.152**	1.460	0.221**
Strong Republican	−1.660	0.213**	−0.960	0.262**	1.498	0.306**	1.301	0.348**
Crime PC × Weak Dem	0.922	0.240**	−1.266	0.406**	−0.929	0.259**	0.027	0.302
Crime PC × Pure Ind	1.391	0.314**	1.307	0.610*	−1.424	0.521**	−0.685	0.415+
Crime PC × Weak Rep	0.657	0.283*	−0.593	0.476	−1.523	0.413**	−0.445	0.495
Crime PC × Strong Rep	1.198	0.414**	−0.784	0.473†	−0.824	0.808	0.219	0.809
Gender (0,1)	0.294	0.090**	0.479	0.119**	−0.045	0.071	−0.317	0.114**
Non-white(0,1)	−0.805	0.112**	—	—	−0.034	0.047	—	—
Age	−0.029	0.010**	−0.011	0.009	0.025	0.011*	−0.007	0.012
Age²	0.000	0.000**	0.000	0.000**	0.000	0.000**	0.000	0.000
Education	0.255	0.022**	0.271	0.031**	−0.134	0.027**	−0.131	0.041**
Political awareness	0.017	0.017	0.024	0.027	−0.019	0.015	−0.054	0.019**
Liberal (0,1)	0.454	0.189*	0.437	0.168**	0.335	0.129**	0.546	0.240*
Moderate (0,1)	−0.687	0.213**	−0.711	0.180**	0.698	0.116**	1.172	0.135**
Conservative (0,1)	−0.783	0.226**	−0.992	0.214**	1.484	0.137**	1.912	0.213**
Very conservative (0,1)	−1.265	0.167**	−1.641	0.198**	1.669	0.182**	2.071	0.228**
Urbanicity	−0.153	0.023**	0.001	0.031	0.027	0.037	0.006	0.044
Gun in HH, not owner	−0.089	0.132	0.520	0.225*	−0.694	0.142**	−0.629	0.189**
No guns in HH	0.560	0.059**	0.672	0.072**	−0.692	0.094**	−0.811	0.091**
Cut1	−3.837	0.267	−2.470	0.364	0.027	0.290	−1.034	0.414
Cut2	−3.076	0.272	−1.649	0.351	1.173	0.290	0.100	0.418
Cut3	−1.502	0.296	0.102	0.343	2.946	0.300	2.007	0.413
N	883		653		891		656	
Pseudo R²	0.101		0.114		0.091		0.124	

Notes: Data are from the 2014 UML YouGov survey, $N = 1,000$ sample of American adults aged 18 and older. Models estimated using ordered logit with clustered standard errors.

**$p < .01$. *$p < .05$. †$p < .10$.

Table A6.4 Ordered Logit Models for Attitudes about Open Space, 2016

Variable	Open space perception		Open space bond I		Open space bond II	
	β	S.E.	β	S.E.	β	S.E.
Measures of Context						
Total open space, 2011 (community level)	0.956	0.384*	—	—	—	—
Increase in development (state level)	—	—	−72.132	28.499*	—	—
Open space loss (state level)	—	—	—	—	−81.125	28.659**
Party ID						
Weak/leaning Democrat	−0.139	0.274	−0.893	0.229**	−0.976	0.242**
Independent/unsure	−0.519	0.360	−2.166	0.295**	−2.303	0.274**
Weak/leaning Republican	−0.019	0.320	−2.179	0.305**	−2.383	0.300**
Strong Republican	−0.217	0.366	−1.767	0.374**	−1.875	0.362**
Interaction						
Context × weak Democrat	0.306	0.568	22.733	34.481	35.814	33.879
Context × pure independent	1.755	0.696*	182.834	43.761**	185.147	38.615**
Context × weak Republican	−0.137	0.585	70.118	44.028	101.406	38.561**
Context × strong Republican	−0.322	0.635	106.636	76.022	112.573	64.001†
Controls						
Gender (0,1)	−0.254	0.121*	0.311	0.135*	0.315	0.135*
Non-white(0,1)	0.020	0.147	−0.025	0.152	−0.025	0.148
Age	−0.024	0.023	0.040	0.022†	0.040	0.022†
Age²	0.000	0.000	0.000	0.000	0.000	0.000
Education	0.175	0.044**	0.018	0.055	0.021	0.055
Income	0.041	0.020*	−0.056	0.021**	−0.059	0.021**
Political interest	−0.286	0.073**	0.110	0.068	0.108	0.068
Liberal (0,1)	0.016	0.206	−0.356	0.195†	−0.352	0.195†
Moderate (0,1)	0.132	0.219	−0.662	0.292*	−0.660	0.292*
Conservative (0,1)	0.312	0.271	−1.287	0.271**	−1.288	0.269**
Very conservative (0,1)	0.683	0.304*	−1.726	0.362**	−1.713	0.358**
Owns home (0,1)	0.104	0.143	−0.965	0.141**	−0.962	0.142**
Cut1	−3.693	0.631	−3.989	0.611	−4.079	0.632
Cut2	−2.076	0.598	−2.845	0.604	−2.934	0.625
Cut3	−0.401	0.592	−0.992	0.614	−1.080	0.632
Cut4	1.827	0.595	—	—	—	—
N	1036		1036		1036	
Pseudo R²	.045		0.153		0.154	

Notes: Data are from the 2016 URI YouGov survey, N = 1,605 sample of American adults aged 18 and older. Models estimated using ordered logit with clustered standard errors at the state level.

**p < .01. *p < .05. †p < .10.

Table A6.5 Ordered Logit Models for Attitudes about Affordable Housing and the Minimum Wage, 2016

Variable	Affordable housing bond		Support for $15 minimum wage	
	β	S.E.	β	S.E.
Personal financial struggles	−0.120	0.128	−0.165	0.132
Party ID				
Weak/leaning Democrat	−0.820	0.301	−0.616	0.314*
Independent/unsure	−2.072	0.348**	−2.608	0.355**
Weak/leaning Republican	−2.034	0.326**	−2.734	0.335**
Strong Republican	−1.785	0.362**	−2.727	0.377**
Interaction				
Context × weak Democrat	0.066	0.169	−0.039	0.172
Context × pure independent	0.422	0.185*	0.549	0.185**
Context × weak Republican	0.143	0.169	0.222	0.171
Context × strong Republican	0.245	0.190	0.212	0.195
Controls				
Gender (0,1)	0.406	0.110**	0.426	0.113**
Non-white (0,1)	−0.049	0.132	−0.015	0.132
Age	0.033	0.020†	0.041	0.021*
Age^2	0.000	0.000	0.000	0.000
Education	0.014	0.040	−0.098	0.041*
Income	−0.055	0.019**	0.016	0.020
Political interest	−0.016	0.053	0.121	0.054*
Liberal (0,1)	−0.491	0.228*	−0.614	0.231**
Moderate (0,1)	−0.793	0.227**	−0.836	0.230**
Conservative (0,1)	−1.289	0.262**	−1.854	0.268**
Very conservative (0,1)	−1.805	0.287**	−2.649	0.305**
Owns home (0,1)	−0.893	0.132**	−0.521	0.133**
Cut1	−4.167	0.558	−3.259	0.569
Cut2	−2.985	0.553	−1.984	0.564
Cut3	−1.126	0.547	−0.514	0.563
N	1318		1316	
Pseudo R^2	0.145		.214	

Notes: Data are from the 2016 URI YouGov survey, N = 1,605 sample of American adults aged 18 and older. Models estimated using ordered logit with clustered standard errors at the state level.

**$p < .01$. *$p < .05$. †$p < .10$.

Table A7.1 OLS Models for Political Knowledge, 2020

	Model 1		Model 2		Model 3	
	β	Std. Error	β	Std. Error	β	Std. Error
Age (in years)	0.008**	0.001	0.006**	0.001	0.007**	0.001
Female(0,1)	−0.351**	0.035	−0.337**	0.034	−0.345**	0.035
Black (0,1)	−0.388**	0.063	−0.377**	0.059	−0.377**	0.063
Hispanic(0,1)	−0.138*	0.063	−0.127*	0.059	−0.137*	0.063
Race-other (0,1)	0.033	0.063	0.025	0.059	0.030	0.063
Education	0.192**	0.018	0.198**	0.017	0.189**	0.018
Pol. interest	0.258**	0.028	0.268**	0.026	0.257**	0.028
Leaners (0,1)	0.295**	0.062	0.287**	0.059	0.293**	0.062
Weak partisans (0,1)	0.126*	2.030	0.145*	0.061	0.111	0.062
Strong partisans (0,1)	0.202**	0.059	0.179**	0.057	0.191**	0.059
External efficacy	0.002**	0.000	—	—	0.001**	0.001
Gov corrupt scale	—	—	−0.098**	0.019	−0.080**	0.021
Constant	0.796**	0.093	1.207**	0.116	1.111	0.127
N	6966		7708		6935	
R²	.156		.151		.159	

Notes: Data are from the 2020 American National Election Study. Models are estimated using OLS regression predicting a scale of political knowledge.

**p < .01. *p < .05.

Notes

Introduction

1. But there is some evidence that Democratic elite negativity on social media has caught up to that of Republicans (Russell 2021).

Chapter 1

1. Examples of this narrative can be found in many publications, but we point readers to a few examples, including Alexander and Copeland (2020) and Frum (2019).
2. These are perhaps two striking of examples of what we would call *leading* partisan change, where elites drive the change in partisan attitudes, and *following* partisan change, where candidates respond to the perceived changing center of their political party in order to win a primary election. We address this in greater detail in later chapters.

Chapter 2

1. To be sure, others contended that party decline was just a movement along the scale and that the number of pure independents remained stable, even during the so-called party decline era (Keith et al. 1992).
2. https://www.youtube.com/watch?v=cAvq12Sa3VE
3. https://www.cnn.com/videos/us/2019/01/16/fast-food-hamburgers-twitter-trump-clemson-moos-ebof-vpx.cnn

Chapter 3

1. Obama famously visited the DC landmark Ben's Chili Bowl ahead of his 2009 inauguration and Michelle Obama has shared their family's at-home chili recipe (President Obama's Chili Recipe Recipe n.d.)

Chapter 4

1. The principal components analysis reveals a single eigenvalue larger than 1 at 3.510 with the next largest eigenvalue smaller than 0.5. The average inter-item correlation for these measures is 0.626, and the Cronbach's alpha is 0.893. All measures indicate a single dimension and a high degree of scalability between the four items.
2. The PCA for the discrimination scale reveals a single eigenvalue larger than 1 at 2.619 with the next largest eigenvalue smaller than 0.25. The average inter-item correlation for these measures is 0.810, and the Cronbach's alpha is 0.927. All measures indicate a single dimension and a high degree of scalability between the three items.
3. The PCA for the racial resentment scale reveals a single eigenvalue larger than 1 at 2.423 with the next largest eigenvalue smaller than 0.4. The average inter-item correlation for these measures is 0.711, and the Cronbach's alpha is 0.880. All measures indicate a single dimension and a high degree of scalability between the three items.
4. https://plato.stanford.edu/entries/affirmative-action/

Chapter 5

1. Admittedly, we never expected there to be such vast differences in actually getting the vaccine, given the death rates at the time we were designing the survey, but we foresaw that there could be debates about the role of the government in providing the vaccine for free.
2. Lerman's et al.'s article opens with the story of a lifelong Republican, Luis Lang, who was outspoken with the media that he would not comply with the ACA's health insurance mandate. But soon after foregoing health insurance, he suffered a medical emergency and exhausted his financial savings. Lerman et al. explain: "He subsequently tried to enroll through a health insurance exchange established under the ACA, only to discover that the annual enrollment window had closed. (Lang might have qualified for Medicaid, but his home state of South Carolina had chosen not to participate in the ACA Medicaid expansion.) In order to treat bleeding in his eyes and a partially detached retina, which if left untreated would result in blindness, Lang began to solicit online donations from the public to cover his medical expenses. In interviews with the media, Lang voiced regret about failing to sign up for one of the insurance options made available to him by President Obama's health reform. At the time, though, as one reporter surmised, 'the ideological satisfaction of resisting "big government" outweighed the practical benefit of access to medical care'" (Lermen et al. 2017, p. 755).
3. Importantly, we are not the first to apply prospect theory to Covid-19 vaccine decisions (Blondel et al. 2021; Fridman, Gershon, and Gneezy 2021; Zhu, Grün, and Dolnicar 2021); however, none of the studies to date investigated partisan elite framing and vaccination intentions or support.

Chapter 6

1. County is obviously not the ideal measure of context here. We would like to have (1) a smaller and (2) a more geographically size-consistent measure to get at neighborhood

effects of locality on behavior. In some states, such as Texas, there are more than 250 counties, while in other states, like Washington, there are fewer than 40. Still, we are limited here by the availability of crime data from the FBI's database and note that the measure, while imprecise, is the best-known comprehensive measure of crime that we could append to a national survey.

2. The versions of the models for all respondents on the dependent variables *concern about gun violence* and *assault weapon ban* are excluded here, as they appear in a previous publication (Pearson-Merkowitz and Dyck 2017). Here we present only the subset model that includes only white respondents. In both versions of the model, the effect of context is significant for pure independents but is muted for partisans.

3. One possibility here is that there simply is not enough variation to explain attitudes toward expanding background checks. On this question, for instance, 79% support background checks, either strongly or not strongly, including 69% support among pure independents.

Chapter 7

1. We exclude all web respondents from the 2012 and 2016 ANES because they have higher political knowledge scores due the ease of looking up the answers to the questions while taking an online self-administered survey.

2. Strong Republicans experienced a dip in external efficacy in 2020, likely because of the 2020 election itself. Over the time trend, it is clear there are some election- or incumbent-related shifts in efficacy related to *who* the governing party or *what* their messaging is (e.g., populism). Still, independents consistently remain the least efficacious group over the entire time period.

3. While we also examined trust in government in the preceding section, there is some evidence in the cross-tabulation of the measure tapping *incumbent-based trust in government*. That is, Republicans espouse a higher level of trust than Democrats because the sitting President is a Republican. This means that some of the covariation in trust/distrust is caught up with a contemporaneous evaluation of the political order rather than a long-term view of politics and government more generally. This conflation of regime-based and incumbent-based trust leads us to prefer an alternative measure of alienation in the analysis.

4. In Table A7.1 in the appendix, we present separate models with these measures included individually and then present a model with both variables simultaneously to confirm that any observed results are not the result of multicollinearity. Figure 7.4 only presents Model 3 results, with all the variables rescaled from 0 to 1 for ease of interpretation.

Chapter 8

1. From the 1933 to 1994, Republicans only had control of the Congress for 4 years (1947–48 and 1953–54).

References

Abramowitz, Alan I. 2021. "It's the Pandemic, Stupid! A Simplified Model for Forecasting the 2020 Presidential Election." *PS: Political Science & Politics* 54(1): 52–54.

Abramowitz, Alan I., and Steven W. Webster. 2016. "The Rise of Negative Partisanship and the Nationalization of US Elections in the 21st Century." *Electoral Studies* 41: 12–22.

Abramowitz, Alan I., and Steven W. Webster. 2018. "Negative Partisanship: Why Americans Dislike Parties but Behave Like Rabid Partisans." *Political Psychology* 39: 119–35.

Agranov, Marina, Matt Elliott, and Pietro Ortoleva. 2021. "The Importance of Social Norms against Strategic Effects: The Case of COVID-19 Vaccine Uptake." *Economics Letters* 206: 109979.

Alberini, Anna. 1995. "Testing Willingness-to-Pay Models of Discrete Choice Contingent Valuation Survey Data." *Land Economics* 71(1): 83–95.

Aldrich, John H. 1995. *Why Parties? The Origin and Transformation of Political Parties in America*. Chicago: University of Chicago Press.

Aldrich, John H. 2011. *Why Parties? A Second Look*. Chicago: University of Chicago Press.

Alexander, R., and Lauren Copeland. 2020. "Mike Bloomberg Could Be the Candidate Democrats Have Been Looking For" (Opinion). CNN, February 2. https://www.cnn.com/2020/02/02/opinions/bloomberg-democrats-best-chance-against-trump-alexander-copeland/index.html (accessed January 6, 2022).

Allcott, Hunt, Levi Boxell, Jacob Conway, Matthew Gentzkow, Michael Thaler, and David Yan. 2020. "Polarization and Public Health: Partisan Differences in Social Distancing during the Coronavirus Pandemic." *Journal of Public Economics* 191: 104254.

Allport, Gordon W. 1954. *The Nature of Prejudice*. Reading, MA: Addison-Wesley.

Allport, Gordon W., and Bernard M. Kramer. 1946. "Some Roots of Prejudice." *Journal of Psychology* 22(1): 9–39.

American National Election Studies. 2021. *ANES 2020 Time Series Study Full Release* (dataset and documentation). July 19. www.electionstudies.org.

American National Elections Studies. 2021. *Time Series Cumulative Data File (1948–2020)*.(dataset and documentation) July 19. https://electionstudies.org/data-center/anes-time-series-cumulative-data-file/ (accessed November 4, 2021).

American Political Science Association Committee on Political Parties. 1950. "Toward a More Responsible Two-Party System. A Report of the Committee on Political Parties of the American Political Science Association". *American Political Science Review* 44(3): 1–96.

Americans for Tax Reform. 2022. "About the Pledge." https://www.atr.org/about-the-pledge (accessed January 7, 2022).

Anderson, Bryan. 2021. "Critical Race Theory Is a Flashpoint for Conservatives, but What Does It Mean?" *PBS NewsHour*, November 2. https://www.pbs.org/newshour/education/so-much-buzz-but-what-is-critical-race-theory (accessed February 2, 2022).

Antonio, Anthony Lising, Mitchell J. Chang, Kenji Hakuta, David A. Kenny, Shana Levin, and Jeffrey F. Milem. 2004. "Effects of Racial Diversity on Complex Thinking in College Students." *Psychological Science* 15(8): 507–10.

Bafumi, Joseph, and Robert Y. Shapiro. 2009. "A New Partisan Voter." *Journal of Politics* 71(1): 1–24.

Bail, Christopher A., Lisa P. Argyle, Taylor W. Brown, John P. Bumpus, Haohan Chen, M. B. Fallin Hunzaker, Jaemin Lee, Marcus Mann, Friedolin Merhout, and Alexander Volfovsky. 2018. "Exposure to Opposing Views on Social Media Can Increase Political Polarization." *Proceedings of the National Academy of Sciences* 115(37): 9216–21.

Bail, Christopher A. 2021. *Breaking the Social Media Prism*. Princeton, NJ: Princeton University Press.

Banda, Kevin, Jennifer Benz, Bruce Desmarias, Virginia Gray, Jeff Harden, Geoff Layman, Justin Kirkland, and Shanna Pearson-Mekrowitz. 2018. "In Memoriam: Thomas M. Carsey." *PS: Political Science & Politics* 51(3): 674–82.

Banda, Kevin K., Thomas M. Carsey, and Serge Severenchuk. 2020. "Evidence of Conflict Extension in Partisans' Evaluations of People and Inanimate Objects." *American Politics Research* 48(2): 275–85.

Barberá, Pablo. 2020. "Social Media, Echo Chambers, and Political Polarization" In *Social Media and Democracy: The State of the Field, Prospects for Reform*, edited by Nathaniel Persily and Joshua A. Tucker, 34–55. New York: Cambridge University Press.

Bartels, Larry M. 2005. "Homer Gets a Tax Cut: Inequality and Public Policy in the American Mind." *Perspectives on Politics* 3(1): 15–31.

Beer, Tommy. 2021. "Trump Called BLM Protesters 'Thugs' but Capitol-Storming Supporters 'Very Special.'" *Forbes*, January 6. https://www.forbes.com/sites/tommyb eer/2021/01/06/trump-called-blm-protesters-thugs-but-capitol-storming-support ers-very-special/ (accessed July 6, 2021).

Berelson, Bernard R., Paul F. Lazarsfeld, and William N. McPhee. 1954. *Voting: A Study of Opinion Formation in a Presidential Campaign*. Chicago: University of Chicago Press.

Berg, Justin Allen. 2020. "Assessing the Effects of Intergroup Contact on Immigration Attitudes." *Social Science Journal*: 1–17. https://www.tandfonline.com/doi/full/ 10.1080/03623319.2020.1814982 (Published online ahead of print).

Berry, Jeffrey M., and Sarah Sobieraj. 2011. "Understanding the Rise of Talk Radio." *PS: Political Science & Politics* 44(4): 762–67.

Bialik, Kirstin, and A. W. Geiger. 2016. "Republicans, Democrats Find Common Ground on Many Provisions of Health Care Law." Pew Research Center. December 8. https:// www.pewresearch.org/fact-tank/2016/12/08/partisans-on-affordable-care-act-provisi ons/ (accessed January 19, 2023).

Binder, Sarah A. 1997. *Minority Rights, Majority Rule: Partisanship and the Development of Congress*. Cambridge: Cambridge University Press,

Bisgaard, Martin, and Rune Slothuus. 2018. "Partisan Elites as Culprits? How Party Cues Shape Partisan Perceptual Gaps." *American Journal of Political Science* 62(2): 456–69.

Blondel, Serge, François Langot, Judith E. Mueller, and Jonathan Sicsic. 2021. "Preferences and Covid-19 Vaccination Intentions." https://hal.archives-ouvertes.fr/hal-03381425 (accessed January 25, 2022).

Boin, Jessica, Mirjana Rupar, Sylvie Graf, Sybille Neji, Olivia Spiegler, and. Hermann Swart. 2021. "The Generalization of Intergroup Contact Effects: Emerging Research, Policy Relevance, and Future Directions." *Journal of Social Issues* 77(1): 105–31.

Bolsen, Toby, James N. Druckman, and Fay Lomax Cook. 2014. "How Frames Can Undermine Support for Scientific Adaptations: Politicization and the Status-Quo Bias." *Public Opinion Quarterly* 78(1): 1–26.

Brenan, Megan. 2020. "Americans' Face Mask Usage Varies Greatly by Demographics." Gallup, July 13. https://news.gallup.com/poll/315590/americans-face-mask-usage-var ies-greatly-demographics.aspx (accessed December 16, 2021).

Broockman, David, and Joshua Kalla. 2022. "The Manifold Effects of Partisan Media on Viewers' Beliefs and Attitudes: A Field Experiment with Fox News Viewers." *OSF Preprints* 1: 1–35.

Brophy, Ira N. 1945. "The Luxury of Anti-Negro Prejudice." *Public Opinion Quarterly* 9(4): 456–66.

Browne. 2019. "Trump Administration to Cut Its Financial Contribution to NATO | CNN Politics." CNN, November 28. https://www.cnn.com/2019/11/27/politics/trump-nato-contribution-nato/index.html (accessed January 18, 2022).

Brownstein, Ronald. 2022. "Republicans Are Trying to Suppress More Than Votes." *The Atlantic.* January 28. https://www.theatlantic.com/politics/archive/2022/01/critical-race-theory-voting-rights-gop/621383/ (accessed January 22, 2023).

Buchanan, James M., and Gordon Tullock. 1962. *The Calculus of Consent.* Ann Arbor: University of Michigan Press.

Bullock, John G., Alan S. Gerber, Seth J. Hill, and Gregory A. Huber. 2015. Partisan Bias in Factual Beliefs about Politics. *Quarterly Journal of Political Science* 10(4): 519–78.

Burbank, Matthew J. 1995. "How Do Contextual Effects Work? Developing a Theoretical Model." In *Spatial and Contextual Models in Political Research*, edited by Munroe Eagles, 165–78. London: Taylor and Francis.

Campbell, Angus, Philip E. Converse, Warren E. Miller, and Donald E. Stokes. 1960. *The American Voter.* New York: John Wiley & Sons.

Campbell, James E. 2008. "Do Swing Voters Swing Elections?" In *The Swing Voter in American Politics*, edited by William G. Mayer, 118–32. Washington, DC: Brookings Institution Press.

Carlisle, M. 2020. N.H. Dems Prefer Death by Meteor over Trump Re-election: Poll. *Time*, February 8. https://time.com/5780556/meteor-poll-trump-new-hampshire/ (accessed January 6, 2022).

Carmines, Edward G., and James A. Stimson. 1980. "The Two Faces of Issue Voting." *American Political Science Review* 74(1): 78–91.

Carmines, Edward G., and James A. Stimson. 1989. *Issue Evolution: Race and the Transformation of American Politics.* Princeton, NJ: Princeton University Press. https:// doi.org/10.1515/9780691218250 (accessed July 5, 2021).

Carsey, Thomas M., and Geoffrey C. Layman. 2006. "Changing Sides or Changing Minds? Party Identification and Policy Preferences in the American Electorate." *American Journal of Political Science* 50(2): 464–77.

Castle, Jeremiah J., Geoffrey C. Layman, David E. Campbell, and John C. Green. 2017. "Survey experiments on candidate religiosity, political attitudes, and vote choice." *Journal for the Scientific Study of Religion* 56(1): 143–61.

Castronuovo, Celine. 2020. "Trump Privately Blamed Black Americans for Lacking Initiative: Report." *The Hill*, September 23. https://thehill.com/homenews/administrat ion/517813-trump-privately-blamed-black-americans-for-lacking-initiative-report (accessed July 6, 2021).

Centers for Disease Control. 2021. "CDC: COVID-19 Integrated County View." https://covid.cdc.gov/covid-data-tracker/#county-view?list_select_state=all_states&list_select_county=all_counties&data-type=Risk (accessed December 31, 2021).

Chiacu, Doina, and Susan Cornwell. 2021. "Tempers Flare in U.S. Congress as COVID-19 Mask Mandates Return." Reuters, July 29. https://www.reuters.com/world/us/congressional-republicans-lash-out-against-new-covid-19-mask-guidance-2021-07-28/ (accessed December 14, 2021).

CNN Political Unit. 2013. "Poll: 'Obamacare' vs. 'Affordable Care Act.'" CNN, September 27. https://politicalticker.blogs.cnn.com/2013/09/27/poll-obamacare-vs-affordable-care-act/ (accessed January 7, 2022).

Converse, P. E. 1964. "The Nature of Belief Systems in Mass Publics." In *Ideology and Its Discontent*, edited by D. E. Apter, 1–74. New York: The Free Press of Glencoe.

Coppock, Alexander, and Donald P. Green. 2022. "Do Belief Systems Exhibit Dynamic Constraint?" *Journal of Politics* 84(2): 725–38.

Cornish, Audie. 2012. "McGovern Campaign Marked Beginning of Direct Mail." NPR, August 1. https://www.npr.org/2012/08/01/157739995/mcgovern-campaign-marked-beginning-of-direct-mail (accessed November 17, 2021).

Covert, Bryce. 2015. "We All Get 'Free Stuff' from the Government" (Opinion). *New York Times*, October 8. https://www.nytimes.com/2015/10/08/opinion/we-all-get-free-stuff-from-the-government.html (accessed July 6, 2021).

Craig, Stephen C., Richard G. Niemi, and Glenn E. Silver. 1990. "Political Efficacy and Trust: A Report on the NES Pilot Study Items." *Political Behavior* 12(3): 289–314.

Davies, Kristin, Linda R. Tropp, Arthur Aron, Thomas F. Pettigrew, and Stephen C. Wright. . 2011. "Cross-Group Friendships and Intergroup Attitudes: A Meta-Analytic Review." *Personality and Social Psychology Review* 15(4): 332–51.

Davis, Leslie, and Hannah Hartig. 2019. "Two-Thirds of Americans Favor Raising Federal Minimum Wage to $15 an Hour." Pew Research Center, July 30. https://www.pewresearch.org/fact-tank/2019/07/30/two-thirds-of-americans-favor-raising-federal-minimum-wage-to-15-an-hour/ (accessed January 6, 2022).

Dawson, Michael, and Lawrence Bobo. 2004. "The Reagan Legacy and the Racial Divide in the George W. Bush Era." *Du Bois Review* 1: 209–12.

DellaVigna, Stefano, and Ethan Kaplan. 2007. "The Fox News Effect: Media Bias and Voting." *Quarterly Journal of Economics* 122(3): 1187–1234.

Delli Carpini, Michael X., and Scott Keeter. 1996. *What Americans Know about Politics and Why It Matters*. New Haven, CT: Yale University Press.

De Tezanos-Pinto, Pablo, Christopher Bratt, and Rupert Brown. 2010. "What Will the Others Think? In-Group Norms as a Mediator of the Effects of Intergroup Contact." *British Journal of Social Psychology* 49(3): 507–23.

Deutsch, Morton, and Mary Evans Collins. 1951. *Interracial Housing: A Psychological Evaluation of a Social Experiment*. Minneapolis: University of Minnesota Press.

Dias, Nicholas, and Yphtach Lelkes. 2021. "The Nature of Affective Polarization: Disentangling Policy Disagreement from Partisan Identity." *American Journal of Political Science* 66(3): 775–90.

Dickson, E. J. 2021. "How Joe Rogan Became a Cheerleader for Ivermectin." *Rolling Stone*, September 2. https://www.rollingstone.com/culture/culture-features/joe-rogan-covid19-misinformation-ivermectin-spotify-podcast-1219976/ (accessed February 2, 2022).

Dimock, Michael. 2020. *How Americans View Trust, Facts, and Democracy Today.* Pew Research Center, February 19. https://pew.org/38gSYyx (accessed November 16, 2021).

Dionne, E. J., Jr., Norman J. Ornstein, and Thomas E. Mann. 2017. *One Nation after Trump: A Guide for the Perplexed, the Disillusioned, the Desperate, and the Not-Yet Deported.* New York: St. Martin's Press.

Downs, Anthony. 1957. "An Economic Theory of Political Action in a Democracy." *Journal of Political Economy* 65(2): 135–50.

Dreisbach, Tom, Meg Anderson, and Barbara Van Woerkom. 2022. "5 Takeaways from the Capitol Riot Criminal Cases, One Year Later." NPR, January 5. https://www.npr.org/2022/01/05/1070199411/5-takeaways-from-the-capitol-riot-criminal-cases-one-year-later (accessed February 2, 2022).

Duch, Raymond M., Harvey D. Palmer, and Christopher J. Anderson. 2000. "Heterogeneity in Perceptions of National Economic Conditions." *American Journal of Political Science* 44(4) (October): 635–52.

Dyck, Joshua J., John Cluverius, and Jeffrey N. Gerson. 2019. "Sports, Science, and Partisanship in the United States: Chronic Traumatic Encephalopathy and the Polarisation of an Apolitical Issue." *International Journal of Sport Policy and Politics* 11(1): 133–52.

Dyck, Joshua J., and Shanna Pearson-Merkowitz. 2014. "To Know You Is Not Necessarily to Love You: The Partisan Mediators of Intergroup Contact." *Political Behavior* 36(3): 553–80.

Dyck, Joshua J., and Shanna Pearson-Merkowitz. 2019. "Ballot Initiatives and Status Quo Bias." *State Politics & Policy Quarterly* 19(2): 180–207.

Eady, Gregory, Jonathan Nagler, Andy Guess, Jan Zilinsky, and Joshua A. Tucker. 2019. "How Many People Live in Political Bubbles on Social Media? Evidence from Linked Survey and Twitter Data." *SAGE Open* 9(1). https://doi.org/10.1177/2158244019832705

Eagles, Munroe. 1995. *Spatial and Contextual Models in Political Research.* London: Taylor & Francis.

Egan, Patrick J. 2013. *Partisan Priorities: How Issue Ownership Drives and Distorts American Politics.* New York: Cambridge University Press.

Eggers, Andrew C., Haritz Garro, and Justin Grimmer. 2021. "No Evidence for Systematic Voter Fraud: A Guide to Statistical Claims about the 2020 Election." *Proceedings of the National Academy of Sciences* 118(45): 1–7. https://www.pnas.org/doi/abs/10.1073/pnas.2103619118

Ellison, Christopher G., Heeju Shin, and David L. Leal. 2011. "The Contact Hypothesis and Attitudes toward Latinos in the United States." *Social Science Quarterly* 92(4): 938–58.

Ellison, Nancy. "Donald Trump Loves His Mother's Meatloaf." *One for the Table.* http://oneforthetable.com/stories/6755-donald-trump-loves-his-mothers-meatloaf (accessed January 7, 2022).

Enten, Harry. 2021. "Analysis: Statistically, Democrats and Republicans Hate Each Other More than Ever." CNN, November 20. https://www.cnn.com/2021/11/20/politics/democrat-republican-hate-tribalism/index.html (accessed December 17, 2021).

Escandell, Xavier, and Alin M. Ceobanu. 2009. "When Contact with Immigrants Matters: Threat, Interethnic Attitudes and Foreigner Exclusionism in Spain's Comunidades Autónomas." *Ethnic and Racial Studies* 32(1): 44–69.

Evans, Michael, and Shanna Pearson-Merkowitz. 2012. "Perpetuating the Myth of the Culture War Court? Issue Attention in Newspaper Coverage of US Supreme Court Nominations." *American Politics Research* 40(6): 1026–66.

Everson, Zack. 2021. "Congressman Thomas Massie's Christmas-Card Arsenal Is Probably Worth Tens of Thousands." December 24. *Forbes*. https://www.forbes.com/sites/zacheverson/2021/12/24/congressman-thomas-massies-christmas-card-arsenal-is-probably-worth-tens-of-thousands/?sh=783570653054 (accessed January 18, 2023).

"Executive Order on Advancing Racial Equity and Support for Underserved Communities through the Federal Government." 2021. The White House, January 20. https://www.whitehouse.gov/briefing-room/presidential-actions/2021/01/20/executive-order-advancing-racial-equity-and-support-for-underserved-communities-through-the-federal-government/ (accessed January 14, 2022).

Faherty, Dave. 2022. "'I Will Die Free': Unvaccinated Burke County Man Denied Kidney Transplant by Hospital." https://www.wsoctv.com/news/local/i-will-die-free-unvaccinated-burke-county-man-denied-kidney-transplant-by-hospital/OJGAFURR4FGERJB7VT24P5RED4/ (accessed May 24, 2022).

Federico, Christopher M., and Jim Sidanius. 2002. "Sophistication and the Antecedents of Whites' Racial Policy Attitudes: Racism, Ideology, and Affirmative Action in America." *Public Opinion Quarterly* 66(2): 145–76.

Feldman, Stanley. 1982. "Economic Self-Interest and Political Behavior." *American Journal of Political Science* 26(3): 446–66.

Filindra, Alexandra, and Noah J. Kaplan. 2016. "Racial Resentment and Whites' Gun Policy Preferences in Contemporary America." *Political Behavior* 38(2): 255–75.

Fiorina, Morris P. 1978. "Economic Retrospective Voting in American National Elections: A Micro-Analysis." *American Journal of Political Science* 22(2): 426–43.

Fiscella, Kevin. 2016. "Why Do So Many White Americans Oppose the Affordable Care Act?" *American Journal of Medicine* 129(5): e27.

Fischel, William A. 2005. *The Homevoter Hypothesis: How Home Values Influence Local Government Taxation, School Finance, and Land-Use Policies*. Cambridge, MA: Harvard University Press.

Fischel, William A. 2017. "The Rise of the Homevoters: How the Growth Machine Was Subverted by OPEC and Earth Day." In *Evidence and Innovation in Housing Law and Policy*, edited by Lee Anne Fennell and Benjamin J. Keys, 13–37. Cambridge: Cambridge University Press.

Fisher, Max. 2011. "Did Sarah Palin's Target Map Play Role in Giffords Shooting?" *The Atlantic*, January 10. https://www.theatlantic.com/politics/archive/2011/01/did-sarah-palin-s-target-map-play-role-in-giffords-shooting/342714/ (accessed February 1, 2022).

Fishkin, James, Alice Siu, Larry Diamond, and Norman Bradburn. 2021. "Is Deliberation an Antidote to Extreme Partisan Polarization? Reflections on 'America in One Room.'" *American Political Science Review* 115(4): 1464–81.

Folley, Aris. 2019. "Obama's Tan Suit Controversy Hits 5-Year Anniversary." *The Hill*, August 28. https://thehill.com/blogs/in-the-know/in-the-know/459155-barack-obamas-tan-suit-controversy-hits-5-year-anniversary (accessed January 7, 2022).

Frank, Thomas. 2007. *What's the Matter with Kansas? How Conservatives Won the Heart of America*. New York: Picador.

Franklin, Charles H., and John E. Jackson. 1983. "The Dynamics of Party Identification." *American Political Science Review* 77(4): 957–73.

Frey, William. 2022. "Anti-CRT Bills Are Aimed to Incite the GOP Base—Not Parents." Brookings. March 30. https://www.brookings.edu/research/anti-crt-bills-are-aimed-to-incite-the-gop-base-not-parents/ (accessed January 22, 2023).

Fridman, Ariel, Rachel Gershon, and Ayelet Gneezy. 2021. "COVID-19 and Vaccine Hesitancy: A Longitudinal Study." *PLOS ONE* 16(4): e0250123.

Friedersdorf, Conor. 2011. "Barack Obama: Affirmative Action's Best Poster Child?" *The Atlantic*, April 28. https://www.theatlantic.com/politics/archive/2011/04/barack-obama-affirmative-actions-best-poster-child/237990/ (accessed August 2, 2021).

Frum, David. 2019. "Howard Schultz May Save the Democratic Party from Itself." *The Atlantic*, January 28. https://www.theatlantic.com/ideas/archive/2019/01/how-howard-schultz-may-save-democratic-party/581443/ (accessed January 6, 2022).

Gainous, Jason, and Kevin M. Wagner. 2013. *Tweeting to Power: The Social Media Revolution in American Politics*. New York: Oxford University Press.

Gallup Inc. 2021. "Presidential Approval Ratings—Donald Trump." Gallup.com. https://news.gallup.com/poll/203198/presidential-approval-ratings-donald-trump.aspx (accessed January 6, 2022).

Gamson, William A. 1968. "Stable Unrepresentation in American Society." *American Behavioral Scientist* 12(2): 15–21.

Gelman, Andrew, Daniel Lee, and Yair Ghitza. 2010. "Public Opinion on Health Care Reform." *The Forum* 8(1). https://doi.org/10.2202/1540-8884.1355

Gerber, Alan S., and Gregory A. Huber. 2009. "Partisanship and Economic Behavior: Do Partisan Differences in Economic Forecasts Predict Real Economic Behavior?" *American Political Science Review* 103(3): 407–26.

Gil de Zúñiga, Homero, Teresa Correa, and Sebastian Valenzuela. 2012. "Selective Exposure to Cable News and Immigration in the U.S.: The Relationship between FOX News, CNN, and Attitudes toward Mexican Immigrants." *Journal of Broadcasting & Electronic Media* 56(4): 597–615.

Gilens, Martin, Paul M. Sniderman, and James H. Kuklinski. 1998. "Affirmative Action and the Politics of Realignment." *British Journal of Political Science* 28(1): 159–83.

Gimpel, James G., and Iris S. Hui. 2015. "Seeking Politically Compatible Neighbors? The Role of Neighborhood Partisan Composition in Residential Sorting." *Political Geography* 48: 130–42.

Gimpel, James Graydon, and Jason E. Schuknecht. 2009. *Patchwork Nation: Sectionalism and Political Change in American Politics*. Ann Arbor: University of Michigan Press.

Goldberg, Michelle. 2021. "What 'My Body, My Choice' Means to the Right" (Opinion). *New York Times*, November 29. https://www.nytimes.com/2021/11/29/opinion/abortion-vaccine-mandate.html (accessed January 6, 2022).

Gramlich, John. 2020. "Q&A: How Pew Research Center Evaluated Americans' Trust in 30 News Sources." Pew Research Center, January 24. https://www.pewresearch.org/fact-tank/2020/01/24/qa-how-pew-research-center-evaluated-americans-trust-in-30-news-sources/ (accessed December 5, 2021).

Green, Donald, Bradley Palmquist, and Eric Schickler. 2008 *Partisan Hearts and Minds*. New Haven, CT: Yale University Press.

Green, Jon, Jared Edgerton, Daniel Naftel, Kelsey Shoub, and Skyler J. Cranmer. 2020. "Elusive Consensus: Polarization in Elite Communication on the COVID-19 Pandemic." *Science Advances* 6(28): eabc2717.

Greenwood, Max. 2021. "One-Third of Americans Believe Biden Won Because of Voter Fraud: Poll." *The Hill*, June 21. https://thehill.com/homenews/campaign/

559402-one-third-of-americans-believe-biden-won-because-of-voter-fraud-poll (accessed August 3, 2021).

Gregorian, Dareh. 2021. "Rep. Marjorie Taylor Greene Says She's Not Vaccinated, Rips 'Vaccine Nazis.'" NBC News, November 2. https://www.nbcnews.com/politics/congress/rep-marjorie-taylor-greene-says-she-s-not-vaccinated-rips-n1283008 (accessed December 14, 2021).

Grossmann, Matt, and David A. Hopkins. 2016. *Asymmetric Politics: Ideological Republicans and Group Interest Democrats.* New York: Oxford University Press.

Guess, Andy, Kevin Aslett, Joshua Tucker, Richard Bonneau, and Jonathan Nagler. 2021. "Cracking Open the News Feed: Exploring What Us Facebook Users See and Share with Large-Scale Platform Data." *Journal of Quantitative Description: Digital Media* 1.

Hacker, Jacob S., and Paul Pierson. 2005. "Abandoning the Middle: The Bush Tax Cuts and the Limits of Democratic Control." *Perspectives on Politics* 3(1): 33–53.

Hacker, Jacob S., and Paul Pierson. 2015. "Confronting Asymmetric Polarization." In *Solutions to Political Polarization in America*, edited by Nathaniel Persily, 59–72. New York: Cambridge University Press.

Haerpfer, C., R. Inglehart, A. Moreno, C. Welzel, K. Kizilova, J. Diez-Medrano M. Lagos, P. Norris, E. Ponarin, & B. Puranen (eds.). 2020. *World Values Survey: Round Seven—Country-Pooled Datafile.* Madrid, Spain, & Vienna, Austria: JD Systems Institute & WVSA Secretariat. https://doi.org/10.14281/18241.13

Hajnal, Zoltan, and Michael U. Rivera. 2014. "Immigration, Latinos, and White Partisan Politics: The New Democratic Defection." *American Journal of Political Science* 58(4): 773–89.

Hamel, Liz, Lunna Lopes, and Grace Sparks, Ashley Kirzinger, Audrey Kearney, Mellisha Stokes, and Mollyann Brodie. 2021. "KFF COVID-19 Vaccine Monitor: September 2021." KFF, September 28. https://www.kff.org/coronavirus-covid-19/poll-finding/kff-covid-19-vaccine-monitor-september-2021/ (accessed January 25, 2022).

Hanel, Paul H. P., Uwe Wolfradt, Gregory R. Maio, and Antony S. R. Manstead. 2018. "The Source Attribution Effect: Demonstrating Pernicious Disagreement between Ideological Groups on Non-Divisive Aphorisms." *Journal of Experimental Social Psychology* 79: 51–63.

Harbridge, Laurel, Neil Malhotra, and Brian F. Harrison. 2014. "Public Preferences for Bipartisanship in the Policymaking Process." *Legislative Studies Quarterly* 39(3): 327–55.

Hare, Christopher, and Keith T. Poole. 2014. "The Polarization of Contemporary American Politics." *Polity* 46(3): 411–29.

Healy, Andrew, and Neil Malhotra. 2013. "Retrospective Voting Reconsidered." *Annual Review of Political Science* 16(1): 285–306.

Heese, Jonas, and Vishal P. Baloria. 2017. "Research: The Rise of Partisan Media Changed How Companies Make Decisions." *Harvard Business Review.* https://hbr.org/2017/10/research-the-rise-of-partisan-media-changed-how-companies-make-decisions (accessed November 16, 2021).

Heseltine, Michael, and Spencer Dorsey. 2022. "Online Incivility in the 2020 Congressional Elections." *Political Research Quarterly* 75(2): 512–26. https://doi.org/10.1177/10659129221078863

Hibbing, John R., and Elizabeth Theiss-Morse. 2002. *Stealth Democracy: Americans' Beliefs about How Government Should Work.* Cambridge: Cambridge University Press.

Hochschild, Jennifer L., and Katherine Levine Einstein. 2015. *Do Facts Matter? Information and Misinformation in American Politics*. Norman: University of Oklahoma Press.

Hodson, Gordon, Richard J. Crisp, Rose Meleady, and Megan Earle. 2018. "Intergroup Contact as an Agent of Cognitive Liberalization." *Perspectives on Psychological Science* 13(5): 523–48.

Homer, Collin, Jon Dewitz, Limin Yang, Suming Jin, Patrick Danielson, George Xian, John Coulston, Nate Herold, James Wickham, and Kevin Megown. 2015. "Completion of the 2011 National Land Cover Database for the Conterminous United States—Representing a Decade of Land Cover Change Information." *Photogrammetric Engineering & Remote Sensing* 81(5): 345–54.

Hopkins, Daniel J. 2018. *The Increasingly United States: How and Why American Political Behavior Nationalized*. Chicago: University of Chicago Press.

Howell-Moroney, Michael. 2004a. "Community Characteristics, Open Space Preservation and Regionalism: Is There a Connection?" *Journal of Urban Affairs* 26(1): 109–18.

Howell-Moroney, Michael. 2004b. "What Are the Determinants of Open-Space Ballot Measures? An Extension of the Research." *Social Science Quarterly* 85(1): 169–79.

Huckfeldt, R. Robert. 1986. *Politics in Context: Assimilation and Conflict in Urban Neighborhoods*. New York: Algora Publishing.

Huckfeldt, R. Robert, and John Sprague. 1995. *Citizens, Politics and Social Communication: Information and Influence in an Election Campaign*. Cambridge: Cambridge University Press.

Hurwitz, Jon, and Jeffery J. Mondak. 2002. "Democratic Principles, Discrimination and Political Intolerance." *British Journal of Political Science* 32(1): 93–118.

Iyengar, Shanto, and Masha Krupenkin. 2018. "The Strengthening of Partisan Affect." *Political Psychology* 39: 201–18.

Iyengar, Shanto, Gaurav Sood, and Yphtach Lelkes. 2012. "Affect, Not Ideology: A Social Identity Perspective on Polarization." *Public Opinion Quarterly* 76(3): 405–31.

Jacobson, Gary C. 1991. "Explaining Divided Government: Why Can't the Republicans Win the House?" *PS: Political Science & Politics* 24(4): 640–43.

Jefferson, Hakeem. 2020. "The Curious Case of Black Conservatives: Construct Validity and the 7-Point Liberal–Conservative Scale" (working paper). Available at https://ssrn.com/abstract=3602209 or http://dx.doi.org/10.2139/ssrn.3602209.

Jenkins, Jennifer. 2021. "Perspective | I'm a Florida School Board Member. This Is How Protesters Come after Me." *Washington Post*, October 20. https://www.washingtonpost.com/outlook/2021/10/20/jennifer-jenkins-brevard-school-board-masks-threats/ (accessed January 25, 2022).

Jennings, M. Kent, Laura Stoker, and Jake Bowers. 2009. "Politics across Generations: Family Transmission Reexamined." *Journal of Politics* 71(3): 782–99.

Jones, Jeff, and Lydia Saad. 2017. *Gallup Poll Social Series: Governance Toplines*. Gallup News Service.

Joyella, Mark. 2021. "Fox News Channel's Sean Hannity Has the Week's Most-Watched Show as CNN's Cuomo Loses Viewers." *Forbes*, August 24. https://www.forbes.com/sites/markjoyella/2021/08/24/fox-news-channels-sean-hannity-has-the-weeks-most-watched-show-as-cnns-cuomo-loses-viewers/ (accessed November 17, 2021).

Jurkowitz, Mark, Amy Mitchell, Elisa Shearer, and Mason Walker. 2020. "U.S. Media Polarization and the 2020 Election: A Nation Divided." Pew Research Center's Journalism Project, January 24. https://www.pewresearch.org/journalism/2020/

01/24/u-s-media-polarization-and-the-2020-election-a-nation-divided/ (accessed December 5, 2021).

Jones, Jeffrey. 2019. "Subgroup Differences in Trump Approval Mostly Party-Based." Gallup.com, March 29. https://news.gallup.com/poll/248135/subgroup-differences-trump-approval-mostly-party-based.aspx (accessed January 6, 2022).

Kahneman, Daniel, and Amos Tversky. 1979. "Prospect Theory: An Analysis of Decision under Risk." *Econometrica* 47(2): 263–92.

Kalmoe, Nathan P., and Lilliana Mason. 2022. *Radical American Partisanship: Mapping Violent Hostility, Its Causes, and the Consequences for Democracy.* Chicago: University of Chicago Press.

Kamenetz, Anya. 2021. "A Look at the Groups Supporting School Board Protesters Nationwide." NPR, October 26. https://www.npr.org/2021/10/26/1049078199/a-look-at-the-groups-supporting-school-board-protesters-nationwide (accessed January 25, 2022).

Kaplan, Richard L. 2002. *Politics and the American Press: The Rise of Objectivity, 1865–1920.* Cambridge: Cambridge University Press.

Karol, David. 2009. *Party Position Change in American Politics: Coalition Management.* New York: Cambridge University Press.

Kaufmann, Karen M., John R. Petrocik, and Daron R. Shaw. 2008. *Unconventional Wisdom: Facts and Myths about American Voters.* New York: Oxford University Press.

Keith, Bruce E., David B. Magleby, Candice J. Nelson, Elizabeth Orr, Mark C. Westyle, and Raymond E. Wolfinger. 1992. *The Myth of the Independent Voter.* Berkeley: University of California Press.

Key, V. O. 1949. *Southern Politics in State and Nation.* New York: Alfred A. Knopf.

Key, Valdimer Orlando. 1956. *American State Politics: An Introduction.* New York: Knopf.

Kinder, Donald R., and Lynn M. Sanders. 1996. *Divided by Color: Racial Politics and Democratic Ideals.* Chicago: University of Chicago Press.

Kinder, Donald R., and Nathan P. Kalmoe. 2017. *Neither Liberal nor Conservative.* Chicago: University of Chicago Press.

Kirzinger, Ashlea, Alex Montero, Liz Hamel, and Mollyann Brodie. 2022. "5 Charts about Public Opinion on the Affordable Care Act." KFF, April 14. https://www.kff.org/health-reform/poll-finding/5-charts-about-public-opinion-on-the-affordable-care-act-and-the-supreme-court/ (accessed November 10, 2022).

Klar, Samara, and Yanna Krupnikov. 2016. *Independent Politics: How American Disdain for Parties Leads to Political Inaction.* New York: Cambridge University Press.

Kline, Jeffrey, and Dennis Wichelns. 1994. "Using Referendum Data to Characterize Public Support for Purchasing Development Rights to Farmland." *Land Economics* 70(2): 223–33.

Kluger, Jeffrey. 2020. "Accidental Poisonings Increased after President Trump's Disinfectant Comments." *Time,* May 12. https://time.com/5835244/accidental-poisonings-trump/ (accessed February 2, 2022).

Koch, Ashley. 2021. "Once Considered Mundane, School Board Meetings Becoming Heated, Violent." *KGW,* October 25 (updated October 26). https://www.kgw.com/article/news/local/the-story/school-board-meetings-heated-violent/283-a4e359e7-4620-493a-aafd-fe2b2c5a0fa0 (accessed January 25, 2022).

Kotchen, Matthew J., and Shawn M. Powers. 2006. "Explaining the Appearance and Success of Voter Referenda for Open-Space Conservation." *Journal of Environmental Economics and Management* 52(1): 373–90.

Kotchen, Matthew J., Zachary M. Turk, and Anthony A. Leiserowitz. 2017. "Public Willingness to Pay for a US Carbon Tax and Preferences for Spending the Revenue." *Environmental Research Letters* 12(9): 094012.

Krupnikov, Yanna, and John Barry Ryan. 2022. *The Other Divide: Polarization and Disengagement in American Politics*. Cambridge: Cambridge University Press.

Kunda, Ziva. 1990. "The Case for Motivated Reasoning." *Psychological Bulletin* 108(3): 480.

Laar, Colette Van, Shana Levin, Stacey Sinclair, and Jim Sidanius. 2005. "The Effect of University Roommate Contact on Ethnic Attitudes and Behavior." *Journal of Experimental Social Psychology* 41(4): 329–45.

Landis, Dan, Richard O. Hope, and Harry R. Day. 1983. *Training for Desegregation in the Military*. Indiana Univ-Purdue Univ at Indianapolis Center for Applied Research and Evaluation. https://apps.dtic.mil/sti/citations/ADA129448 (accessed January 14, 2023)..

Lang, Corey. 2018. "Assessing the Efficiency of Local Open Space Provision." *Journal of Public Economics* 158: 12–24.

Lang, Corey, and Shanna Pearson-Merkowitz. 2015. "Partisan Sorting in the United States, 1972-2012: New Evidence from a Dynamic Analysis." *Political Geography* 48: 119–29.

Lang, Corey, and Shanna Pearson-Merkowitz. 2022. "Aggregate Data Yield Biased Estimates of Voter Preferences." *Journal of Environmental Economics and Management* 111: 1–18.

Lang, Corey, Michael Weir, and Shanna Pearson-Merkowitz. 2021. "Status Quo Bias and Public Policy: Evidence in the Context of Carbon Mitigation." *Environmental Research Letters* 16(5): 054076.

Layman, Geoffrey. 2001. *The Great Divide: Religious and Cultural Conflict in American Party Politics*. New York: Columbia University Press.

Layman, Geoffrey C., and Thomas M. Carsey. 2002a. "Party Polarization and 'Conflict Extension' in the American Electorate." *American Journal of Political Science* 46(4): 786–802.

Layman, Geoffrey C., and Thomas M. Carsey. 2002b. "Party Polarization and Party Structuring of Policy Attitudes: A Comparison of Three NES Panel Studies." *Political Behavior* 24(3): 199–236.

Layman, Geoffrey C., Thomas M. Carsey, John C. Green, Richard Herrera, and Rosalyn Cooperman. 2010. "Activists and Conflict Extension in American Party Politics." *American Political Science Review* 104(2): 324–46.

Lee, Frances E. 2009. *Beyond Ideology*. Chicago: University of Chicago Press.

Lee, Frances E. 2016. *Insecure Majorities: Congress and the Perpetual Campaign*. Chicago: University of Chicago Press.

Leffler, Warren K. 1964. "[Ku Klux Klan Members Supporting Barry Goldwater's Campaign for the Presidential Nomination at the Republican National Convention, San Francisco, California, as an African American Man Pushes Signs Back]" (photograph). https://www.loc.gov/pictures/item/2003673964/ (accessed July 5, 2021).

Lemmer, Gunnar, and Ulrich Wagner. 2015. "Can We Really Reduce Ethnic Prejudice Outside the Lab? A Meta-Analysis of Direct and Indirect Contact Interventions." *European Journal of Social Psychology* 45(2): 152–68.

Leonhardt, David. 2021. "Red Covid." *New York Times*, September 27. https://www.nytimes.com/2021/09/27/briefing/covid-red-states-vaccinations.html (accessed December 14, 2021).

Lerman, Amy E., Meredith L. Sadin, and Samuel Trachtman. 2017. "Policy Uptake as Political Behavior: Evidence from the Affordable Care Act." *American Political Science Review* 111(4): 755–70.

Levendusky, Matthew. 2009. *The Partisan Sort*. Chicago: University of Chicago Press.

Levine, Dan. 2017. "Democrats and Republicans Have Virtually Switched Sides on States' Rights." *Business Insider*, January 26. https://www.businessinsider.com/democrats-and-republicans-switched-sides-on-states-rights-2017-1 (accessed January 6, 2022).

Levy, Jack S. 1992. "An Introduction to Prospect Theory." *Political Psychology* 13(2): 171–86.

Lewis, Jeffrey B., Keith Poole, Howard Rosenthal, Adam Boche, Aaron Rudkin, and Luke Sonnet 2022. "Voteview: Congressional Roll-Call Votes Database." https://voteview.com/. (accessed January 1, 2022).

Lewis-Beck, Michael S. 1985. "Pocketbook Voting in US National Election Studies: Fact or Artifact?" *American Journal of Political Science* 29(2): 348–56.

Liesman, Steve. 2013. "What's in a Name? Lots When It Comes to Obamacare/ACA." CNBC, September 26. https://www.cnbc.com/2013/09/26/whats-in-a-name-lots-when-it-comes-to-obamacareaca.html (accessed January 6, 2022).

Linskey, Annie. 2020. "Democratic Convention Embraces Black Lives Matter." *Washington Post*, August 18. https://www.washingtonpost.com/politics/democratic-convention-embraces-black-lives-matter/2020/08/18/f1de2ce8-e0f7-11ea-b69b-64f7b0477ed4_story.html (accessed July 6, 2021).

Lipmann, Walter. 1925. *The Phantom Public*. Piscataway, NJ: Transaction Publishers.

Livingston, Gretchen, and Anna Brown. 2017. "Public Views on Intermarriage." Pew Research Center's Social & Demographic Trends Project, May 18. https://www.pewresearch.org/social-trends/2017/05/18/2-public-views-on-intermarriage/ (accessed July 13, 2021).

Lodge, Milton, and Charles S. Taber. 2013. *The Rationalizing Voter*. New York: Cambridge University Press.

Lowry, William R. 2018. "The Exceptionalism of the Open Space Issue in American Politics." *Social Science Quarterly* 99(4): 1363–76.

Lupia, Arthur. 1994. "Shortcuts versus Encyclopedias: Information and Voting Behavior in California Insurance Reform Elections." *American Political Science Review* 88(1): 63–76.

Lupia, Arthur. 2016. *Uninformed: Why People Know So Little about Politics and What We Can Do about It*. New York: Oxford University Press.

Luskin, Robert C. 1991. "Explaining Political Sophistication." *Political Behavior* 12(4): 331–361.

Madison, James. 1787. "The Federalist No. 10.". In *The Federalist*, edited by George W. Carey and James McClellan, 351–52. Indianapolis, IN: Liberty Fund.

Mann, Thomas E., and Norman J. Ornstein. 2016. *It's Even Worse than It Looks: How the American Constitutional System Collided with the New Politics of Extremism*. New York: Basic Books.

Marietta, Morgan, and David C. Barker. 2019. *One Nation, Two Realities: Dueling Facts in American Democracy*. New York: Oxford University Press.

Mark, David. 2008. "Helms Was Ahead of Campaign Curve." POLITICO, July 7. https://www.politico.com/story/2008/07/helms-was-ahead-of-campaign-curve-011577 (accessed November 17, 2021).

Mason, Lilliana. 2015. "'I Disrespectfully Agree': The Differential Effects of Partisan Sorting on Social and Issue Polarization." *American Journal of Political Science* 59(1): 128–45.

Mason, Lilliana . 2018. *Uncivil Agreement: How Politics Became Our Identity.* Chicago: University of Chicago Press.

McCarty, Nolan. 2011. "The Policy Effects of Political Polarization." In *The Transformation of American Politics*, edited by Paul Pierson and Theda Skocpol, 223–55. Princeton, NJ: Princeton University Press.

McLeod, Poppy Lauretta, Sharon Alisa Lobel, and Taylor H. Cox, Jr. 1996. "Ethnic Diversity and Creativity in Small Groups." *Small Group Research* 27(2): 248–64.

McTague, John, and Shanna Pearson-Merkowitz. 2013. "Voting from the Pew: The Effect of Senators' Religious Identities on Partisan Polarization in the US Senate." *Legislative Studies Quarterly* 38(3): 405–30.

Meleady, Rose, Richard J. Crisp, Gordon Hodson, and Megan Earle. 2019. "On the Generalization of Intergroup Contact: A Taxonomy of Transfer Effects." *Current Directions in Psychological Science* 28(5): 430–35.

Mercer, Jonathan. 2005. "Prospect Theory and Political Science." *Annual Review of Political Science* 8(1): 1–21.

Milbank, Dana. 2022. "Opinion: How Fox News and Republican Officials Devised One Biden Smear." *Washington Post*, January 21. https://www.washingtonpost.com/opini ons/2022/01/21/fox-news-lie-school-board-domestic-terrorists/ (accessed January 22, 2022).

Miles, Eleanor, and Richard J. Crisp. 2014. "A Meta-Analytic Test of the Imagined Contact Hypothesis." *Group Processes & Intergroup Relations* 17(1): 3–26.

Miller, Joanne M., Kyle L. Saunders, and Christina E. Farhart. 2016. "Conspiracy Endorsement as Motivated Reasoning: The Moderating Roles of Political Knowledge and Trust." *American Journal of Political Science* 60(4): 824–44.

Mitchell, Amy, Jeffrey Gottfried, Jocelyn Kiley, and Katerina Eva Matsa. 2014. "Political Polarization & Media Habits." Pew Research Center's Journalism Project, October 21. https://www.pewresearch.org/journalism/2014/10/21/political-polarization-media-habits/ (accessed November 18, 2021).

MIT Election Data and Science Lab. 2018. "County Presidential Election Returns 2000–2020." *Harvard Dataverse.* https://dataverse.harvard.edu/dataset.xhtml?persistentId= doi:10.7910/DVN/VOQCHQ (accessed January 15, 2022).

Montopoli, Brian, and Jill Jackson. 2010. "'Pledge to America' Unveiled by Republicans (Full Text)." https://www.cbsnews.com/news/pledge-to-america-unveiled-by-republic ans-full-text/ (accessed January 7, 2022).

Moore-Berg, Samantha L., Lee-Or Ankori-Karlinsky, Boaz Hameiri, and Emile Bruneau. 2020. "Exaggerated Meta-Perceptions Predict Intergroup Hostility between American Political Partisans." *Proceedings of the National Academy of Sciences* 117(26): 14864–72.

Morrison, Elizabeth Wolfe, and Joyce Mardenfeld Herlihy. 1992. "Becoming the Best Place to Work: Managing Diversity at American Express Travel Related Services." In *Diversity in the Workplace*, edited by Susan Jackson and Associates (pp. 203–26). New York: Guilford.

Murphy, Reg, and Hal Gulliver. 1971. *The Southern Strategy.* New York: Scribner.

Mutz, Diana C. 2002. "The Consequences of Cross-Cutting Networks for Political Participation." *American Journal of Political Science* 46(4): 838–55.

Mutz, Diana C. 2006. *Hearing the Other Side: Deliberative versus Participatory Democracy*. New York: Cambridge University Press.

Nesdale, Drew, Anne Maass, Kevin Durkin, and Judith Griffiths. 2005. "Group Norms, Threat, and Children's Racial Prejudice." *Child Development* 76(3): 652–63.

Neumann, Rico, and Patricia Moy. 2018. "You're (Not) Welcome: The Impact of Symbolic Boundaries, Intergroup Contact, and Experiences with Discrimination on Immigration Attitudes." *American Behavioral Scientist* 62(4): 458–77.

Newman, Benjamin J. 2014. "My Poor Friend: Financial Distress in One's Social Network, the Perceived Power of the Rich, and Support for Redistribution." *Journal of Politics* 76(1): 126–38.

Newman, Benjamin J., Yamil Velez, Todd K. Hartman, and Alexa Bankert. 2015. "Are Citizens 'Receiving the Treatment'? Assessing a Key Link in Contextual Theories of Public Opinion and Political Behavior." *Political Psychology* 36(1): 123–31.

Nolte, John. 2021. "Nolte: Howard Stern Proves Democrats Want Unvaccinated Trump Voters Dead." *Breitbart*, September 10. https://www.breitbart.com/entertainment/2021/09/10/nolte-howard-stern-proves-democrats-want-unvaccinated-trump-voters-dead/ (accessed December 14, 2021).

Norman, Herb. 1998. "The Talk of the Town: The Saga of Bob Grant." *Journal of Popular Culture* 32(1): 91–98.

Nyhan, Brendan, Jason Reifler, Sean Richey, and Gary L. Freed. 2014. "Effective Messages in Vaccine Promotion: A Randomized Trial." *Pediatrics* 133(4): e835–42.

Oakes, J. Michael. 2004. "The (Mis)Estimation of Neighborhood Effects: Causal Inference for a Practicable Social Epidemiology." *Social Science & Medicine* 58(10): 1929–52.

Obama, Barack. 2008. "Transcript: Barack Obama's Speech on Race." NPR, March 18. https://www.npr.org/templates/story/story.php?storyId=88478467 (July 6, 2021).

Ocasio-Cortez, Alexandria. 2020. "@AOC Twitter Thread." Twitter, December 2. https://twitter.com/aoc/status/1334184644707758080?lang=en (accessed January 14, 2022).

Oliphant, James, and Chris Kahn. 2021. "Half of Republicans Believe False Accounts of Deadly U.S. Capitol Riot—Reuters/Ipsos Poll." Reuters, April 5. https://www.reuters.com/article/us-usa-politics-disinformation-idUSKBN2BS0RZ (accessed October 7, 2021).

Orr, Lilla V., and Gregory A. Huber. 2020. "The Policy Basis of Measured Partisan Animosity in the United States." *American Journal of Political Science* 64(3): 569–86.

Osmundsen, Mathias, Alexander Bor, Peter Bjerregaard Vahlstrup, Anja Bechmann, and Michael Bang Petersen. 2021. "Partisan Polarization Is the Primary Psychological Motivation behind Political Fake News Sharing on Twitter." *American Political Science Review* 115(3): 999–1015.

Osmundsen, Mathias, Michael Bang Petersen, and Alexander Bor. 2021. "How Partisan Polarization Drives the Spread of Fake News." *Brookings*, May 13. https://www.brookings.edu/techstream/how-partisan-polarization-drives-the-spread-of-fake-news/ (accessed December 5, 2021).

Passarelli, Francesco, and Alessandro Del Ponte. 2020. "Prospect Theory, Loss Aversion, and Political Behavior." In *Oxford Research Encyclopedia of Politics*, edited by William R. Thompson.. Oxford University Press. https://doi.org/10.1093/acrefore/9780190228637.013.947

Pearson-Merkowitz, Shanna, and Joshua J. Dyck. 2017. "Crime and Partisanship: How Party ID Muddles Reality, Perception, and Policy Attitudes on Crime and Guns." *Social Science Quarterly* 98(2): 443–54.

Pearson-Merkowitz, Shanna, Alexandra Filindra, and Joshua J. Dyck. 2016. "When Partisans and Minorities Interact: Interpersonal Contact, Partisanship, and Public Opinion Preferences on Immigration Policy." *Social Science Quarterly* 97(2): 311–24.

Pearson-Merkowitz, Shanna, and Corey Lang. 2020. "Smart Growth at the Ballot Box: Understanding Voting on Affordable Housing and Land Management Referendums." *Urban Affairs Review* 56(6): 1848–75.

Pengelly, Martin. 2020. "Civil Rights Groups Sue Trump over Assault on Peaceful Protesters near White House." *The Guardian*, June 4. http://www.theguardian.com/us-news/2020/jun/04/aclu-lawsuit-trump-protesters-church-white-house (accessed July 6, 2021).

People Staff. 2023. "Florida Gov. Ron DeSantis' Administration Blocks AP African American History Course from High Schools." *People*, January 20. https://people.com/politics/florida-gov-ron-desantis-blocks-ap-african-american-history-course/ (accessed January 20, 2023).

Perry, Samuel L. 2013. "Racial Composition of Social Settings, Interracial Friendship, and Whites' Attitudes toward Interracial Marriage." *Social Science Journal* 50(1): 13–22.

Petrocik, John R. 1996. "Issue Ownership in Presidential Elections, with a 1980 Case Study." *American Journal of Political Science* 40(3): 825–50.

Pettigrew, Thomas F. 1998. "Intergroup Contact Theory." *Annual Review of Psychology* 49(1): 65–85.

Pettigrew, Thomas F. 2009. "Secondary Transfer Effect of Contact: Do Intergroup Contact Effects Spread to Noncontacted Outgroups?" *Social Psychology* 40(2): 55–65.

Pettigrew, Thomas F. 2021. "Advancing Intergroup Contact Theory: Comments on the Issue's Articles." *Journal of Social Issues* 77(1): 258–73.

Pettigrew, Thomas F., and Linda R. Tropp. 2006. "A Meta-Analytic Test of Intergroup Contact Theory." *Journal of Personality and Social Psychology* 90(5): 751–83.

Pew Research Center. 2016. *The New Food Fights: US Public Divides over Food Science* (report). Pew Research Center—Food Science, December 1. https://www.pewresearch.org/science/2016/12/01/the-new-food-fights/ (accessed January 3, 2022).

Pew Research Center. 2019. *Political Independents: Who They Are, What They Think* (report). Pew Research Center—U.S. Politics & Policy, March 14. https://www.pewresearch.org/politics/2019/03/14/political-independents-who-they-are-what-they-think/ (accessed January 3, 2022).

Pew Research Center. 2020. "Republicans, Democrats Move Even Further Apart in Coronavirus Concerns." Pew Research Center—U.S. Politics & Policy, June 25. https://www.pewresearch.org/politics/2020/06/25/republicans-democrats-move-even-further-apart-in-coronavirus-concerns/ (accessed December 16, 2021).

Pew Research Center. 2021. "Voters' Reflections on the 2020 Election." Pew Research Center—U.S. Politics & Policy, January 15. https://www.pewresearch.org/politics/2021/01/15/voters-reflections-on-the-2020-election/ (accessed October 7, 2021).

Phillips, Joseph. 2022. "Affective Polarization: Over Time, through the Generations, and during the Lifespan." *Political Behavior* 44(September): 1–26.

Piven, Frances Fox, Lorraine Carol Minnite, and Margaret Groarke. 2009. *Keeping Down the Black Vote: Race and the Demobilization of American Voters*. New York: New Press.

Popkin, Samuel L. 1991. *The Reasoning Voter*. Chicago: University of Chicago Press.

Prendergast, Patrick, Shanna Pearson-Merkowitz, and Corey Lang. 2019. "The Individual Determinants of Support for Open Space Bond Referendums." *Land Use Policy* 82: 258–68.

"President Obama's Chili Recipe." *PBS Food*. https://www.pbs.org/food/recipes/presid ent-obamas-chili-recipe/ (accessed January 7, 2022).

Prothro, James W., and Charles M. Grigg. 1960. "Fundamental Principles of Democracy: Bases of Agreement and Disagreement." *Journal of Politics* 22(2): 276–94.

Quinnipiac University Poll. 2017. *American Voters Believe Trump Is Abusing His Powers, Quinnipiac University National Poll Finds; Job Approval Remains at Historic Low.* Quinnipiac University Poll, May 24. https://poll.qu.edu/Poll-Release-Legacy?releas eid=2460 (accessed January 7, 2022).

Quinnipiac University Poll. 2018. *U.S. Voters Believe Comey More than Trump, Quinnipiac University National Poll Finds; Support for Marijuana Hits New High.* Quinnipiac University Poll, April 26. https://poll.qu.edu/Poll-Release-Legacy?releaseid=2539 (accessed January 7, 2022).

Rabb, Nathaniel, Jake Bowers, David Glick, Kevin H. Wilson, and David Yokum. 2021. "The Influence of Social Norms Varies with 'Others' Groups: Evidence from COVID-19 Vaccination Intentions." *Proceedings of the National Academy of Sciences, 119*(29): 1–8.

Relman, Eliza. 2020. "Joe Biden Addresses Black Lives Matter Protests and Draws Contrast with Trump." *Business Insider*, June 2. https://www.businessinsider.com/joe-biden-black-lives-matter-protests-speech-trump-video-2020-6 (accessed July 7, 2021).

Richardson, Bruce. 2021. "Letters: Critical Race Theory Will Lead to Bullying of White Males, Christians." *The Columbus Dispatch*, June 14 https://www.dispatch.com/story/opinion/letters/2021/06/14/letters-critical-race-theory-attack-white-males-needed-examination-racist-atrocities/7583156002/ (accessed January 14, 2022).

Rouse, Stella M., and Ashley D. Ross. 2018. *The Politics of Millennials: Political Beliefs and Policy Preferences of America's Most Diverse Generation.* Ann Arbor: University of Michigan Press.

Ruggeri, Kai et al. 2020. "Replicating Patterns of Prospect Theory for Decision under Risk." *Nature Human Behaviour* 4(6): 622–33.

Russell, Annelise. 2018. "U.S. Senators on Twitter: Asymmetric Party Rhetoric in 140 Characters." *American Politics Research* 46(4): 695–723.

Russell, Annelise. 2021. "Minority Opposition and Asymmetric Parties? Senators' Partisan Rhetoric on Twitter." *Political Research Quarterly* 74(3): 615–27.

Schattschneider, Elmer Eric. 1942. *Party Government.* New York: Farrar and Rinehart.

Schmid, Katharina, Miles Hewstone, Beate Küpper, Andreas Zick, and Ulrich Wagner. 2012. "Secondary Transfer Effects of Intergroup Contact: A Cross-National Comparison in Europe." *Social Psychology Quarterly* 75(1): 28–51.

Schwalbe, Michael C., Geoffrey L. Cohen, and Lee D. Ross. 2020. "The Objectivity Illusion and Voter Polarization in the 2016 Presidential Election." *Proceedings of the National Academy of Sciences* 117(35): 21218–29.

Sears, David O., Richard R. Lau, Tom R. Tyler, and Harris M. Allen. 1980. "Self-Interest vs. Symbolic Politics in Policy Attitudes and Presidential Voting." *American Political Science Review* 74(3): 670–84.

Settle, Jaime E. 2018. *Frenemies: How Social Media Polarizes America.* Cambridge: Cambridge University Press.

Settle, Jaime E., and Taylor N. Carlson. 2019. "Opting Out of Political Discussions." *Political Communication* 36(3): 476–96.

Sigelman, Lee, Carol K. Sigelman, and David Bullock. 1991. "Reconsidering Pocketbook Voting: An Experimental Approach." *Political Behavior* 13(2): 129–49.

Silver, Nate. 2017. "The Comey Letter Probably Cost Clinton the Election." *FiveThirtyEight*, May 3. https://fivethirtyeight.com/features/the-comey-letter-probably-cost-clinton-the-election/ (accessed January 7, 2022).

Skocpol, Theda, and Vanessa Williamson. 2016. *The Tea Party and the Remaking of Republican Conservatism*. New York: Oxford University Press.

Stangor, Charles, Gretchen B. Sechrist, and John T. Jost. 2001a. "Changing Racial Beliefs by Providing Consensus Information." *Personality and Social Psychology Bulletin* 27(4): 486–96.

Stangor, Charles, Gretchen B. Sechrist, and John T. Jost. 2001b. "Social Influence and Intergroup Beliefs: The Role of Perceived Social Consensus." In *Social Influence: Direct and Indirect Processes*, edited by Joseph P. Forgas and Kipling D. Williams, 235–52. New York: Taylor & Francis.

Steeh, Charlotte, and Maria Krysan. 1996. "Trends: Affirmative Action and the Public, 1970–1995." *Public Opinion Quarterly* 60(1): 128–58.

Stettner, Andrew. 2021. "Fact Sheet: What's at Stake as States Cancel Federal Unemployment Benefits." *The Century Foundation*, May 13. https://tcf.org/content/commentary/fact-sheet-whats-stake-states-cancel-federal-unemployment-benefits/ (accessed December 14, 2021).

Sussman, Anna Louie. 2020. "The Loneliness of the Pro-Choice Republican Woman." *The New Yorker*, October 30. https://www.newyorker.com/news/us-journal/the-loneliness-of-the-pro-choice-republican-woman (accessed September 30, 2021).

Tam Cho, Wendy K., James G. Gimpel, and Iris S. Hui. 2013. "Voter Migration and the Geographic Sorting of the American Electorate." *Annals of the Association of American Geographers* 103(4): 856–70.

Tausch, Nicole, Miles Hewstone, Jared B. Kenworthy, Charis Psaltis, Katharina Schmid, Jason R. Popan, Ed Cairns, and Joanne Hughes. 2010. "Secondary Transfer Effects of Intergroup Contact: Alternative Accounts and Underlying Processes." *Journal of Personality and Social Psychology* 99(2): 282.

Taylor, Keeanga-Yamahtta. 2019. *Race for Profit: How Banks and the Real Estate Industry Undermined Black Homeownership*. Chapel Hill: University of North Carolina Press.

Theriault, Sean M. 2013. *The Gingrich Senators: The Roots of Partisan Warfare in Congress*. New York: Oxford University Press.

Thrush, Glenn, Jo Becker, and Danny Hakim. 2021. "Tap Dancing with Trump: Lindsey Graham's Quest for Relevance." *New York Times*, August 14. https://www.nytimes.com/2021/08/14/us/politics/lindsey-graham-donald-trump.html (accessed January 6, 2022).

Tobler, Waldo R. 1970. "A Computer Movie Simulating Urban Growth in the Detroit Region." *Economic Geography* 46 (supplement): 234–40.

Tredoux, Colin, and Gillian Finchilescu. 2010. "Mediators of the Contact: Prejudice Relation among South African Students on Four University Campuses." *Journal of Social Issues* 66(2): 289–308.

Tropp, Linda R., and Fiona Kate Barlow. 2018. "Making Advantaged Racial Groups Care about Inequality: Intergroup Contact as a Route to Psychological Investment." *Current Directions in Psychological Science* 27(3): 194–99.

"Tucker: Biden Is Giving the Left More Power to Harass Their Political Enemies." 2022. Fox News, January 17. https://www.foxnews.com/transcript/tucker-biden-is-giving-the-left-more-power-to-harass-their-political-enemies (accessed January 25, 2022).

U.S. Department of Justice, Office of the Attorney General. 2021. "Partnership among Federal, State, Local, Tribal, and Territorial Law Enforcement to Address Threats against School Administrators, Board Members, Teachers, and Staff" (memorandum), October 4. https://www.justice.gov/ag/page/file/1438986/download (accessed January 25, 2022).

Verba, Sidney, Kay Lehman Schlozman, and Henry E. Brady. 1995. *Voice and Equality: Civic Voluntarism in American Politics*. Cambridge, MA: Harvard University Press.

Villarreal, Daniel. 2020. "Trump Says the Black Lives Matter Movement Is 'Destroying Many Black Lives.'" *Newsweek*, September 25. https://www.newsweek.com/trump-says-black-lives-matter-movement-destroying-many-black-lives-1534411 (accessed July 6, 2021).

Wallace, David Foster. 2005. "Host." *The Atlantic* (April). https://www.theatlantic.com/magazine/archive/2005/04/host/303812/ (accessed November 16, 2021).

Walsh, Joe. 2021. "Rush Limbaugh's Biggest—and Most Controversial—Moments." *Forbes*, February 17. https://www.forbes.com/sites/joewalsh/2021/02/17/rush-limbaughs-biggest-and-most-controversial-moments/ (accessed November 17, 2021).

Walshe, Shushannah. 2014. "How Little-Known MIT Professor Jonathan Gruber Shook Up Washington This Week." ABC News, November 14. https://abcnews.go.com/Politics/obamacare-architect-jonathan-gruber-fire/story?id=26919286 (accessed January 18, 2022).

Wattenberg, Martin P. 1999. *The Decline of American Political Parties, 1952–1996*. Cambridge, MA: Harvard University Press.

Wattenberg, Martin P. 2002. *Where Have All the Voters Gone?* Cambridge, MA: Harvard University Press.

Webster, Steven W. 2020. *American Rage: How Anger Shapes Our Politics*. Cambridge: Cambridge University Press.

Weintraub, Karen. 2020. "A COVID-19 Vaccine at What Price? Should All Americans Be Able to Get a Shot for Free?" *USA TODAY*, July 21. https://www.usatoday.com/story/news/health/2020/07/21/should-government-funded-covid-19-vaccine-free-all-americans/5426531002/ (accessed December 14, 2021).

White, Fiona A., Islam Borinca, Loris Vezzali, Katherine J. Reynolds, Johanna K. Blomster Lyshol, Stefano Verrelli, and Juan M. Falomir-Pichastor. 2020. "Beyond Direct Contact: The Theoretical and Societal Relevance of Indirect Contact for Improving Intergroup Relations." *Journal of Social Issues* 77(1): 132–53 .

Whitt, Sam, Alixandra B. Yanus, Brian McDonald, John Graeber, Mark Setzler, Gordon Ballingrud, and Martin Kifer. 2021. "Tribalism in America: Behavioral Experiments on Affective Polarization in the Trump Era." *Journal of Experimental Political Science* 8(3): 247–59.

Williams, Robin M., Jr. 1947. "The Reduction of Intergroup Tensions: A Survey of Research on Problems of Ethnic, Racial, and Religious Group Relations." *Social Science Research Council Bulletin* 57: xi, 153.

Wojcieszak, Magdalena. 2010. "'Don't Talk to Me': Effects of Ideologically Homogeneous Online Groups and Politically Dissimilar Offline Ties on Extremism." *New Media & Society* 12(4): 637–55.

Wojcieszak, Magdalena, Bruce Bimber, Lauren Feldman, and Natalie Jomini Stroud. 2016. "Partisan News and Political Participation: Exploring Mediated Relationships." *Political Communication* 33(2): 241–60.

Wolak, Jennifer. 2020. *Compromise in an Age of Party Polarization*. New York: Oxford University Press.

Yang, Qi, Khizar Qureshi, and Tauhid Zaman. "Mitigating the Backfire Effect Using Pacing and Leading." Complex Networks & Their Applications X: Volume 2, Proceedings of the Tenth International Conference on Complex Networks and Their Applications COMPLEX NETWORKS 2021 10. Springer International Publishing, 2022.

Zaller, John R. 1992. *The Nature and Origins of Mass Opinion*. Cambridge: Cambridge University Press.

Zhou, Shelly, Elizabeth Page-Gould, Arthur Aron, Anne Moyer, and Miles Hewstone. 2019. "The Extended Contact Hypothesis: A Meta-Analysis on 20 Years of Research." *Personality and Social Psychology Review* 23(2): 132–60.

Zhu, Oscar Yuheng, Bettina Grün, and Sara Dolnicar. 2021. "Tourism and Vaccine Hesitancy." *Annals of Tourism Research* 92(January): 1–5.

Index

For the benefit of digital users, indexed terms that span two pages (e.g., 52–53) may, on occasion, appear on only one of those pages.

Tables and figures are indicated by *t* and *f* following the page number

affective partisan polarization. *See* polarization
affirmative action, 92–94
Affordable Care Act (ACA) (Obamacare) (2010)
  compromises and, 58–59
  Democratic Party and, 15–16, 58–59
  difference in support based on framing of, 20–21, 58–59
  model for, 15–16
  prospect theory and, 105–6
  Republican Party and, 16, 20–21, 58–59, 105–6
  voter responsiveness and, 144
affordable housing development, 140–44, 143*f*
Allport, Gordon, 70, 72–73, 94–96, 178
American National Election Study (ANES), 6, 25–26, 28, 30–31, 38, 41, 59, 150–54, 158–59
American Political Science Association (APSA) Committee on Political Parties, 174
American Voter, The (Campbell), 118–19, 147
Anderson, Cooper, 39
AOC. *See* Ocasio-Cortez, Alexandria
Arab Spring, 37–38

Bail, Chris, 43–44
Bannon, Steve, 103–4
Beck, Glenn, 39
Berelson, Bernard, 121
Biden, Joe
  BLM and, 81
  Covid-19 and, 104–5, 107–10

elites and, 81
inequality and civil rights policy and, 81
information environment and, 11
stolen election claims and, 96, 166, 177
taxation and, 107–8
bipartisanship, 56–63, 164
Black community, government role in helping, 89–92, 91*f*
Black Lives Matter (BLM), 7, 80–81
Bloomberg, Michael, 10
Bobo, Lawrence, 76–77
Bor, Alexander, 44–45
Breitbart (website), 39, 42–43, 113
Broockman, David, 43
Brownstein, Ronald, 97
Buchanan, Pat, 92–93
Bullock, John, 21
Burbank, Matthew, 121
Bush, George W., 16, 96

campaign information sources, 38, 39*f*, 40*f*
Campbell, Angus, 17
Campbell, James E., 117
Capitol insurrection (January 6th)
  causes of, 11–12, 166, 177
  elites and, 177
  Republican Party and, 11–12, 177
  stolen election claims and, 96, 166, 177
  support for, 11–12, 177
Carlson, Tucker, 1
Carmines, Edward, 122–23
Carswell, Chad, 109–10
Chauvin, Derek, 80–81
Civil Rights Act (1964), 76, 77
civil rights policy, 80–82, 87–89, 89*f*
Clinton, Bill, 78–79, 96, 120

Clinton, Hillary, 35, 47, 93
Collins, Susan, 13
Comey, James, 47–48
compromises
    ACA and, 58–59
    decreasing potential for, 4, 165, 167–70
    Democratic Party and, 63, 170
    elites and, 167–70
    gridlock and, 168–69
    instability and, 169
    intergroup contact theory and, 69–70
    lack of motivation for, 177–78
    negative partisanship and, 56–57, 63
    polarization and, 59, 177–78
    policy preferences and, 56–63, 57f,
        67–68
    Republican Party and, 63, 169–73
Cooperative Congressional Election study
    (2014), 49
Covid-19 pandemic
    Democratic Party and, 104–10, 105f, 170
    discussion of study on, 113–14
    elites and, 103–4, 105–6, 109–10
    information environment and, 43,
        166–67
    Ivermectin promotion during, 166–67
    prospect theory and, 100, 103–13, 105f
    Republican Party and, 103–10, 105f, 166
    risk-taking during, 103–13
    support for vaccination policy
        experiment, 106–10, 107t, 109f
Crime Bill (1994), 78
critical race theory (CRT), 82, 97, 166–67
Cruz, Ted, 37
Cullman, Susan, 13

Dawson, Michael, 76–77
Dean, Howard, 120–21, 131
DellaVigna, Stefano, 36
Delli Carpini, Michael, 147
Democratic National Committee, 81, 120
Democratic Party
    ACA and, 15–16, 58–59
    affirmative action and, 92–94
    affordable housing development and,
        140–44, 143f
    Black community and, government role
        in helping, 89–92, 91f

campaign information sources and, 38,
    39f, 40f
civil rights policy and, 80–82, 87–89, 89f
compromises and, 63, 170
Covid-19 pandemic and, 104–10, 105f, 170
elites and, 3–4, 5–6, 78–79, 80, 105,
    171–73
gun violence/gun control and, 129–34,
    130f, 133f
ideology and, 13–16, 30–32, 105
information environment and, 36, 39–
    41, 171–73
intergroup contact theory and, 74–75,
    82–94, 83f, 170–71
land availability and preservation and,
    134–40, 137f, 139f
majority status effect on candidate
    preference and, 60–63, 61f
minimum wage and, 140–44, 143f
motivated reasoning and, 165
negative partisanship and, 5–6, 20–21,
    28–32, 29f, 30f, 31f, 33f, 54, 62–63, 170
non-political preferences and, 63–65
partisan identity measured in, 25–27, 26f
polarization and, 5–6, 39–41, 62–63,
    103, 126–27, 171, 173–78
policy preferences and, 49–50, 51–55
political disaffection and, 156–58, 157t,
    158t
political knowledge and, 151–55, 152t,
    153f, 154t
prospect theory and, 103
racial equality and, 80–82, 84–87, 86f
racialization of, 75–80, 170–71
social sorting and, 27–28, 65–67
taxation and, 110–13, 111t, 112f
trust in media and, 41–43, 41f
voter responsiveness and, 120, 124–25,
    126–27, 140–41
Dionne, E. J., 172
disaffection, political, 155–58, 157t, 158t
disinformation, 8, 18, 144–45, 161
Drutman, Lee, 168–69

elites
    compromises and, 167–70
    Covid-19 pandemic and, 103–4, 105–6,
        109–10

Democratic Party and, 3–4, 5–6, 78–79, 80, 105, 171–73
expressive responding and, 165–67
ideology and, 12–13, 15, 48
independents and, 5
information environment and, 36–37, 43–44, 45–46
instrumental behavior and, 165–67
intergroup contact theory and, 74–75, 80–82, 92–94
misinformation created by, 2
motivated reasoning and, 69–70
overview of, 2, 3–4, 163–65, 179
polarization and, 3–4, 45, 62–63
policy preferences and, 4, 48–51
political behavior and, 16–17, 18–19, 20
prospect theory and, 105–6, 108–10
Republican Party and, 3–4, 5–6, 11, 62–63, 82, 97, 103–4, 105–6, 108–10, 165–67, 170–71, 177
voter responsiveness and, 116, 122–23, 144
way forward and, 165–68, 178
Epstein, Joseph, 93
Erickson, Doug, 166
Ernby, Kelly, 166

Facebook, 36–37
fake news, 42–43, 44–45
Farhart, Christina, 119
Federico, Christopher, 119, 148
Feldman, Stanley, 140–41
Floyd, George, 80–81, 96–97
Fox News, 34, 35–36, 42–43, 82, 171–72
Frank, Thomas, 124–25, 175
Friedersdorf, Conor, 93–94

Garland, Merrick, 1
Gelman, Andrew, 58–59
Gerber, Alan, 110
Gil de Zúñiga, Homero, 36
Gilens, Martin, 92
Gingrich, Newt, 172
Goldwater, Barry, 13, 76
Gosar, Paul, 163
government role in helping Black community, 89–92, 91f
Graham, Lindsay, 11

Grant, Bob, 34–35
Greene, Marjorie Taylor, 103–4
Grossmann, Matt, 62–63
Gruber, Jonathan, 144
gun violence/gun control, 125–34, 128f, 130f, 132f, 133f

Hannity, Sean, 35–36, 39–40, 42–43
Harbridge, Laurel, 59–60
Harrison, Brian, 59–60
Hastert, Dennis, 172–73
Healy, Andrew, 24
Helms, Jesse, 37
Heritage Foundation, 58–59
Hibbing, John, 57–58
Hice, Jody, 103–4
Hopkins, David, 62–63
House of Representatives polarization, 32, 33f
Huber, Gregory, 110
Hurwitz, Jon, 176–77

ideology
critiques of research on, 12–13
definition of, 10–11, 12–13
Democratic Party and, 13–16, 30–32, 105
elites and, 12–13, 15, 48
entrenchment of, 63
information environment and, 33–34
motivated reasoning and, 119
negative partisanship and, 22
partisanship as larger factor than, 12–15
polarization and, 12–15, 32
policy preferences and, 63
political behavior and, 10–11, 12–15
Republican Party and, 13–15, 16, 30–32
voter responsiveness and, 122–23
immigration, 14, 16, 54, 71, 74
independents
as behavior, 150
data for studies on, 151–59
definition of, 149–50
elites and, 5
information environment and, 38, 41, 146–47
intergroup contact theory and, 83
motivated reasoning and, 119

independents (*cont.*)
  negative partisanship and, 30, 146–47,
    155–56
  number of, 27
  overview of, 146–47, 160–62
  paradox of, 149
  perception of, 115
  polarization and, 155–56, 156*f*
  political behavior and, 117–18
  political disaffection and, 155–58, 157*t*,
    158*t*
  political knowledge and, 116, 118–20,
    150–59, 152*t*, 153*f*, 154*t*, 160–62
  prospect theory and, 111, 112–13
  pure independents, 5, 8, 30, 146–47,
    149–50, 155, 161–62
  trust in media and, 41–42, 41*f*
  undertheorization of, 5
  voter responsiveness and, 5, 8, 19, 116–
    18, 119–20, 124–25, 131–34, 136–40,
    139*f*, 142, 143*f*, 145
information environment
  campaign information sources and, 38,
    39*f*, 40*f*
  changing nature of, 25–27, 33–45
  choice of cable news channel and, 43–44
  consequences of changes in, 37–45
  Covid-19 pandemic and, 43, 166–67
  Democratic Party and, 36, 39–41,
    171–73
  echo chambers and silos and, 44
  elites and, 36–37, 43–44, 45–46
  fairness doctrine and, 34
  fake news and, 42–43, 44–45
  ideology and, 33–34
  independents and, 38, 41, 146–47
  intergroup contact theory and, 74–75, 92
  marketplace of ideas and, 38
  misinformation and, 2
  motivated reasoning and, 144–45, 148
  negative partisanship and, 33
  overview of, 23–25, 45–46
  partisan news and, 33–36
  polarization and, 12, 24–25, 33, 39–41,
    40*f*, 45
  political behavior and, 10, 15–18
  political knowledge and, 148
  regulation of, 34–35

  Republican Party and, 63, 78, 171–73
  social media and, 1, 3–4, 36–38, 43–44,
    45–46
  talk radio and, 35
  trust in media and, 41–43, 41*f*
  voter responsiveness and, 116, 122–23,
    144–45
information shortcuts, 17–18, 116, 118–
  19, 144
Ingraham, Laura, 166–67
intergroup contact theory
  affirmative action and, 92–94, 95*f*
  civil rights policy and, 80–82, 87–89, 89*f*
  compromises and, 69–70
  definition of, 70–72
  Democratic Party and, 74–75, 82–94,
    83*f*, 170–71
  development of, 70
  discussion of study on, 94–98
  elites and, 74–75, 80–82, 92–94
  government role in helping Black
    community and, 89–92, 91*f*
  importance of partisan cues and, 92–94
  independents and, 83
  information environment and, 74–75,
    92
  institutional support and, 72–73, 94–96
  party messaging and, 80–82
  polarization and, 72–75, 82, 96
  police shootings and budgets and, 87–
    89, 89*f*, 90*f*
  policy preferences and, 71–72, 74–75
  racial equality and, 80–82, 84–87, 86*f*
  racialization of political parties and,
    75–80
  Republican Party and, 74–75, 82–93,
    83*f*, 97, 170–71
  research design for study on, 82–92,
    83*f*, 86*f*
  secondary transfer effects and, 70–71
  tertiary transfer effects and, 71

Jacobson, Gary, 56
January 6th insurrection. *See* Capitol
    insurrection (January 6th)
Jenkins, Jennifer, 1–2
Johnson, Lyndon, 76, 77–78
Justice Department, 1–2

Kahneman, Daniel, 101–2, 106, 111–12
Kaiser Family Foundation, 104–5
Kalla, Joshua, 43
Kalmoe, Nathan, 167
Kaplan, Ethan, 36
Kaplan, Richard, 33–34
Keeter, Scott, 147
Keith, Bruce, 155, 156
Key, V. O., 121
Klar, Samara, 149–50
knowledge, political. *See* political
    knowledge
Kornacki, Steve, 47
Krehbiel, Keith, 168
Krupnikov, Yanna, 149–50
Kunda, Ziva, 17

Laar, Colette, 70–71
land availability and preservation, 134–40,
    137*f*, 139*f*
Lazarsfeld, Paul, 121
Lee, Frances, 15, 20, 168–69, 178–79
Lerman, Amy, 105–6
Levendusky, Matthew, 174
Limbaugh, Rush, 34, 35, 39, 42
Lippmann, Walter, 147
Lupia, Arthur, 144, 154–55, 161–62

Maddow, Rachel, 40
Madison, James, 167–68, 176
majority status effects on candidate
    preference, 60–63, 61*f*
Malhotra, Neil, 24, 59–60
Mann, Thomas, 172
Martin, Treyvon, 80–81
Mason, Lilliana, 21, 27–28, 167
Massie, Thomas, 163
Mayhew, David, 168
McCain, John, 163
McConnell, Mitch, 13
McPhee, William, 121
media. *See* information environment
Miller, Joanne, 119
minimum wage, 140–44, 143*f*
Mondak, Jeffrey, 176–77
Morrison, Toni, 78–79
motivated reasoning
    definition of, 17

Democratic Party and, 165
elites and, 69–70
ideology and, 119
independents and, 119
information environment and, 144–45,
    148
non-political preferences and, 63–64
political behavior and, 15–18, 19–22
political knowledge and, 18
prospect theory and, 100, 113
Republican Party and, 154–55, 165
spread of, 63–64, 69–70, 97–98, 100, 165
voter responsiveness and, 119, 126–27, 129
MSNBC, 34, 36, 171–72
Murkowski, Lisa, 13
Mutz, Diana, 118

negative partisanship
    civic engagement and, 21
    compromises and, 56–57, 63
    criticism of, 110, 165
    definition of, 20–21, 28
    Democratic Party and, 5–6, 20–21, 28–
        32, 29*f*, 30*f*, 31*f*, 33*f*, 54, 62–63, 170
    ideology and, 22
    immigration and, 54
    independents and, 30, 146–47, 155–56
    information environment and, 33
    measurement of, 28–32, 29*f*, 30*f*, 31*f*, 33*f*
    non-political attitudes and, 65
    political behavior and, 19–22
    Republican Party and, 5–6, 20–21, 28–
        32, 29*f*, 30*f*, 31*f*, 33*f*, 54, 62–63, 170
    rise of, 3–4, 19–22, 27–32, 40–41, 45
    social sorting and, 27–28
news. *See* information environment
Nixon, Richard, 75–76, 120, 170–71
Nolte, John, 99, 113

Obama, Barack
    information environment and, 35–36
    non-political preferences and, 63–64
    racialization of political parties and,
        78–80
Obamacare. *See* Affordable Care Act
    (Obamacare)
Ocasio-Cortez, Alexandria, 37, 43–44, 69,
    81, 163

On the Nature of Prejudice (Allport), 70
Ornstein, Norman, 172
Osmundsen, Mathias, 44–45

Palin, Sarah, 163
pandemic. *See* Covid-19 pandemic
partisanship. *See* motivated reasoning;
    negative partisanship; polarization
party elites. *See* elites
Pelosi, Nancy, 13, 81
Petersen, Michael, 44–45
Peterson, Collin, 13
Pettigrew, Thomas, 72–73
Phyllis Schlafly Report, The, 37
polarization
    compromises and, 59, 177–78
    constitutional crisis as result
        of, 177–78
    contribution of present volume on, 3–5
    criticism of research on, 165
    data for present volume on, 6
    Democratic Party and, 5–6, 39–41, 62–
        63, 103, 126–27, 171, 173–78
    distribution across party of, 5–6, 62–63,
        103, 126–27, 171
    elites and, 3–4, 45, 62–63, 174
    factions and, 176
    growth of, 3–4, 175
    House of Representatives and, 32, 33*f*
    ideology and, 12–15, 32
    independents and, 155–56, 156*f*
    information environment and, 12, 24–
        25, 33, 39–41, 40*f*, 45
    intergroup contact theory and, 72–75,
        82, 96
    methodology for present volume on, 6
    organization of present volume on, 6–9
    overview of, 3–5
    political knowledge and, 5, 148
    reinforcement across party of, 173
    Republican Party and, 5–6, 39–41, 62–
        63, 103, 126–27, 171, 173–78
    spillover effects of, 3–4
    voter responsiveness and, 5, 122–23,
        126–27
    way forward on, 178–79
police shootings and budgets, 87–89, 89*f*,
    90*f*

policy preferences
    bipartisanship and, 56–63
    compromises and, 56–63, 57*f*, 67–68
    definition of, 48–55
    Democratic Party and, 49–50, 51–55
    elites and, 4, 48–51
    ideology and, 63
    intergroup contact theory and, 71–72,
        74–75
    majority status effects on candidate
        preference, 60–63, 61*f*
    measurement of influence on, 48–55,
        50*t*, 52*t*
    non-political preferences and, 63–65,
        66*t*
    overview of, 47–48, 65–68
    party identification and, 63–65
    Republican Party and, 49–50, 51–55
    voter responsiveness and, 138
political behavior
    elites and, 16–17, 18–19, 20
    ideology and, 10–11, 12–15
    independents and, 117–18
    information environment and, 10,
        15–18
    motivated reasoning and, 15–18, 19–22
    negative partisanship and, 19–22
    overview of, 10–12
    party cues as information shortcuts and,
        18–19
    party shifts over time and, 21–22
    political knowledge and, 18
    prospect theory and, 102–3, 114
political disaffection, 155–58, 157*t*, 158*t*
political knowledge
    definition of, 147–48
    Democratic Party and, 151–55, 152*t*,
        153*f*, 154*t*
    external efficacy and, 158, 159*f*
    independents and, 116, 118–20, 151–55,
        152*t*, 153*f*, 154*t*, 160–62
    information environment and, 148
    motivated reasoning and, 18
    partisan issue constraint conflated
        with, 18
    polarization and, 5, 148
    political behavior and, 18
    political disaffection and, 158–59, 160*f*

as proxy for acceptance of two-party
    regime, 150
Republican Party and, 151–55, 152*t*,
    153*f*, 154*t*
retrospective voting model and, 24
prejudice. *See* intergroup contact theory
prospect theory
    ACA and, 105–6
    Covid-19 pandemic and, 100, 103–13, 105*f*
    definition of, 101–2
    Democratic Party and, 103
    discussion of study on, 113–14
    elites and, 105–6, 108–10
    expected utility theory contrasted with,
        101–2
    independents and, 111, 112–13
    motivated reasoning and, 100, 113
    overview of, 99–101
    political behavior and, 102–3, 114
    Republican Party and, 100, 103, 170
    status quo bias and, 102–3
    support for vaccination policy
        experiment and, 106–10, 107*t*, 109*f*
    taxation and, 110–13, 111*t*, 112*f*

racial equality, 80–82, 84–87, 86*f*, 97
Reagan, Ronald, 24, 26–27, 34, 76–78
reasoning, motivated. *See* motivated
    reasoning
Republican Party
    ACA and, 16, 20–21, 58–59, 105–6
    affordable housing development and,
        140–44, 143*f*
    campaign information sources and, 38,
        39*f*, 40*f*
    civil rights policy and, 82, 87–89, 89*f*
    compromises and, 63, 169–73
    Covid-19 pandemic and, 103–10, 105*f*,
        166
    critical race theory and, 82, 166–67
    elites and, 3–4, 5–6, 11, 82, 97, 103–4,
        105–6, 108–10, 165–67, 170–71, 177
    fake news and, 42–43, 44–45
    flip-flopping and, 11–12
    government role in helping Black
        community and, 89–92, 91*f*
    gun violence/gun control and, 129–34,
        130*f*, 133*f*

ideology and, 13–15, 16, 30–32
importance for addressing partisanship
    of, 170–73
information environment and, 63, 78,
    171–73
intergroup contact theory and, 74–75,
    82–93, 83*f*, 97, 170–71
land availability and preservation and,
    134–40, 137*f*, 139*f*
majority status effects on candidate
    preference, 60–63, 61*f*
minimum wage and, 140–44, 143*f*
motivated reasoning and, 154–55, 165
negative partisanship and, 5–6, 20–21,
    28–32, 29*f*, 30*f*, 31*f*, 33*f*, 54, 62–63,
    170
non-political preferences and, 63–65
partisan identity measured in, 25–27,
    26*f*
polarization and, 5–6, 39–41, 62–63,
    103, 126–27, 171, 173–78
policy preferences and, 49–50, 51–55
political disaffection and, 157*t*, 158*t*
political knowledge and, 151–55, 152*t*,
    153*f*, 154*t*
prospect theory and, 100, 103, 170
racial equality and, 82, 84–87, 86*f*, 97
racialization of, 75–80
RINOs and, 32
social sorting and, 27–28
stolen election claims and, 96, 166, 177
taxation and, 110–13, 111*t*, 112*f*, 171
trust in media and, 41–43, 41*f*
voter responsiveness and, 120, 121–22,
    124–25
responsiveness of voters. *See* voter
    responsiveness
Rogan, Joe, 166–67
Romney, Mitt, 16, 77–78
Russell, Annelise, 173
Ryan, Paul, 69

Sanders, Bernie, 117, 120, 131
Saunders, Kyle, 119
Schattschneider, E. E., 15
Schultz, Howard, 10
Sidanius, Jim, 119, 148
social media, 1, 3–4, 36–38, 43–44, 45–46

social sorting, 27–28, 65–67, 164–65
Stefanik, Elise, 1
Stimson, James, 122–23
stolen election claims, 96, 166, 177

taxation, 110–13, 111*t*, 112*f*
Telecommunications Act (1996), 34–35
Theiss-Morse, Elizabeth, 57–58
Trump, Donald
    attacks on media by, 42–43
    BLM and, 80–81
    Capitol insurrection and, 96, 166, 177
    as challenging assumptions about
        political behavior, 10–11
    Covid-19 pandemic and, 103–4, 108–
        10, 166–67
    elite adaptation to, 11
    ideology and, 10–11
    inequality and civil rights policy under,
        80–81
    information environment and, 35–36,
        37, 78
    misinformation and, 11–12
    policy preferences and, 49
    racialization of political parties under,
        77–78
    social media use by, 43–44
    stolen election claims by, 96, 166, 177
    trust in media, 41–43, 41*f*
Tversky, Amos, 101–2, 106, 111–12
Twitter, 35–36, 37, 43–44, 163, 173

voter responsiveness
    ACA and, 144
    affordable housing development and,
        140–44, 143*f*
    causal inference problem and, 121–22
    contextual effects and, 121–24
    data for study on, 125–27

Democratic Party and, 120, 124–25,
    126–27, 140–41
designing two tests for, 123–44
discussion of study on, 144–45
easy vs hard issues on, 122–23, 141
elites and, 116, 122–23, 144
geographic context and, 121, 123–24,
    140, 142–44
gun violence/gun control and, 125–34,
    128*f*, 130*f*, 132*f*, 133*f*
ideology and, 122–23
independents and, 5, 8, 19, 115, 116–18,
    119–20, 124–25, 126–29, 128*f*, 131–
    34, 132*f*, 136–40, 139*f*, 142, 143*f*, 145
information environment and, 116,
    122–23, 144–45
land availability and preservation and,
    134–40, 137*f*, 139*f*
lived environment as test case of,
    120–23
minimum wage and, 140–44, 143*f*
motivated reasoning and, 119, 126–27,
    129
overview of, 115–17
personal financial context and, 140–44
polarization and, 5, 122–23, 126–27
policy preferences and, 138
Republican Party and, 120, 121–22,
    124–25
research design for study on, 125–27
results of study on, 127–34, 128*f*, 130*f*,
    132*f*, 133*f*, 136–40, 137*f*, 139*f*, 141–
    44, 143*f*
socio-economic status and, 124–25

Wallace, David Foster, 34
Wattenberg, Martin, 25–26
Webster, Steven, 167
Wolak, Jennifer, 59